My War at Home

D0107265

My War at Home

Masuda Sultan

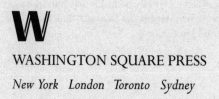

WASHINGTON SQUARE PRESS

New York London Toronto Sydney

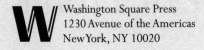 Washington Square Press
1230 Avenue of the Americas
New York, NY 10020

ISBN-13: 978-0-7434-8047-5
ISBN-10:   0-7434-8047-3

First Washington Square Press trade paperback edition February 2006

10 9 8 7 6 5 4 3 2 1

WASHINGTON SQUARE PRESS and colophon are
registered trademarks of Simon & Schuster, Inc.

Manufactured in the United States of America

For information regarding special discounts for bulk purchases,
please contact Simon & Schuster Special Sales at 1-800-456-6798
or business@simonandschuster.com

To my parents and family, including those who would be called "extended family" or "relatives" in the West. In places like Afghanistan they are just family.

Acknowledgments

My special thanks to Hannibal Travis. I deeply appreciate your patience and wisdom throughout this book. Thank you to Vic Sarjoo and Deborah Bell for your encouragement and insight. You have saved me much in therapy costs, as Vic would say, and no matter how much you insist otherwise, I know I would not have done this without you. Babai, Sara, and Aziza, I will always cherish you as my siblings and friends who can understand. And Aziza, I will never forget you staying up the last night before my due date to read as much as you could and sharing your special wisdom.

My editors, Tracy Behar and Wendy Walker, at Simon & Schuster have been fabulous. Thanks also to Susan Brown for helping to sharpen the vision for this book.

Eileen Cope, you will always be the person that kicked this off and believed in it first, even before I did when I avoided you at twenty-three. I could not have asked for a better agent or one with more heart and love.

The ultimate honor is to be asked to share your story, the story of your family, and the story of your people.

Contents

Chapter 1

The Second Most Important Day

The pleasure of God is the pleasure of the parents.

—Islamic saying

At sixteen, I finally had the guts to make the call to my new husband. With my reluctant acceptance, my parents had arranged my marriage to a doctor fourteen years my senior.

I had been planning to call him for weeks now, trying to find the right opportunity, and backing out at the moment it was no longer a fantasy but a step closer to hearing his voice. I had to hurry because my mother was going to be back soon, and my younger sisters could come out into the living room at any moment.

As I dialed the operator, I felt a flash of hot fire spread across my face. It rushed through my body. "I'd like to make a collect call," I said uncertainly to the operator—I hoped she would tell me I couldn't and put me out of my misery. I had found the number under "Doctor" in the neatly written phone book my father kept next to the telephone. I hated that this was the way I was first to speak with my husband. I felt cheap, but there was no other way I could call him without my parents finding out. What if he didn't recognize who I was? They only ask your name on a collect call, and this wouldn't give me enough time to say, "I'm

Masuda, the girl you married three months ago, remember?"

What if he knew who I was and still refused my call? Would he think I was a shameless American girl? After all, he had called my parents about once a week after the ceremony to see how everyone was doing, but had made my mother proud by never asking about me. That meant that he was either very conservative, too shy to ask my parents about me, or both. In any case, it was a very appropriate way to behave, according to Pashtun culture.

"Masuda Sultan." I rushed to say my full name before the operator's recorder stopped. Ring . . . Ring . . . I tapped the top of the black wooden entertainment system on which the phone was resting. I was somewhat disappointed he wasn't home on a Sunday afternoon. Could he be out with a woman? I knew nothing about his personal life but wondered about it.

On the third ring, he picked up. I rushed to fill the copper wires that connected us. "*Salaamwalaikum*. This is Masuda. I'm sorry to call you this way, but I just felt that we should be speaking, and um—if it's a problem I can hang up and we can pretend this never happened." I was so frightened that I wished I had never called.

"No, no, it's fine. Don't worry." I wanted to jump in the air. "So how are you?" he asked.

"Oh, not bad, just um, home."

He was sweet. I was ecstatic that he was happy to hear from me. This was my husband, but it felt like I was calling a secret boyfriend, which made it all the more fun. We went on to talk about his long hours at work as a doctor at the clinic.

I explained that it was already becoming too late for me to apply to college, but that my college counselor at school felt I had a really good shot at some top schools. My parents told me not to apply, to wait and see what happens. I brought up the college issue in particular to see if he really was comfortable with my attending school.

A few months back, when my parents asked me if I would agree to marry their choice, I had objected at first, saying that at sixteen it was too early for me to get married, and I wanted to go to college. My parents asked me who I would marry later on, and if I already had a boyfriend. "Of course not!" I said, feeling defensive, and under suspicion.

"Then who will you marry, if not our choice? Maybe you are too young, but this is an opportunity you may never have again. We think you're mature enough."

They were worried they would not find a good match for me if we waited any longer, because I would then be way too educated for most Afghan men from families my parents would have known in southern Afghanistan before the war.

Eventually, I caved in, seeing the merits of my parents' choice, and not having anyone else in mind. I only asked that I be allowed to continue my education through college. My parents agreed to request that Nadir's brother, who had approached them to ask for my hand in marriage, talk to Nadir about this one condition. Nadir's brother reported back to say this was acceptable.

Because there had been so many people involved in the agreement, I wanted to be sure that Nadir really valued my college education. I was relieved that he did, although he didn't give me much direction about where to apply. It was only our first call, and I had done a lot simply by achieving contact.

I had just had my first conversation with my new husband, and he suggested I call him back collect as often as I wanted. As I hung up the phone, I turned around to see my sisters in the living room. They were looking up at me curiously. I couldn't ask them what they heard or knew, because I didn't want to bring attention to it. I only hoped that they didn't notice anything, even though my face must have been red from the feeling of hot flames emanating from it.

. . .

I longed to know who my husband really was. I blamed the discomfort I had felt at times, the dead silence on the phone, on the way in which we had met. Or perhaps it was because I was a complete amateur and had never been in a relationship before. Maybe he was being nice by not saying much, and giving me an opening with his silence to talk about myself and ponder any random thought I desired. Nadir was probably the smartest man I'd ever met, so I trusted his instincts. I also knew that our children would be very intelligent, if nothing else. But I wished that he could have told me how much he enjoyed speaking to me, that he looked forward to our wedding, and our life together.

I remembered the first time I met him. He came over to my parents' home for dinner, with his brother and his brother's wife. As in most *melmastias*, or occasions where we had guests, we had spent two days preparing for their arrival. The first day my father, or Agha, had shopped for fresh *halal* meats and groceries, while the rest of us cleaned all day, making the entire house spotless. The day of the *melmastia*, we rose to the comforting aroma of sautéed onions, a task that Moor, or mother, had begun long before we had come to our senses. We soon joined in, washing sprigs of mint and cilantro, using the mortar and pestle to squash garlic into a paste, and stuffing chopped meat into *mantoo*, spicy Afghan dumplings over which mint yogurt is poured before serving. We spent the day cooking enough food for at least twice the number of guests expected, fretting over whether it would be too little. The worst embarrassment in *melmastia* is not having enough food. That point is not marked by people leaving hungry, or whether the food is finished, but by whether anyone eating must question their desire to reach for a particular dish because there may be someone else who wants some. In other words, the guests must eat freely and to the greatest extent possible. Guests must also never exert themselves or be left wanting anything. They must sit and be catered to, although female guests who feel close to the family often insist on helping to clean up.

I greatly enjoy serving guests, probably because our whole family has always considered it a pleasure. Like an orchestra, our family would manage all of the details and minor crises together. This is when our sense of being a team was perhaps strongest. When it's time to serve dinner, Agha checks on the food constantly as Moor heats it up, and we are all assigned tasks. In the race to get all the dishes out at the same time so that they remain as hot as possible, we maneuver around one another in the kitchen. As I duck to avoid the large tray of aromatic basmati rice being passed over my head, run a mitten over to my mother to handle the pot, and ask Agha to remove the Afghan bread toasting in the oven before it burns, we each try to be our best and most efficient. All this is done with the goal of making minimal noise and trying to appear smooth to our guests. Sara decorates the eggplant and tomatoes with chopped peppers and fresh cilantro, like a skilled artist proud of her craft. I try to catch what's been forgotten, like bringing out the pickled lemons Agha has jarred weeks ago in preparation. My youngest sister, Aziza, helps with the easiest chores, like preparing the salad, while nagging our mother for more adult responsibilities, such as preparing a whole stew of chicken and curry.

The night of Nadir's visit, my mother asked me to bring drinks to our guests, so I walked to the living room balancing a tray of glasses filled with orange juice and placed on saucers with a napkin folded into a triangle under them. One never served a drink to a guest in our house without a saucer and napkin for the glass to rest on, and the glass on top of a decorated silver tray. On another occasion, I had carried a glass of water to a guest with my bare hands, only to see the look of desperate shame on my father's face. He shrunk before my eyes, but I felt I couldn't turn back. I was already standing in front of the guest with the glass of water.

As I walked over to Nadir with the tray of orange juice, I noticed the front of his foot was perched on the coffee table, his toes curled around the top corner. How rude! I thought. While it was customary to take off our shoes inside the house, putting your foot on the coffee table was bad manners by any standard. As I got closer I hoped he'd make room for my tray, but he didn't budge. I couldn't bear to look at his face. I stared at his foot as I walked closer and closer, getting nervous about what I would do if he didn't move. I fixated on his big toe, which was clean and well groomed, but hairy. I didn't want to have to tell him to move his foot. That would have been confrontational, and I was too shy to point it out.

Finally, as I stopped and stood before him, his big toe moved. This was my introduction to Nadir. The next time I saw him, we were married, through an Islamic ceremony called *nikkah*.

Once, when I was ten and my extended family came to my parents' home for a wedding party, a wise elder relative told me that marriage is holy within Islam. The women of the family were lounging around Afghan mattresses set on the floor, lying on our sides with our arms thrown over large velvet pillows. My mother's grandmother Koko leaned in close and whispered to me: "There are three days that are the most important in your life. The day you were born, the day you are married, and the day you die. These dates are marked by God and cannot be changed. Only God knows when they will occur."

My mind began to race. I certainly couldn't remember the day I was born, and I might not be conscious when I'm dying—but the day I got married would be the most important day I could live through. At ten I already knew this, but Koko confirmed it, and learning the role of God made it more profound.

Koko's words rang in my head every time I performed another ritual that brought us closer to the end of our journey.

Being married at sixteen had been awkward but filled with

mystery. In some ways, we were only engaged. We weren't living together and had yet to perform the ceremony at which I would wear my white gown and read passages from the Qur'an with Nadir while our families held a large green shawl over our heads like the roof of our new home. But we had already done our *nikkah*, or Islamic wedding ceremony, where I wore a green dress and agreed to accept Nadir as my husband.

This was the most confusing thing for my friends. Under Islam, we had been married, but culturally, we were merely engaged. In Afghan culture, this is a special time in a relationship when you can get to know the other person, but you are expected to refrain from intimate relations. Depending on the attitudes of their families, couples would date, speak on the phone, or have no contact at all.

Our families held our *nikkah* ceremony in a hotel in Flushing, Queens. The green dress I wore was the color of Islamic devotion, as well as the color of prosperity. I sat in a room with the other women, waiting to be asked my approval to marry Nadir. My father had asked to represent me as my *wakil*, or person to whom I give my permission to be married. Some Muslims believe that the marriage contract should be agreed upon between the groom and the closest male relatives of the bride, rather than between a man and his wife. My family believes that the bride should agree to the marriage, but should be represented by a male relative during the ceremony, rather than appear in person before the groom, which would be immodest.

At the ceremony, my father had arranged for two witnesses, male members of our extended family, to come to my room. Speaking to these witnesses would be my only participation in the ceremony. Although women under classical Islam are allowed to represent themselves in marriage, conservative families appoint witnesses as go-betweens to confirm the intent of the bride to the *mullah*, or religious leader. I couldn't confirm my own intent to the *mullah* because traditional Pashtun culture does not permit unmarried women to show themselves before men, even their religious leaders.

My two witnesses spoke a very formal phrase of Pashto, asking whom I would appoint to represent me in the ceremony. I was very nervous, and I didn't quite understand all the words they were speaking, although I knew what they were asking. But Agha had told me the formal, proper way to say that he could represent me, so I repeated what he taught me. Then my witnesses left. A few minutes later, my mother, sisters, and other relatives in the room collapsed in joy, hugging one another and crying because a girl of their family had finally grown up and "reached her place," in my mother's words.

A minute later my new husband entered the room and the music started playing. We did the traditional first walk as a married couple, slowly and in time with the music, entering the main room to join our families and guests. I did not show expression, and kept a serious straight face as we walked through the crowd of people. I could not bear to look at anyone's face, but I knew all eyes were on me. On stage my mother and father gave my new husband a gold ring and watch, and his family gave me a set of gold and bejeweled earrings, necklace, and a ring. Without ever speaking, we had been married.

Right after the ceremony, Nadir literally had to run to the airport to return to the hospital where he worked as an internist. He shook my hand and said good-bye. I hadn't spoken one word to him on the day of our engagement, or at any other time for that matter. The whole episode had been arranged by our families. My father and grandfather knew his father in Kandahar, and our families met again in Brooklyn as refugees from the Soviet bombing of Kandahar in the 1980s. Our fathers and grandfathers, and their fathers and grandfathers, were fellow members of the Popalzai tribe, the tribe of the current president of Afghanistan, Hamid Karzai. Our families made a great match, but would we?

• • •

I could barely see out of the white veil in front of my face. I may as well have been unconscious. I couldn't feel anything. Drowning in harsh lights pointed at me, all I saw were brightly colored blurs of people crossing in front of me. All I could hear were snippets of laughter and *tashakors* (thank-yous) in Pashto.

It was the second most important day of my life, the day of my formal wedding. This time, my husband and I would go home together.

We were in Karachi, Pakistan. I was seventeen, and it was the summer after I graduated high school. I had done well and graduated a year earlier than scheduled, and it was time to get married. Almost a thousand people attended the open-air garden wedding of the last remaining bachelor of six brothers. It was my wedding, but none of it was mine.

One woman came up to me and called me an American doll. I got up when they wanted me to, sat down when they wanted me to, and remained as still as possible.

The light on the large video camera set up in front of me felt unbearable in the sticky Karachi heat. Every so often, the light would be pointed away from me, and I could feel a cool breeze on my arms and neck.

I made sure not to look up too much, lest I should appear to be without shame. Sometimes I would look up, especially when my older brother, Babai, was taking a picture, not only because I wanted to be looking at the camera for the pictures but because I wanted to show the other Afghan girls that it was okay to look around. Besides, I had grown up in America, and American girls couldn't possibly be held to the same standards.

But I didn't want to look up too much. I wanted to show the groom's family that the fact that I had grown up in America didn't mean I would be arrogant or a bad wife to their brother.

Nadir's eldest sister, Bibi, was the master of ceremonies in Karachi. His mother had died a refugee in Pakistan. With his mother gone, Nadir's eldest sister was the obvious choice to organize the wedding. She had a high, squeaky voice, so her true power in the family did not come across at first. Her long nose reminded me of the bird Toucan Sam from the Froot Loops commercials.

Sometimes Moor would call me a Bibi. It was like being called an angel. Bibis are the most respected women in Pashtunwali. They are full of a deep sense of shame, almost always complying with the wishes of their husbands and families, and are essentially good-hearted for trying to keep the peace in their relationships. They don't complain, and they certainly don't fight. Everyone loves them. I had always aspired to be a Bibi, though the title was often bestowed by the mother-in-law. It is the mothers-in-law who pose the most significant challenge to a young wife's Bibi-dom.

Older women are almost always called Bibi, followed by their name or another term of affection, like Gul, meaning "flower." I don't know how so many old women became Bibis, but perhaps it's because their mothers-in-law died and the standards were relaxed. Many older women who arrived in America, brought over by their U.S.-citizen sons and daughters, had the first name Bibi, followed by the family name. An American woman once remarked how incredible it was that there were so many women named Bibi in Afghanistan.

To a clapping audience, Bibi displayed all of the new gold jewelry sets, bangles, rings, and earrings that Nadir's sisters and aunts had adorned me with. Over the previous six months, I had traveled with my mother to most of the shopping areas we knew in New York City to buy things for my wedding, including sparkling beaded evening gowns and matching shoes on Thirty-seventh Street in Manhattan, and elegant Indian outfits from Jackson Heights in Queens.

After arriving in Pakistan for the wedding, my mother and I had visited Sadar, the gold market in Karachi, to buy jewelry for the wedding. There we passed beggars on the street as we left our car. Outside the store there were men with automatic rifles who opened the door for me. Inside, the store was glowing in the reflection of beautiful, rich gold. For Muslim women, gold is the prized possession that is a sign of wealth. In fact, gold is usually the only storage of value and financial security for a woman, especially in poor societies. Gold is also considered holy, so my seemingly superficial shopping experience felt strangely spiritual as well. I loved feeling connected to my ancestors through this beautiful natural element. The shopkeepers, sensing that they were going to make a big sell with these foreigners, especially a young girl like myself, spared not an iota of energy in showing me all their wares. They could tell we weren't local Afghans, but had come from the West. As soon as they knew what we wanted, they stacked rows and rows of gorgeous red velvet jewelry boxes and opened them for me one by one. I would either nod, indicating it should be put to the side, or shake my head in disapproval. I picked out the most expensive items in the store. Most of the gold in the bazaar was 22-karat, something usually unheard of for most girls I knew in the United States. I was never able to do this in America. Here, I was royalty.

Among Pashtun families, the bride typically didn't pick her own jewelry, especially not the jewelry bought by in-laws as wedding gifts. But in my case, we suggested that I help choose the jewelry, because I knew that Nadir's family would buy me a huge gold necklace reaching to my waist, which I would have no use for. I was lucky. I was one of the few girls allowed to pick out her own jewelry, and I felt like a princess the whole time.

I didn't have to do anything at the wedding except be careful not to laugh, or even smile, or move my eyes too much. I had promised my mother back in New York that I wouldn't smile. We had just purchased my veil and were standing on the street waiting for my father to pick us up when she warned me not to do it. I wanted to cry, but instead I insisted I knew that rule already. Of course I wouldn't smile at my wedding.

In Kandahar in my mother's day, the more a bride cried, the more she was loved. The sadder she was about leaving her family, the more she loved them. For me, it wasn't sadness about leaving my family that hurt, but the sadness of feeling that every bit of my fate would be decided for me, and yet not knowing what would happen to my life. It was for the best, I thought, because I would certainly make everyone happy. I wanted to be perfect in that way. Besides, adults had wisdom that I could not understand. Maybe I would love my husband. I had always wanted to marry an Afghan man who would respect our family and embrace our culture.

The wedding was a typical mix of Western and Afghan customs. The women and the men were kept separate, and the wedding party was held in the women's section. The women wore traditional *shalwar kameez*, a long shirt with loose pants. Their outfits were all very festive—like the hard candy your grandma keeps in a jar. Red, yellow, purple, green, with gold embroidery, mirrors, and large chiffon silk shawls over the head, and around the neck and shoulders.

I noticed a woman in a black sparkly pantsuit walk around me and stand next to me for a picture. When she walked away, I realized it was Homira, my new sister-in-law. I had never seen Homira in a pantsuit, even at weddings in the States. In fact, I had only seen her in traditional ethnic clothes.

Following tradition, I lifted a pinch of salt into Nadir's mouth, and we briefly gazed at each other in the mirror for the first time as husband and wife. Then we read passages from the Qur'an in Arabic about how God created men and women from "one soul," and placed love and care in their hearts toward each other. The mirror and Qur'an ceremony (*aina mosaf*) is the centerpiece of most Afghan weddings I have attended. Many Afghan couples, including many in my parents' generation, had never seen each other prior to this ceremony. In the old days brides may not even have seen themselves before looking into the mirror at their wedding. For a bride who had already seen herself in a mirror, the ceremony let her see how beautiful she looked all made up on her wedding night. Even then she may hardly recognize herself, as most Afghan brides do not pluck their eyebrows or wear a speck of makeup before their wedding day.

I felt a hand pressing down on my right shoulder. "Sit down!" Another hand propped me up by my left arm. "Noooo!" Nadir and I were standing in front of our chairs on a raised platform, facing the wedding guests, preparing to be seated.

This was one of the rituals to determine who would be more powerful in the marriage. It was often a fun game for the in-laws, trying to persuade the groom or bride of the other side to sit down. I was sure my mother wanted me to sit first, to show that I would be an obedient wife. But I wouldn't. I held my shoulders up and planted my body as firmly as possible. I wouldn't let a good old competition go without a battle. Everyone was cheering, shouting words of encouragement to either the bride or groom, depending on whose side of the family they belonged to.

When the cheers became very loud, Nadir bent his knees and leaned to sit. I followed, but made sure to go slow so that I'd sit down after he had reached sitting position. As soon as I sat down, everyone burst into applause. I won. Although I felt a real sense of accomplishment, I knew that simply winning this game did not prove that I would be the dominant spouse. And I hoped his family would understand that I could still be a good wife.

Nadir sank into his chair and complained of the heat. Pearly beads of sweat had formed on his forehead and above his upper lip. The heat in Karachi was as thick as Moor's rice pudding. The humidity made it feel like a sauna. Women's beautiful new silk clothes would stick to their bodies, sometimes leaving the mark of the dye of their clothes on their skin. An outfit only once worn would look like it had weathered a storm.

My eldest brother-in-law told the women to hurry up. "We have to rush. It's almost midnight." Weddings were banned from lasting after midnight at the time, due to civil unrest in Karachi. A few gestures and motions later, my father walked up to me, kissed me on the forehead, and tied a festive emerald and gold sash around my waist. Earlier, when I had asked why a green belt was needed for my wedding night, I was told it was to make me strong. Next, a large white chiffon scarf, with scattered green sequined dots sewn on, folded thick with many layers, was draped over my head, covering my face.

The corners of the scarf, each tied in neat knots, were opened by the men of my family. Inside the scarf's layers, there was fresh cardamom, raisins, sugar-covered almonds, and even some dollar bills. The gifts were meant to signify prosperity in my future.

Now that my face was covered, I could barely see anything. Midnight was at hand, and my eldest brother-in-law was now telling the entire wedding party to rush. We were whisked away into a white sedan decorated with pink and white ribbons and flowers. When we drove away, I caught my last glimpse of the men armed with automatic rifles, some still standing on the rooftop of the entrance to the wedding garden. The guards were necessary due to the strife in Karachi that was killing hundreds of people each month that year.

As we drove, humid air rushed in through the window but could barely penetrate the veil covering my face. I gently lifted the white chiffon and let the cooling breeze kiss my neck. I hoped no one would object. The drive felt very long, even though we ran red lights and didn't slow down unless a car was clearly in our way. In Karachi, nobody stopped at the occasional red light. When we had first arrived in the city, my father remarked that all the traffic goes by the grace of God. We had all laughed at that.

As long as it seemed, the ride ended before I was ready, as the car pulled up to a modern-looking apartment building. I was nervous, and I could not concentrate. In fact, I didn't want to think about what my night would be like. Bursts of color and shots of emotion crisscrossed through my mind. There was a solid part of me that felt it would be a good opportunity to really get to know my new husband. As I stepped out of the car a jug of water was spilled by my feet, a ritual to wish good luck to a guest. I was welcomed as a new addition to their family. They made me feel honored and wanted.

As the other cars pulled up, everyone became more excited. I looked up at the building that would be my new home while in Pakistan. Once white, it had turned a light gray. I held my dress up so that I wouldn't trip, and my father and husband helped as I walked up the many flights of stairs, in the open air, to get to the top floor, where my temporary new home would be.

As I walked through the doors, many smiling faces of women greeted me. The women guided me to a red velvet mattress on the floor and offered the best seat in the house, with a large matching red velvet pillow pressed against the wall on which to rest my back. My new husband came and sat next to me. And as the rest of the large extended family, both mine and his, filtered into the room, warm expressions of *mubarak*, or congratulations, were shared.

"*Mubarak* seven thousand times!" they exclaimed, one louder than the other.

"May God give you seven sons!" another woman cried. The jolly women tried to outdo one another with well-wishes.

Although it was one o'clock in the morning, trays of hot tea, cookies, and sweets were brought out to serve all the guests. Many guests insisted that they should leave, for the bride and groom must be tired. As is customary, a few close female members of my family would stay overnight, sleeping nearby to make sure I wasn't completely alone in a house full of strangers. My mother, her sister Lailuma, and Shakoko, my father's older sister, stayed with me.

As I sat in my new bedroom for some last pictures before my relatives left, with the skirt and train of my wedding dress swirled around the bed, I wondered what it would be like when Nadir and I were in the room alone. Finally, the moment I had thought about for as long as I could remember was approaching.

Chapter 2

Marriage, Then Love?

When someone with whose religion and character you are satisfied asks for your daughter in marriage, accede to his request.

—Saying attributed to the Prophet Muhammad
(Peace Be Upon Him)

In the years before coming to Karachi, I would imagine lying next to my new husband, still in my wedding dress, and asking him all sorts of questions. "So, what's your real name? What is your favorite color? Do you know how to cook? What is your dream?"

There were endless questions. I could go on for days asking them. This was how I imagined my first night with my husband. I did not know how to imagine the rest. I knew that it would hurt to be together for the first time, but I hoped that I would be able to keep quiet.

My mother walked into the bedroom where I was sitting, surrounded by a sea of white. She held out a piece of white cotton cloth, about the size of two handkerchiefs, the edges embroidered by hand. "Take this," she said. I froze for a second, completely embarrassed. Then I took it, said nothing, and put it aside. Although we had not discussed it, I knew that the cloth wasn't for her. It was so that my mother could prove my purity to my in-laws. Despite the fact that I had grown up in America, we still had to observe this practice. I did not look in her eyes, but kissed her three times Afghan style. Kiss on one cheek, then the other, then the other, and we said good night.

That night, we spoke about our wedding day. He told me I looked better with less makeup, and I hoped that meant I was naturally pretty, not that I looked less than my best on my wedding day. Before we fell asleep, he kissed me on the forehead. I imagined him saying, "Welcome aboard. You're gonna be all right."

We woke up to birds chirping outside our window, and it felt as if we were in a romantic movie shot on an island, waking up to the sounds of birds. I thought that we would have a nice breakfast together and speak about our plans for the rest of the day, but Nadir woke up and left the room to shower.

The women knocked on my door. My aunt kissed me on both cheeks and asked how my evening was. Other cousins and relatives were nervously waiting to hear what had happened. "Did you sleep well?" one cousin asked playfully, fully aware that a no would have meant the evening was quite a success. "I slept great!" I told them, not wanting to give away any clues or details to feed the inevitable gossip.

My mother walked in the room and immediately noticed that my makeup was still perfectly in place. She asked very matter-of-factly how my evening had gone, and I said, "Fine." That was all she needed to hear. Her question was more of a formality than an expression of curiosity.

While cousins joked about how little sleep I had probably really gotten, I escaped from the room so that I could quickly freshen up for tea with Nadir. After my shower, though, there was no sign of Nadir. I had been looking forward to having our tea together, but he had left to join his brothers. He wouldn't return until around midnight, as would be the case for the rest of our stay in Karachi.

For ten straight days, we dined at the homes of my many in-laws. Usually only the women were invited, but sometimes men were invited too—they ate in a different apartment. This was my time to be pretty, to wear all my new Indian and Afghan outfits, and makeup to match. I was expected to change into a new outfit at least once a day, if not two or three times. "We want to see you in all your new clothes before you go," said one of Nadir's younger sisters, visiting from Saudi Arabia.

I found it quite uncomfortable to constantly change into new outfits, including new shoes and makeup, and sometimes even a new hairstyle. A typical morning was spent curling my hair with a curling iron, smearing tons of liquid color on my face, and trying on incredibly beautiful and festive outfits with gold trim, embroidery, and mirrors. After lunch, I would change looks all over again, this time with the help of at least four or five of Nadir's female relatives. In the evening, back at home, I would put on a slightly less festive outfit for dinner, with less glitter and shimmer. I remembered the comment on my wedding night about being a doll.

Nadir's sisters were very helpful, offering to do my makeup and encouraging the younger girls to iron my clothes. I became a fashion model for anyone working on me, because it would have been rude to refuse an offer of beauty help. Sometimes I would have aqua-blue eye shadow painted over my eyes with a streak of hot pink in the middle, while other women would try a few more shades before arriving at a choice. No matter how awful the makeup artist, I smiled and told her how pretty she made me look.

During these ten days, I was paraded around and oohed and ahhed at, almost worshipped. I decided to enjoy it. When my parents planned dinner at an expensive restaurant in Karachi that catered to tourists, I hoped to get my hair done up in a salon to look more glamorous than ever. The morning of the event, I asked Homira, the sister-in-law who had lived in the United

States and who wore Western clothes to my wedding, which salon I should go to.

"What do you mean? Did you ask Bibi?" she wanted to know.

"No, but I can."

"Of course, you have to ask Bibi. You cannot go to the salon without asking her first, at least that's how we do it."

I squeezed my toes, feeling like I would fall. I knew Bibi had the role of the elder woman in the home, but I had no idea she had this much power.

"Shouldn't you have to ask your husband?" I asked, knowing that in traditional families this was the norm.

"No, no, Bibi is the person to go to. Our husbands don't care. They tell us to ask Bibi."

"Why don't they care?"

"Because they trust her. She's the eldest sister. She's like their mother."

It surprised me that a woman had been given a role of authority in such a conservative environment. But I realized some men wanted their wives controlled, and they didn't mind that they didn't have to do it. As long as someone did.

Homira must have seen the confused look on my face.

"Bibi gets my spending money too, and I have to go to her when I need to buy something. I'm sure she takes her cut."

I was stunned—and relieved that Bibi would soon be thousands of miles away from me after my return to the United States. Over the course of my stay, I learned how much all of my sisters-in-law resented her, but that they had no choice because their husbands had designated her as the point person for just about every issue. When their husbands were traveling, spending money for groceries and other necessities was left with Bibi, and she would assign the driver to go shopping for everyone. Women rarely left the house—and they were certainly never expected to do their own shopping. Some American women might consider this a privilege, but to me it was the kind of privilege I had as a child.

I did not envy the lives of my sisters-in-law at all. All five of them were married to men who saw their wives' roles very clearly. The women were certainly never expected, or allowed, to work. They were not responsible for finances, nor do I think they even knew what their husbands were worth.

At home, all the women married into the family were expected to eat together, along with the children. This made for some messy and loud meals for the wives. Meanwhile, their husbands ate in a separate room, occasionally joined by their sisters. The other room became this forbidden place that I longed to enter. It was the room that had the fresher bread, no children to shove their hands in the yogurt bowls, and lively conversation about the state of politics in Pakistan. It was also the room that my new husband was in. I would not share a meal with him until we went to my aunt's apartment a week later.

My aunt insisted that men and women sit together, and did not invite Nadir's family into their small apartment. As soon as I sat down, my white-bearded uncle told me to throw my head scarf away. I thought he was testing me. "No, take it off," he insisted. "You are with our family now. I tell them they don't have to wear it at home." My aunt gently tugged at my scarf and I gleefully took it off, feeling like a bear coming out of hibernation after a long winter. I instantly felt lighter. For the first time, I thought of my family as liberal, and I was proud to show off to Nadir that we were less concerned about the scarf than his family was.

My parents didn't say anything. I knew that even though they felt it was all right for me to take my scarf off, they did not want to encourage me to do the same in the presence of my in-laws. By not condoning the removal of my scarf at that moment, they were also avoiding the risk that I would seek their approval in doing the same under less liberal conditions later. Handling issues such as dress and modesty was a game with my parents. I knew their expectations, but I often tried to get them to find it in their hearts to be a little more lenient. It usually didn't work.

When traveling between homes, however, my in-laws told me to cover my face by draping two layers of black chiffon over it, a measure I had not taken when going out with my own family. My sisters-in-law joked that with my fair skin, I might be kidnapped in Karachi, never to be seen again. They told me the story of a beautiful Afghan refugee, with three children, who was captured one day in broad daylight in the bazaar. She never returned home and it was suspected that the Pakistani authorities or perhaps even rebels had their way with her in the mountains of the countryside.

The days and nights in Karachi got damper and darker as they passed. I began to get tired of making myself up, and changing outfits, and doing it all over again. Besides, my new husband wasn't even around to see the fruits of my labor. When I developed a sore throat and ran a temperature, there was no one to take care of me. My mother and other family had gone to Quetta to visit my aunt Khala Sherina, who was unable to make my wedding and come to Karachi, so Moor met her halfway. I felt so alone without my relatives—as if I had been left to the care of strangers. I asked my sisters-in-law for medicine, but because of civil unrest all the shops in the bazaar were closed for three days. Yet Nadir was somehow always gone. Finally, one of my sisters-in-law, married to the most conservative brother, recalled having some *joshanda*, or herbal Pakistani medicine, and as I drank it I squirmed but felt better as the chunks of bitter herbs scratched their way down my throat. Mostly, I felt better that someone was finally paying attention and giving me something—anything.

Soon we would leave Pakistan, and I would be back home in the United States. I wondered what life would be like with Nadir in our new home. I wondered what it looked like, what it smelled like, what home would feel like. When I made it home, I would be comfortable enough to fulfill my duties as a new wife.

Nadir's relatives encouraged me to remain in Pakistan. One day I was told that my father-in-law was to visit me, so I had to put on a huge scarf, cover my entire body, and sit waiting for him to arrive. After he told me how tiny I was, he asked me whether I liked Karachi or New York better. I just smiled and giggled, as I was expected to. He told me that I and my new husband would not be able to resist his entreaty to live in Pakistan like all his other sons, even the one who married a Japanese woman. If a Japanese woman could adjust to Pakistan, how could it be very hard for me, an Afghan?

We came back to the States to live in Pittsburgh because Nadir had found a job in a clinic there. It was to be the first day of the life my husband and I would share on our own, without other family around us. After my family left Nadir and me alone, my mother realized she had forgotten her keys and returned a little while later to get them. I still remember the look of surprise on my mother's face when I opened the door for her, holding the keys in the air. She had expected me to be in tears, perhaps like stories I had heard of newlywed brides being left by their family for the first time. The American teenager inside of me had decided that I was ready to be free from my parents and that I was prepared for my first full day as a real adult.

But in all the time we would spend together, Nadir and I lived as strangers. For the first year of our life together in Pittsburgh, we never once went to the park, the movies, or out for dinner alone together. He directed me not to visit him at the hospital, even though he was on thirty-six-hour shifts, during which I was alone in our apartment. I missed him and wondered why he was so embarrassed by me. I think now that it must have been my young age. I'm sure it would have raised eyebrows to have a seventeen-year-old girl show up for a thirtysomething doctor on his break. When Nadir left to go to the bathroom on a visit to the bank to open up an account, the female bank clerk asked me if he was my father, somewhat concerned. I politely answered no, but I never told Nadir.

For almost six months, I did nothing but play what I call an MAP, or "Muslim American Princess." I received numerous calls from extended family in New York, all agog over my husband's work. I had married a *doctor*.

Due to passport issues, I had remained in Pakistan a week longer than anticipated, and would therefore miss the start of classes. I missed the opportunity to attend the first semester of college, so I was told to relax and enjoy my new life. When I brought up my desire to find a job to keep me busy until the semester started, I was reminded that I was set—for life. Traditional Afghan women were not expected nor allowed to work. Besides, I was told, why would you want to work a menial job in retail? So instead of working or continuing my education, I turned my attention toward cooking, and watching TV. Most days I would watch the talk shows I could never watch for long while living with my parents, with topics such as "My Trampy Mother Slept with My New Boyfriend," "Teen Girls Gone Man-Crazy," or "Your Man Is Gay, Get Used to It."

Even during my first semester of school that spring, at Allegheny Community College, professors frequently complimented my schoolwork, asking me why I was not at Carnegie Mellon. While my teachers in high school thought I would attend a prestigious university, the uncertainty, geography, and cost of the education were factors that led me to community college. Some of my American peers who appeared to be struggling for a future seemed to be envious that I was "taken care of." I was truly privileged. I was a doctor's wife.

During that time, I would frequently take long walks around Carnegie Mellon University and shop for bargains on Walnut

Street. But walking down Walnut Street, the whitest neighbor-hood I had ever lived in after Flatbush, Brooklyn, and Flushing, Queens, passing by Victoria's Secret and the Gap, I'd wonder what it felt like to be like the affectionate and happy blond couples hugging, holding hands, and even kissing on the street.

What would it be like if Nadir and *I* had held hands on Walnut Street, then sat in front of the ice cream shop and shared a cone? Would it ever happen? Would I ever be normal? I felt invisible among the passing families. When I didn't feel invisible I felt like an outcast. I felt they looked at me strangely, probably because I must have been looking too closely, wanting to observe their most private moments. A woman on a bench caressing her husband's cheek with her fingertips, a young father lovingly chatting with his daughter about school or bike riding, or an older couple holding hands and laughing on a Sunday afternoon walk. Observing them was the only thing that made me feel I existed. I secretly shared in their intimacy and hated them for not inviting me in.

If only I could feel a part of something like that. I could only see how people lived, I would never get to feel it. I wanted so desperately to know in my heart what that was like, just to try it once. I had parents and a family in New York that loved me, but I was growing more and more distant from them as my growing anger toward them made me feel like a shriveled old piece of fruit.

On days like that, I would come home, tidy up the house, and cook a low-fat dinner, pasta or sautéed salmon with an Afghan-style vegetable dish, prepared by adding fried onions and tomatoes to the dish. I was very careful not to add too much oil.

Nadir hated to find oil in the pot. Besides, it wasn't good for me either. I was on a strict diet to lose at least ten pounds. Nadir had already told me I needed to take off some weight if I wanted him to be attracted to me. The first time he said that, it didn't hurt too much. I wanted to lose some weight too. But soon I realized he expected me to take it seriously. One autumn, he ordered me out for a walk on a cold Sunday while it was raining, as he popped *Pulp Fiction* into the VCR. I walked around the neighborhood for over two hours, feeling sorry for myself and crying underneath the large protective trees outside the mansions near the university.

The complaints worked. Nadir bought me a NordicTrack treadmill and I was on it regularly. But mostly, I stopped eating. Within a few months, I went from a dress size of 8/10 down to 0/2. I was so happy when I first squeezed into a pair of size 0 pants. You could not get smaller than 0. It was as if you didn't even exist.

When my brother, Babai, visited and learned of my inability to feel close to Nadir, he explained that Muslim men sometimes have difficulty expressing themselves. He told me to cook well. The way to a man's heart is through his stomach, he explained. I should reach out to Nadir, show him and tell him that I love him. Babai also asked me questions about my love for Nadir, and my answer was the same as it had always been—I loved him but I was not in love with him. "Have you told him that you love him?" he asked, and I confessed that I had not.

The night that Babai left, I resolved to tell Nadir that I loved him. How would I say it? We barely spoke to each other. It would certainly be awkward. What if there was silence? What if he said nothing back? I had never said those words to anyone and it was embarrassing to think of uttering them.

That night, in bed, I stared toward the ceiling in the dark, egging myself on to say it. Just say it. It will make life better. He will open up. This has to end.

I tried to speak, but the words were empty. I struggled to swallow the lump in my throat. I tried but I couldn't seem to say anything. Finally I took a breath of air, said *"Bismillah-ir-Rahman-ir-Raheem"* to myself (which means "In the name of Allah, the Most Compassionate, the Most Merciful"), and let it out.

"I love you."

Silence. I looked over to see his reaction, but by then he was snoring. I rolled over and tried to sleep, feeling like an idiot. I was so embarrassed, but I thought it was better that he had not heard me. At least he had been spared the shame.

One time, I went to the hairdresser and agreed to let her try highlights. I came back with a full head of completely blond hair. When Nadir came home, he asked me what I had done to myself. Attempting to show him it wasn't something to get excited about, I told him I liked it. And besides, I asked, "What is wrong with it?" He replied, "Just look in the mirror. I would be embarrassed to walk down the street with you looking like that."

I wasn't sure why *he* should be embarrassed walking down the street with *me*. I had enough self-confidence to realize I was the young pretty thing, the trophy wife that made people on the street wonder who he must be to get *me*. Yet it still stung. He let out a laugh. "How could you do that to yourself?"

What he didn't understand was that I was not only trying out something new that I thought was fun, but hoping that this would make me beautiful in his eyes.

That was the one thing I longed for above all else—to be wanted, valuable. I had never received a compliment from him, and I quickly learned my new act wouldn't get me one.

It was at this point that I realized it didn't matter what I did— I would never be acceptable, attractive, or wanted in his eyes. And even if I was, I would never be told or truly appreciated. I wished that he would pay attention to me, give me a compliment. I wished that he would love me.

I entered a period of what Americans call soul-searching. Where I come from, it is called turning my face to God. I had tried in the past, quite unsuccessfully. My desire to prove wrong the American stereotypes about arranged marriage was driving me further into my misery. My marriage was supposed to be a source of warmth, but it was ice-cold. For a while, I felt I would rather burn slowly than freeze to death, alone.

I started to keep a journal, in which I struggled with God. At that time, I viewed God as another male that had made my life miserable. I was convinced that He was as eager to control me as my husband and father were. I wanted not to run, but to hide in a corner under a blanket and not to be seen by anyone. I wanted to become an object, to not know that feeling of being without warmth, happiness, or pain. I wished to dissolve under my blanket.

I began wanting to read the Qur'an in English. I started to explore religion. Growing up, I was taught that our interpretation of Islam and Qur'an was the *only* one. While exploring if there were other legitimate interpretations, I chanced upon a ridiculous one based on numerology. I found a few copies of the Qur'an at the local library, but gasped at their placement on the lowest shelf of the bookcase. Didn't the librarians realize how important this book was and that the proper place was higher on the shelf, preferably over everyone's head? I was so insulted that I hurriedly moved them all to the top shelf and left with one.

I began to read it that night, hoping that the Qur'an would give me answers to my life. I was lonely, and I sought the companionship of God. But I found the book hard to understand. The words were in Old English and it seemed outdated to me. Still, what I read raised questions about the way I was living my life. The Qur'an said that among the signs of God's greatness is that "He created for you mates from among yourselves that you may dwell in tranquility with them and He has put love and mercy between your hearts."

Sometimes, driving on the expressway, I imagined crossing over into the next lane and colliding head-on with an approaching car, or pressing on the accelerator as hard as I could and hitting a wall. I wouldn't make the tight rounded turn to the right onto the Long Island Expressway in Queens. Rather, I would look straight at the wall, fixate on a point, and be transported by sheer anger and misery directly into the depths of that solid piece of cement, never to be conscious again. For a few seconds, my body would feel the rush of the moment, then sharp pain, then nothing.

My soul was decayed; there was no longer any reason for it to occupy my body. I wanted it all to disappear. I wanted to feel nothingness.

My family would get a call from a concerned figure of authority on the other end, perhaps a police officer. "Ma'am, we're very sorry to tell you this, but your daughter has sustained severe injuries in a head-on collision. We don't think she'll make it." Suicide was a sin in Islam, but I questioned whether God would punish me. Surely He had to understand what I was going through, and know how much I had tried to make my life work. My God was one that would understand that, and have the capacity to forgive.

I craved an end to my loneliness and misery. I didn't want to be with anyone else, I couldn't think much beyond wanting my life to be over. Divorce simply wasn't an option—then.

A year after starting our life in Pittsburgh, we moved closer to New York City to be near our families. But even though there was less physical distance between us, I felt even more cut off from my family. I saw them almost once a week, when we would drive over to their Flushing apartment for an elaborate Afghan meal with rice and chicken *khourma*, a stew made with tomatoes and sautéed onions, the staple of almost every Afghan dish. I would always help out in the kitchen, or at least attempt to look busy while Nadir would chat wth my father. Oddly, these were some of our best times. These were the times I would learn what Nadir thought about the news and politics. He would laugh and be polite to my family. I suspected that my family didn't realize how

29

miserable I was, because this part of our life was very normal.

They couldn't understand what I was going through. They desperately wanted my marriage to work, and refused to believe that their choice for me made me unhappy. Later I learned that my mother had suspected I was unwell, but was afraid to say anything, lest she raise questions in my mind and make the situation even worse.

My mother said, "If I see a wound I try to heal it, not lodge my fingers into it and tear it into a gash." This was typical behavior for an Afghan family. When a woman has marital problems, friends and family try to ease her pain by minimizing its importance or seeking solutions that cause minimal disruption to the husband, even if the husband's words or actions cause immense pain for the woman. The truth was no one could confront the idea of my leaving Nadir, including myself. Nadir was, after all, a good man who worked hard and came home every night. Besides, there was no one else for me to marry because I would be much less eligible as a divorcée, and I had been too educated and ambitious to begin with. No, a divorce would put me in a whole new category, like the cold, leftover basmati rice you don't want to eat but feel too guilty to throw out.

Chapter 3

A Stranger's Garden

My heart is like a child: it cries,
and demands flowers from a stranger's garden.

—Afghan poet

I was young, beautiful, smart, funny, charming, and completely miserable. A doctor, not my husband, told me that I was in the prime of my life, physically and mentally. Learning and accepting that I was miserable was the hardest thing to do. What made the idea of divorce seem so impossible was that my parents were so proud that I was married to a doctor, and that my community was so envious of my "catch." I heard that many mothers wished their daughters could be married to such an accomplished person from a respectable family. My aunt recommended I wear a blue eye to ward off their jealous looks. Their envy could translate into evil toward me.

I felt like a child. Even though I was an adult at nineteen, attending college and maintaining the household, I didn't have control of my own life. A conversation between my mother and a relative in my kitchen played in my head. The woman was related to my mother and described her niece's prospects for college. The young woman's parents had decided to permit her to attend college away from home, recognizing that education was the key to their daughter's future, and that she should get the best there is. I knew the girl and knew *I* was a better student. If I tried really hard, maybe I could make it to a good college—maybe even to law school. I knew I'd never make it to Harvard, but I longed to try for the Ivy League. I also knew her parents, and always figured they were as conservative as mine. I was surprised to learn that they would let her go away to college and did not restrict her to living at home with them. I secretly wished they would restrict her. After all, that's what my parents did to me. I wanted to say how inappropriate it was for this girl to go away to school, but I also knew how ridiculous that was given I didn't actually *believe* it was inappropriate at all. I just wanted the same opportunity. I was surprised at how envious and bitter I felt. This must be how petty, evil people feel inside.

I would later write in my diary, "God, I so wish I could go to law school. . . . I think I can get into some of the best ones. I'm so damn tired of everyone limiting me. Maybe *I'm* limiting myself by listening to them."

I couldn't tell anyone how embarrassing it was to be in such a backward world. In the deepest parts of my mind I felt tired, beaten, cynical, and I knew that it would only get worse when the children came. I knew I would love my children, but that I would also resent them. That would make me even more miserable.

Nadir spoke of the luxury cars we would be able to purchase in less than a year, when he would attain the status of a specialist in the clinic. I imagined myself staring outside the window of a large house on top of a green hill with the Mercedes parked outside and two children running about the lawn, only I was in tears. I didn't want any of that.

If only I could have my own life. Sleeping on a mattress in a cramped space and working at Starbucks would be better than anything I could have with Nadir. At least I could laugh when I wanted to, think I looked pretty even if I wasn't, walk to work smiling at people, and be unafraid to look strangers in the face. I had even become afraid of looking into people's eyes. I could tell they knew I was lost, and I didn't know what to do with their pity. They could not help me.

Two and a half years after my wedding day, I was on my way to class at Queens College, the sun was in my eyes and my red turtleneck was "itching" me, as my younger sister would say. But suddenly, I didn't feel it anymore and felt like I was being directed by some other force. It was as if I lost control of my movements, but I was completely relaxed, and the car did not sway. Without resistance, my arms turned the steering wheel toward the exit. It was time.

In high school, soon after my parents had first asked me if I would agree to marry their choice, I was assigned *Madame Bovary* as a reading assignment for English class. As I read about her life, I couldn't help but feel that I was peering into my future. I wondered where I would get arsenic, if it was still being sold, and whether I might die some other way. I knew I tended to wrap myself in fantasies that had little to do with my life, so I dismissed my feelings as being too weak-minded to resist a dramatic book. While married, I thought of Madame Bovary often. Somehow I knew I would end up just like her—although I decided arsenic poison was too painful a death and a mistaken choice. I lived in a modern world, which called for a painless death.

I clutched the steering wheel and looked at myself in the rearview mirror. I *know* I'm beautiful, I thought. But so miserable. I felt like an adult looking at myself as a child. Weak, powerless, pushed around. I wondered why I hadn't done anything sooner. Fear was yesterday's threat. Today I was becoming an adult.

I drove through the tree-lined streets of Flushing to my parents' house. I parked the car, and without thinking I opened the front door with my keys and walked upstairs. I was on autopilot.

My mother, surprised to see me home, greeted me, *"Salaam-walaikum."* I put my bag down and started sobbing uncontrollably. I held my breath, then looked directly into her eyes. "I'm not going back. It's over."

I had finally accepted that I was miserable. I had failed. I had been in denial for months, perhaps the whole two and a half years we had been married.

"You know it's a mistake." My mother reminded me of the discussion we had had days earlier about my thoughts of leaving. She had said that I would regret leaving such a good man, that I should try harder and think about a happy marriage as the goal of a lifetime, and that it would be hard to find another man from a similar background who was so well educated.

I warned her that I would indeed be making "the mistake." I explained my position. "I know, it's *my* mistake. I'm not going back. I can go somewhere else, but I am returning here to keep your reputation." From my parents' point of view, it was incredibly important that I return to their house, rather than take an apartment or live anywhere else. It was bad enough for the local Afghan community that I was leaving my doctor husband. Anything but going back to my parents' house would have meant that I had been cheating on him and had probably run off with someone else. Even if this wasn't true, living apart would mean that I had been to blame, and my parents would be shamed for life for having raised such a reckless and loose daughter. Besides, I had become so isolated that I had no real friends, only acquaintances.

My father was immediately called at the office. "Come home. Masuda is here and she says she's not going back," my mother told him accusingly.

I hated that feeling of being turned in. I had been a bad girl. My daddy was being told all about it. I wanted to run out of there. I wanted to run, to disappear amid the nameless faces of New York City, never to be found again. But here I was, about to

confront my parents and then the world about the most personal and painful relationship of my life.

My parents pleaded with me not to leave my husband,
demanded to know whether there was someone else, and asked
why I wanted to ruin not only my own life but my husband's
too. My father said he wanted the best for me and had tried to
find the perfect match. They worried that I had come for help
too late to help make the marriage work. They told me to look
at what other Afghan girls were going through with their husbands, marrying men who weren't educated and who would
never let their wives go to college. They accused me of being
arrogant and acting like a queen.

But even my parents knew that there was no love between
Nadir and me after four years of knowing each other and almost
three spent living in the same house. I told my parents I couldn't
go back to empty rooms, long nights alone, weekends spent
barely talking to each other. When I was a little girl I dreamt that
my marriage would be an exciting chance to meet a new friend,
not a sentence to live as a ghost in my own house, tiptoeing
around, trying not to make noise or be heard.

My parents realized that I needed to come home, if just for a
few days to rest, so they agreed to take me in. Soon after, my
aunts and uncles began to visit. Months after she told me to
wear a blue eye to ward off jealousy, my eldest aunt in America,
Shakoko, confirmed that it had been the envy of others that
caused me to consider leaving my husband. She consoled me,
holding my head on her bosom as I released my tears. *"Bas, bas,"*
she said, which meant "Enough, enough."

Over the next few days I cried with more women, as friends and
distant relatives of my parents poured in to visit. After small talk
about family, they would announce the reason for their official
visit. "We're here to ask about Masuda. We are sad and upset." It
would start out as a vague conversation and progress as my

mother told them more details. Many were shocked about my leaving Nadir, not only because it was rare in the community but also because they had become too comfortable with the image of my perfect family.

A few of the women who came, especially those in their late forties and older, were particularly concerned about me. They would put me through the same line of questioning. Did he drink alcohol? I would say no. Did he go with other women? No. Did he beat you? No. Then confusion would overwhelm them. It was very hard for them to understand why I was putting my family through such a crisis if none of their criteria for a bad husband had been fulfilled.

"So you don't *like* him?" Sometimes it was so hard to get through this question that I would start crying. Then they would say *"Bas, bas"* and hold me to their bosom. This would often be followed by stories of how horribly women in Afghanistan had been treated by particular men they knew. It was then that I learned that one very distant relative in Afghanistan brought women home to have affairs with "in broad daylight." His wife knew, but there was nothing she could do. I didn't know how this was supposed to make me feel better.

Janni Gul, a wise elder relative who had more grandchildren than I could count, told me she had had many problems when she got married as well. "Yes, Bibi, it was very hard in the begin-ning. But it takes a man ten years. You have to be patient." I didn't know quite what she meant, but I burst into another orchestra of tears, feeling sorry for myself, with ten years as my only hope. "You have to give a man ten years' time. He will soften up. He will see you have bore him children. And age makes a man tender."

I didn't know whom to feel sorry for, myself or the woman trying to console me. All of us knew that Janni Gul had lived with an extremely temperamental husband, a thin, tall man with a very long white beard. I was being given advice by women who had lived with some of the most difficult men fate could have found for them. Yet they were somehow happy.

That is why I had reluctantly agreed to an arranged marriage in the first place. As one Muslim woman had told me, "In Western weddings you have love then marriage. In the East you have marriage then love." I saw that men and women in arranged marriages tended to be happier than those in "love marriages."

I had once watched an episode of *20/20* about how arranged marriages boast an incredibly low rate of divorce, compared to the almost 50 percent divorce rate in America. John Stossel wondered if Easterners in arranged marriage had it better than Americans. Even then, I felt like yelling at the television, "Of course they have a lower divorce rate! Women can't *get* a divorce!" In Pakistan and Afghanistan, for example, women are denied the easy access to a divorce that men have. They have to apply to a court and show special circumstances that satisfy the strictest brand of Islamic law. Some liberal Islamic scholars argue that, in actuality, it should be easier for women to obtain a divorce because the Prophet Muhammad told women that they could get a divorce if they were unhappy with their husbands. But that is a minority view, especially in poor countries. Also, cultures that practice arranged and especially forced marriage generally have a poor record on women's rights, and the women usually don't have the education or the economic resources to leave their homes.

Many of the elder women from the community felt I had not waited long enough to fall in love. As much as I wanted to believe in the wisdom of my elders, I felt it would never happen.

A few months later, the community attempted to repair my marriage in a very public way. Nadir was sitting across from me on a mattress laid alongside a wall in my parents' home. (Afghans usually place velvet-covered mattresses along the perimeter of their rooms, using them as living and dining room seating, and even for napping.) We were surrounded by his friends, my relatives, and a few elder members of the community.

"Look, I'm sorry. I never wanted to hurt you," Nadir said. It was the first time I had heard his voice since I had left him. It was also the first time I had heard an apology from him. Despite several bouquets of flowers and cards that used the previously undeclared "I love you," I had refused to talk to him.

Now we were arguing before an audience of judges. I didn't say much. The elders spoke about the importance of working on a marriage, especially an arranged one. "We're not American," said Rashid, his friend who had traveled all the way from California with his wife. "We don't just give up and say it's over. You have to try. Marriage requires effort." I felt like jumping out of my seat and screaming that I had never tried harder at anything than my marriage. None of these people knew the truth.

"He really loves you," everyone said. I didn't know what to make of this, but I respected Rashid and his wife, and remembered that he had always been particularly kind to me. During the meeting, Nadir got angry trading accusations with me and stormed out of the house. But Rashid walked out to bring him back in.

Eventually, Nadir looked at me and said, "Maybe this is what it took for me to realize how valuable you are to me—that I do in fact love you." I couldn't believe my ears. I had never imagined Nadir saying those words to me in front of everyone else. In fact, I had never heard him say "I love you," *ever*. I felt embarrassed for him that he had to express his feelings in front of everyone, especially because he was such a private person, but his doing so proved that he did have feelings for me.

A few hours after the delegation left, I spoke with my older brother, Babai. He had become a mediator between me and my parents. Babai was a little over two years older than me, and he understood me better than most of my family. Although he was not an elder, his age and role in the family meant that his opinion mattered. After I left Nadir and refused to get out of bed for months, Babai would try to coax me into going outside. He would do this by claiming to be bored, saying he really needed someone to play tennis with. Along with my mother and sisters, Babai increasingly tried to spend more time with me, knowing that slowly and with their love I would come out of my heaviness. Sitting on Babai's bed, we both said we thought the meeting went well, and what a great ending it would be to go back that night. I went to my room for a few minutes and imagined what would happen if I really said yes. So I agreed to go back, believing that we could build on the day's expressions of love and understanding.

When Moor found out, she called Nadir's family's house. Nadir and his brother were together, talking about politics and life with friends, as they did on many Saturday nights. I summarized my family's reaction in my diary: "Nice surprise for everyone. SHE'S GOING BACK!!! SHE'S GOING BACK!!!"

Everyone was so happy with me. All of a sudden light was brought back into my mother's face. Shakoko was relieved. They were so glad to help me pack my things. "Go home," everybody said. "Go home."

This time I was staying for good, I thought. I deeply wanted my marriage to work. I wished that I could somehow be a better wife. I still loved the security of marriage. I did not want to go out into the big bad world to be harassed by men, without an anchor, without a protector. I would make it work.

Nadir drove over to pick me up. His broad smile revealed his perfect pearly teeth and made me instantly nervous. I was strangely happy for him, but terribly sad for myself. He opened the door of his car for me, something that had never happened before. We had little to talk about, and I realized how uncomfortable the familiar feeling had been. I must have been used to it before, but now it seemed wrong to have to search so hard for words. How could he possibly want me back? I had nothing left to offer him.

Whatever desire I once had to give of myself, and love him as a husband, was gone. Nadir must have thought we were going to start over. There were no comments about the weight I had put on since leaving. He was gentle and asked me about school and my family, but to me he didn't seem genuine. The awkward silences were unbearable. His entire presence was offensive. I wanted to scream, kick, and hurl things at him. But I also felt deeply sorry for him. I cared for him and did not want him to be sad and lonely. Maybe I just needed to try harder.

One night, after I had come back, Nadir was working a thirty-six-hour shift. I had slept through the day on the black leather couch, which seated two. My head was on the armrest when I woke up. I imagined living in Queens, cooking and cleaning the house every day, continuing an education I could never use, never seeing my life change or grow, forgetting what it was like to feel joy or togetherness. I wished I could've slept longer. I had no desire to watch TV, to speak with anyone, even to eat. Mostly, I did not want my mind to be awake. I tried to sleep again, and I closed my eyes. I wished to be discarded. To be thrown away like an empty pack of cigarettes, the foil frayed at the top, bits of tobacco at the bottom. I would lie in the gutter, trampled on, and dissolve into the sewer's dirty water and discarded things—old keys, gum wrappers, bits of paper with addresses on them, the past no longer remembered. I wished to disappear and be absorbed by all that is meant to disappear.

As I was having these thoughts, I suddenly remembered that Nadir had some pills he would take when he needed to sleep. He would take half a pill from the amber-colored cylinder container. I went to the bedroom, sat on his side of the bed, and opened the drawer to the night table. There it was, a deep yellow-orange color. It appeared to glow inside the drawer. I picked it up and read the label. Patient's Name: Nadir. Valium, 10 mg.

Perfect. I longed to sleep. I was so tired. Then, as if I were acting out my fate, I emptied the whole container into the middle of my palm. I only wished there were more pills. I did not count them. I did not wish to analyze what I was doing. I only wanted to be driven by my gut desire to fulfill my fate. I only wanted to act. I wanted my mind to rest. I felt a chill come over my body, but I was calm. It was almost as if I had a sense of peace that I had never experienced before. I was resigned to my fate. And I was actively fulfilling it. This was what I had to do. It was the only thing I could do.

I closed the pill container, now empty, and put it back in the drawer, closing it. I walked over to the kitchen sink and filled a glass with water. Then I carefully swallowed pill after pill and went to the couch to lie down. Not knowing how much time had passed, I came to again and felt dizzy. I remembered there was a large bottle of vodka a doctor had given Nadir as a gift, which had remained untouched and stored in our second bedroom. Somewhere I had heard, perhaps on television, that mixing Valium with alcohol could be deadly.

As I walked to the bedroom, I felt as if I were acting out my role in a play. I was a natural, playing my role without any hesitation or feeling of doubt. Only I noticed the room was spinning. I struggled to keep my balance, reminding myself that the earth was steady. I lifted the large bottle of Stoli clear poison to my mouth. I had never tasted alcohol before, and I cannot remember the taste of the colorless liquid. By then my senses had been numbed. My taste buds were in a coma.

I did not know what happened until I opened my eyes to the vague sound of a familiar voice, shaking me and calling my name. It was Nadir. He was in his purple scrubs and tortoise-shell glasses, a tired and concerned look on his face. The way his deep, black, liquid eyes seemed to reach out to me from his tired face, their gaze unwavering, worried me.

"Are you okay?"

I looked at him, confused. I had failed. I wished that I could have ended it all. It would have been painless. Now it was time to face him.

"You threw up?"

I didn't know what he meant. I had no recollection of what had happened in the last twenty-four hours. I did not want to speak. I wished that he could have been gone longer.

"I'm fine." I walked to the bathroom to get away from him. I needed to collect myself in private. As I walked I noticed a rather large yellowish stain caked on the carpet. I must have thrown up.

When I came out of the bathroom Nadir was rubbing the carpet with a wet hand towel. I didn't know what to say. I was embarrassed by what I had done. I felt like a child. He asked me if I wanted to go to the doctor, almost as if he had to ask. I said no. He did not ask again. He still seemed worried, however. I was not sure if his concern was out of love or some feeling of responsibility. Or if he wanted to protect himself from wrongdoing in case he was questioned in the future. He suggested I could consider therapy.

I left again a few weeks after that. This time for good. As my cousin Agha Jan and my brother drove with me to pick up my belongings from the apartment, Agha Jan went over the rules with me. "Remember," he said, "you have to be sure about this. Don't think that this means you can now go out and do whatever you want. You might want to go out with your girlfriends, your friends, but you will have responsibilities. This does not mean freedom." I nodded, but inside I was rolling my eyes.

I decided to leave the marriage and become a woman because I had no other choice. I had tried it every other way. I also realized that being married was not being an adult. Being an adult was making my decision and facing the consequences.

I resented what I could not do. I thought I would experience youth and American culture *with* my husband. There was the implicit idea that what you cannot do in your father's household, you may be able to do in your husband's household. An Afghan relative once told me, if it's not your father that's controlling you, it will be your husband. I realized that my husband did not want me to experience American culture the way I needed to. I wanted to go to a music concert, dye my hair blond, go to the opera, experience ballet, visit the beach, and have nice dinners together.

I also wanted to have American friends. But none of the American girls my age were married. Mostly they went dating or dancing on girls' night out, and it wouldn't be appropriate for me to join them. I felt so lonely. My husband's social set was small and older, with an average age of forty-five.

At the same time, Nadir didn't want me to be Afghan. He said Afghan women have nothing better to do than gossip all the time. When I wanted to get my hair done in the salon for a wedding, he wanted me to do my own hair. "Afghan women always go to the salon," he complained. They were too concerned with the way they looked. He preferred that we didn't relate to other Afghans, because of their uneducated, backward ways.

I knew I was more valuable than I felt. I had lost the weight, prepared great meals, entertained guests, and achieved perfect grades once I went back to college. I was all I was supposed to be and I didn't get what I wanted to get from my husband. All of the things that I tried, things I was told would work—looking beautiful, being sweet, learning to cook, and cleaning the house—did not get me what I wanted, to be loved by my husband. Because of that, I didn't even love myself.

It was the most intense, soul-searching time that I have ever experienced and probably ever will. I questioned everything—

from my relationship with my parents to my desire for children, my religion, my sexuality, my fears, and my concept of right and wrong. My dilemma became: Was it better to pursue individual freedom at the cost of shaking up a lifelong commitment, and upsetting not only my family but the entire community?

I loved the security of the marriage, but I hated the feeling of choking.

My husband and I were both part Afghan and part American. We both wanted to preserve the best values and traditions that both cultures had to offer. He wanted me to be subservient like an Afghan wife but isolated from my community like an American one. I wanted to live the independence of an American with the connectedness to family and community of a Muslim Afghan. As if mixing flowers from two bouquets, he chose the flowers he wanted me to be, but I wanted what was left.

Chapter 4

The Little, Little Masuda

Every child is born a Muslim.

> —Saying attributed to the Prophet Muhammad
> (Peace Be Upon Him)

When I returned home to live with my parents after my separation, they expected me to also return to being the Masuda they knew before I left to get married. One night, as I was reading in bed, Moor even tucked me in under my old fluffy comforter with the crisp white background and pink-colored flowers and said, "You are the old Masuda again. The little, little Masuda. You are like when you were sixteen." It was clear that she was unrealistically—desperately—hoping that the old rules of growing up would apply. She was unsure of how to navigate the uncharted waters we had now embarked upon.

Moor had good reason to be nervous. She also knew that once a young person experiences a relationship intended to be romantic, whether it goes well or not, some switch has been turned on that is almost impossible to turn off. A saying of the Prophet Muhammad warns Muslims against staying single and instructs them to marry in order to avoid temptation. Indeed, I have observed that young people in America almost never stop dating once they start, whether that is at the age of twelve, fifteen, or eighteen. While I had no desire to have a relationship with anyone at the time or, as I thought, perhaps ever again, in the deepest part of me I knew that this too would pass and life would begin again—as it did, slowly, after months of sleep and rest. I pursued a college degree in economics and business, found a job, and began to make friends. The beginning of my new life coincided with spring, and twenty years after my birth I felt as if I were starting to grow again.

Moor hoped that I would marry again quickly. None of our relatives ever had to deal with a divorced woman. In Afghanistan, men rarely divorced their wives. Rather, they would sort of just stop dealing with them, and the women would continue to live in the in-laws' household, especially if there were children involved. Going back to your "father's house" was a big shame for the woman, her family, and her in-laws. It just didn't happen culturally. It was better to live in misery with your in-laws than to be seen as a woman who was discarded or, worse, as a woman who deserted her obligations as a wife. Women in Afghanistan usually could not get divorces, certainly not under the Taliban, and even now it is extremely difficult. An Afghan police officer told an American reporter in 2002 that Afghan women fleeing from forced marriages performed under the Taliban are still being jailed rather than granted the divorces they seek.[1]

One morning, I thought I heard the sound of a bird singing the Western wedding song in our backyard in Flushing. *Doo-di-doooo-doooo. Doo-di-doooo-doooo.* I wondered if this was a message to me. Would I be getting married soon? Was God trying to tell me something by speaking through these birds? I always wondered if God was speaking to me through messages in newspapers, storefront signs, or other symbols I stumbled upon in everyday life. I always wanted to be alert, to listen, and not to dismiss anything. In my openness to God I sometimes created endless confusion for myself. Like when I was trying to decide whether I should stay with my husband or leave him. I encountered many omens, all of which said different things. It was very frustrating. Why couldn't God just be direct with me? Ultimately I got my answer, but it came from within myself rather than through something else.

The little girl that Moor wanted me to be again was the perfect Pashtun Muslim girl who laughed quietly, spoke even more quietly, and often relied on the opinions of her parents over her own. Moor spent most of my life raising me to be a good wife to a man someday. A good girl, and therefore a good wife, wouldn't complain or make trouble for anyone, could resist temptation and bad influences, and would put up with a heavy load of chores and family responsibilities without objecting or even breathing too loudly. She and my father wanted me to be first and foremost a good Muslim, then a good cook and housecleaner, with sewing and embroidery skills as additional requirements.

My parents wanted my older brother and me to grow up as good Muslims in the land of the infidels, so they enrolled us in a weekend *madrassa*, or religious school, in Brooklyn. The problem was that there was no community of Afghans, and the only thing that came close was an informal operation run by Pakistanis, which they found out about from our Pakistani neighbors, who also sent their children. Every Saturday and Sunday, we were forced to wake up early, miss weekend cartoons and playing with Joon and Jeannie, our Korean brother-sister neighbors, and walk with a group of Pakistani children to an apartment building a few blocks away. Then, we would sit with our legs crossed on large rugs through lectures given in Urdu, and though they reluctantly agreed to speak in English for my brother and me, they ultimately preferred to stick to Urdu because it was more comfortable for them and, they probably felt, more important than speaking in English. Religious instruction seemed more like gibberish to me then, between the Urdu and Arabic that was never translated for us, but my parents considered it vital that their children receive appropriate Islamic training. Sometimes they would cave under the pressure of our complaints and ask our neighbor to tell the teacher to explain things in English, but he would only explain bits and pieces of the conversation after many minutes of speaking.

Perhaps it didn't matter what language they spoke in. Most of the time we dealt in Arabic, learning to read the Qur'an or reciting it by rote. The irony was that for as much as the Qur'an was praised and its importance repeated, we were never actually told to read a translation to understand what it *means*. I later entered a more progressive *madrassa* at a mosque where they quoted the Qur'an in English and gave us a book of stories about the prophets to read. Even the progressive teachers never, not once, gave us the book of God in a language we could understand, or encouraged us to read it.

There were strict rules in the *madrassa* about everything from appearance and dress to conduct. It was a requirement to wear *hijab*, the Islamic head covering, to class. I usually dressed in Pakistani-style *shalwar kameez*, which is Urdu for long shirt and pants, loose-fitting clothes that covered me to my wrists and down to my ankles. I did not wear *hijab* regularly, but would wear it when a conservative family visited my parents' home as guests, whenever I went to the mosque, and at funerals. *Hijab* was also to be worn whenever I prayed or read the Qur'an.

At the *madrassa* it was inappropriate to wear rings or nail polish to class. Knowing it was frowned upon and wanting to be a good student, I was always extremely embarrassed and disappointed when I glanced down at my toes and realized I had forgotten to remove my polish. I hoped they wouldn't notice but they always did, without fail, and handed me the remover and tissue, ordering me to go to the bathroom. According to most Muslims, the required washing in preparation of prayer involves washing of the hands and fingernails; if your nails are painted, then you are unable to wash them and are therefore too unclean to approach God in prayer.

I did not, and do not to this day, understand why color on your fingernails means you cannot be clean enough to pray, especially with an all-knowing God, but questioning Islam is certainly not something we were encouraged to do. My often incessant questioning directed at my father or my teachers got me only so far. When I was ten or eleven, I kept asking why, after being taught that every person's fate is determined by God, I was also taught that those who did not obey God's rules were going to Hell. "If God really wanted a man to be a good Muslim, why couldn't He just make him into one?" I would also ask, "Why do we have to bend over and take so many different physical positions when we pray?" Later, when I learned that there was in fact a dispute in the media among Islamic scholars about whether the Qur'an really required women to wear veils, I asked my relatives about it. Just like all the other times, the answer was, "Those are not real Muslims." The majority knows the truth, my relatives believed. The majority of Muslims are conservative, especially by Western standards, which is why I considered myself to be a Republican until recently. The conservative family values of the Republicans appeal to the Muslim mind's political temperament, similar to the way conservative Christians feel. I even voted for President Bush.

In the new *madrassa* I always listened quietly and attentively, not asking a lot of questions, to the point of being called a brownnoser by the other Afghan kids. One day, toward the end of the year, our teacher said that there was one exceptional student in the class. All the kids craned their necks, thinking the best student would betray himself somehow. But the teacher extended his finger, spun around the room, and stopped when he got to me. I had become the best Qur'anic student in my class, and I was learning how to read and recite in Arabic much faster than before.

My burgeoning ability to recite the Qur'an in Arabic made Agha very proud, because he is recognized in the Afghan community as a Qari, or reciter of the Qur'an for community events such as engagement ceremonies, gatherings at the mosque, and funerals. He even gave the opening Qur'anic reading when the Afghan-American community gathered at Queens College to welcome President Karzai to New York. Although he often worked seven days a week at the time, Agha spent many Sunday afternoons teaching me how to recite the Qur'an in Arabic. On those afternoons, Agha's voice box would exhaust itself and his face would glow red with love for God and the Qur'an. He would recite so loudly that my mother was incapable of speaking on the telephone from anywhere in the apartment, and his eyes would tear up from holding the "heeeeem" in *Bismillah-ir-Rahman-ir-Raheem* (In the name of Allah, the Most Compassionate, the Most Merciful). After holding his note so long, and my wondering whether we were there for me to learn or for him to practice, he would turn to me and tell me to repeat. This was when I tried most to impress him, but I was embarrassed to be as passionate as him when I recited. I would take a deep breath and begin, never quite getting it right.

I didn't realize how proud Agha was of me until we were living in Queens and the Afghan neighbors living below us told Agha how wonderful it was to hear the Qur'anic recitations streaming in through their window live in the summer. He replied by saying, "Put Masuda in a contest with five hundred girls—no, five hundred boys *and* girls, and she will win." While other families taught their children, more often their boys, how to read the Qur'an, Agha taught me how to recite it aloud. Though I have not practiced reciting Qur'an in many years, I still dream of one day reciting it the way my father does. For now, he pours his hopes into my youngest sister, Aziza, who recently finished reading the Qur'an through in Arabic, by no means an easy task, as one billion Muslims know.

• • •

Reciting the Qur'an with Agha was one way to remember God. Throughout my deep depression, in my period of soul-searching, and even as I considered seeking a divorce, I invoked God constantly. In deciding what to do about my marriage I spoke to Him often, asking for a sign, any advice He could give me. I prayed to Him, promising that I would sacrifice many sheep and cows if He helped me to be closer to my husband. "Just make it happen," I pleaded.

I had turned to Islam in my time of most need, and even though I sometimes even cursed God for not being responsive to me, I ultimately begged Him to help me, and in the end He delivered. Although I had to do most of the work, He made sure that my efforts would succeed. Looking back, I realize that God has always answered my prayers. It has always taken Him awhile, and I have usually had to suffer in the meantime, but somehow, eventually, what I have requested always comes true. Once, frustrated while studying the night before final exams in college, I let out a huge sigh and as if I were on autopilot, I let my breath out, saying, "Ohhh God, you know best," in Pashto. I had never uttered those words before and shocked myself the moment I realized I had said them, because this was a phrase commonly used by elders. I had heard it many times from Moor, and somehow it must have registered in my mind. Remembering God was the one duty in Islam that my parents seemed to overfulfill. It was like the vitamin C of Islam—you could never have too much. The Qur'an says that the human heart finds satisfaction in the remembrance of God, and that God remembers those who remember Him.

The importance of remembering God was something I heard about a lot growing up. When I fell down in our backyard in Flatbush, Brooklyn, where I grew up before moving to Queens, scraping my knee against the uneven cement, Moor said that God would make it better. When she would argue with my father, she would say that God knows best, and when she would hear about a crisis happening with the family in Afghanistan, she would say that only God knows their fate. "May God grant them safe passage," she would say.

Praying five times a day was another way to remember God. Although most Muslims believe that it is required to pray five times a day by facing Mecca and reciting certain verses from the Qur'an, I didn't always pray. My parents always begged us to pray regularly and praised us when we did.

My parents have become more religious over the years. Moor often says that "the older people get, the closer to death, the more they turn to God." And the more religious my family gets, the more the community respects us. When Moor, my sister Sara, and my brother went on a pilgrimage to Mecca, known as the *Hajj* in Arabic, members of the community were clearly impressed. How wonderful it is, they commented, that even Sara has become a *Hajjana* at the young age of eighteen. Among Afghans a *Hajjana*, or a woman who has completed *Hajj*, is usually an elder woman preparing for coming face-to-face with her God on Judgment Day by visiting the holy places of the Qur'an. Soon after they returned from their pilgrimage, Sara received a number of wedding proposals from families that now viewed her as a more desirable match for their sons. Certainly, this was another way for the community to judge her purity and innocence, and it helped to offset, in their eyes, some of the bad influence that my life had upon my younger sisters. After my divorce, my parents, particularly my father, were concerned that I would have a negative influence on my sisters. By working, and being independent, I would make them want to do the same, which would steer them away from arranged marriages. Worse, the community would use my actions to judge my sisters. The best indication of a girl's character is the behavior of her family—her mother and sisters, especially. Moor worried that Sara would receive few wedding proposals, but she has done just fine, mostly because she has maintained her own image in the community, and now she is respected for her religious piety and familial devotion.

The experience of going to *Hajj*, as Sara explained it to me, was not nearly as awe-inspiring or even as spiritual as I had expected it to be. Most of it seems to involve overnight buses, standing in endless lines, struggling through enormous crowds, and performing prescribed rituals in a hurry before rushing on to the next set. It is a physically demanding journey, marked by action and sweat and hardship. The pilgrims sleep in tents, eat group meals together, and live among hundreds of thousands of people performing the same rituals over the same number of days. In a way it is like the Woodstock of Islam, multitudes of like-minded people converging to celebrate what really matters to them. I have learned that I cannot expect a journey of any kind, whether to Afghanistan or Mecca, to enlighten me as to my path in life. Rather, I feel I must be ready to observe, gain perspective, and continually be surprised and disappointed. I look forward to the day when I will join the Islamic *umma*, or community, in my pilgrimage to Mecca—but I know that I must be prepared for it. The preparation of my mind and soul for this once-in-a-lifetime journey will be transforming in itself. I also know that it may not bring the answers I have hoped it will. The answers, or at least my version of them, need to be figured out entirely on my own—with help from God.

The Qur'an says of the pilgrimage to Mecca that men will come "on foot and mounted on every kind of camel," on "journeys through deep and distant mountain highways." My father tells me the story of my grandfather riding to *Hajj* on horseback from Afghanistan. It took him two years to return home over the thousands of miles. Presumably, he spent weeks or months at the cities and villages along the way, including Herat, where his first wife was from and where my family still has claim to a home with eleven bedrooms. Sara and I dream of returning someday, spending time in legendary Herat, having picnics and browsing for Persian carpets in the bazaar. Afghans who have seen it speak with veneration of the magnificent nearly five-hundred-year-old mosque in Herat, which is adorned with exquisite geometrical tile work in brilliant blues and has been called one of the most beautiful examples of Islamic architecture in the world. The city's seven-hundred-year-old earthen citadel has eighteen guard towers and is said to have been built on the foundation of an even older fortress erected by Alexander the Great, during his campaign to Afghanistan prior to the birth of Jesus. Someday, Sara and I hope to see this too.

My grandfather would also ride on horseback, with his caravan, to the Soviet Union, where he would sell dried fruits and nuts. He did this regularly, until on one trip he spent most of his fortune on fruits and nuts and headed out with his largest caravan ever, only to find that prices had dropped drastically. He lost much of his fortune on that transaction. My father remembers the time as being very difficult for the family. It greatly influenced my father, causing him to fear that any day could be the day that we lose everything we have worked for over the years.

Growing up, I was always interested in what my father and the other men were saying at family events. While the women were speaking about clothes and family, and gossiping about this one and that one, the men would get loud, arguing about the news and whether the latest development was good for Afghanistan. I wanted to engage them and point out how truthful or idiotic some of their statements were. But this was usually inappropriate. Speaking too openly with men, even in family settings, is seen as flirtation. One time, I joined a conversation among men thinking that the presence of my father and husband was protection enough. However, Nadir told me months later that this behavior had been very inappropriate for a woman. Besides, at mixed events the men are almost always seated at the end of the room opposite the women, and sometimes in an entirely different room, so I would catch their conversation only when walking by or when I successfully tuned out the women's chat. But then I couldn't be too obvious about that because the women would think I was arrogant if I didn't pay attention to them.

I never could understand, nor do I today, why the women wouldn't talk about such topics. If they did, they had very practical views of politics and current affairs. It was often the view that men do what they want no matter what happens, that war destroys everyone, especially women, and that women have to take care of the men, who are often driven by pride or naiveté. It was as if men were children, who got too excited and caught up in their emotions. They believed men started wars because they didn't know how else to handle themselves, not because they had a just cause or a smart plan. I was reminded of these women's words when I read reports in the media that the seventy virgins that suicide bombers and the 9/11 hijackers believed would be their reward in Paradise might really be seventy *raisins*, depending on how you translated the word *houri* from Arabic. Something in me wants to believe that the Islamic world's catastrophes may all result from a minor misunderstanding of one word, which snowballed into anger, conspiracy, and death. But I know that more than one word created the world's problems and divisions.

The Afghan women I have met often speak with deep wisdom about the chaos of the age they have lived through. Many women have said that they saw the world "turned upside down." As my mother once remarked, "Look at so-and-so, they were so wealthy and stylish, but now in America they are barely getting by. But look at this other family, they used to be so poor in Afghanistan, and now they have a nice apartment and two cars."

For many Afghans who planned to live and die in a Muslim country, just living in the land of the infidels was a hardship. My uncle's wife, who came here in her seventies, would often pass judgment on American society. She would call Americans infidels and tell me not to associate with them, ever. I have always wondered why conservative Muslims bothered to come to America at all if they hated the way of life so much. On the one hand, it is great that they see this place as welcoming to all kinds of people, and it reminds me of the early settlers who came here to practice their religions free from persecution. But it angers me to see old people complaining about how free this society is, and trying to "protect" their families from it by constantly telling them how horrible it is that there are half-naked people on television. I really wanted to ask my aunt why she lived in America if she hated its people. I never had the courage to ask her, and she died just two years into her stay here. I think she would have probably answered the way most Afghan elders I know have answered, which is that they're here for their children. *But what are their children here for?*

In the New York City public schools, the challenge was not the Arabic of the Qur'an but the English of our textbooks. I came to the United States when I was five, not knowing a word of English. I remember the first day of school at PS 119 in Brooklyn like it was yesterday. I was so excited to go to school, because I had watched my older brother come and go into a different world with a book bag and important assignments. He brought home news from this legendary place, made friends, and became smart enough to make fun of my parents' pronunciation of English words. Until that time, we always played together, but he had been summoned to do serious work. If only I was allowed to enter the school building with him and given a seat, I would show him, I thought. When my first day of school arrived, Moor dropped me off in the school yard, telling me to line up with the other children and that she would come back to pick me up later. I waited and waited, and occasionally a student would say something to me, but I didn't understand, so I just shook my head, as if to say no. Finally, our teacher appeared, an elegant white lady with yellowish gray hair who smiled and seemed so nice. "Miss-is Druck-er," I repeated to myself over and over again at home so that I would pronounce her name correctly. It was the most important English phrase that I had memorized, but I would learn many more in kindergarten. Within a year or two, I was one of the best students in my class.

Although I learned English quickly, for many years I was mistaken about a number of expressions. While watching Saturday morning cartoons, I would often hear the television calling my name. At the end of a segment they would sing, "After these Masudays, we'll be right back." Obviously, they were saying "messages" rather than "Masudays," the plural version of my name in Pashto. For many years, I also thought that the jingle in the Kentucky Fried Chicken commercials was "We do chicken rice!" Chicken with rice was perhaps the most common dinner in our home. In the winter, after battling through the New York City slush, the smell of Moor's chicken with sautéed onions and thick tomato sauce, or *khourma*, told you that all would soon be well.

The most awkward mistake by far, however, involved very important American words, *prostitute* and *Protestant*. I thought they were one and the same, although I didn't know what either word meant. I had heard people say they were Protestant, but never had a reaction to it because I didn't know the meaning, and I never bothered to ask because it was assumed that I would know. One day, as a young teen, I finally asked my father what a prostitute was, after watching a segment on Peter Jennings's *World News Tonight*. "May you never have to know what that is," he answered. I was confused. I had met people that had told me very proudly that they were prostitutes. The next time I saw a sign on the street that said PROTESTANT, I walked by quickly, ashamed to know anything about them. It took me a few years to realize my error.

I admired Mrs. Drucker more and more as I got to know her,

and I always felt I had a special place in her heart. That belief was confirmed when, in third grade, as a student of her daughter's, I came into class one day with a very short and very bad haircut perpetrated by Moor with a pair of old scissors from Afghanistan. I walked into class with the hood of my coat on, refusing to take it off, even when the kids around me kept asking why I kept it on and insisted that I show my head. Finally, the teacher told me to take off my coat, *and hood*, and when I did all the children started to laugh and call me a boy, exactly as I feared they would. I cried and cried that day. The next day I was told I had a visitor waiting in the hallway. It was Mrs. Drucker! She handed me a little red basket with a miniature-sized strawberry-scented shampoo and conditioner, and told me it was a special gift for me to wash my hair with so that it would grow.

Mrs. Drucker would watch me, the shy girl, eventually run for school president in fifth grade. My campaign platform sucked— I said I would bring back chorus—and I lost to a boy who had more cool appeal. After I saw that my competitor had plastered posters with his picture in the hallways, I instructed my campaign manager to do the same, but by then it was too late—we looked like we were "copying" Dexter. I knew I was in trouble when, on voting day, I sat across from Samantha, the cool girl who wore short skirts, and watched as she danced her pen around my name, then looked up at me as if to make sure I was looking and marked a check next to his. Later, when we were called into the principal's office for the results, she shook my hand, told me I had done a good job, but that I was not the next president. I'm sure my face was flushed, because the embarrassment of losing was awful. I was already not considered cool, and my pathetic campaign would not help my image.

There were many reasons why I wasn't considered cool growing up. My parents had cool radar, only their reaction was always to avoid anything that would make us cool. It was their policy. Mainly, they were afraid that if we focused on looking a particular way, that would take us away from our studies. Also, in their experience, students who were cool also tended to be more popular, and popular students did not do well in school. Their goal was to make sure we didn't become too confident, or too liked, and they knew just how to do that.

I had to dress conservatively in elementary and junior high, which was certainly not going to earn me any cool points. Because none of the shops we frequented sold dresses that were acceptably covering, I often had dresses made at home, by Afghan relatives. The sleeves were often short, because that was allowed for me, but the hemline reached beyond my knee, usually closer to my ankle. The skirt was often three-tiered, the fabric flowered, purchased from the Pakistani fabric sellers that Moor could bargain down to a better price.

I hated the way I was dressed. Mostly, I was embarrassed to be seen. One time, I wore one of those dresses to school picture day, and a girl told me I looked like her grandmother. Oh, the shame! The irony was that I applied the same concept of shame that I had grown up with, an element of Pashtunwali, or the implicit code of conduct among Pashtuns, to situations that involved Westerners. My sense of shame was so profound, it often stopped me from speaking if I thought there was even a remote chance the person would not like what I said. Still I dreamed about what it would be like to wear cool clothes and be judged based on what I said or did, not how I looked in my old-lady dresses.

At elementary school graduation, I wore a red lace dress that was somewhat better, but when I got to school nobody was wearing anything like it, especially not the color red. One of the teachers called me "the lady in red" but I didn't get the reference, thinking that she meant I looked older, like an old lady, in my red dress. At least I had done better than "grandmother" this time. I was asked to give a speech that day, and I delivered, even making the audience laugh at times. I put extra effort into my speech, because I knew I would not look good. At least I might be thought of fondly for delivering a good speech, I hoped. It was only years later that I learned why I was asked to deliver that speech. I was valedictorian of my elementary school class! I had no idea at the time. That I went from not speaking a word of English to being class valedictorian I owe to Mrs. Drucker and all the other great teachers who looked out for me in Brooklyn.

For years, Moor refused to let me wear blue jeans, the ultimate symbol of cool. It was as if blue jeans were some forbidden thing, and putting them on would mean that I had become American and would never be the same. That is pretty much what happened when I got my first pair. I was in seventh grade, and we were in a mall in Virginia visiting an older Afghan couple that had been our neighbors in Brooklyn. We went to the mall, and the woman, Spoozhmai, began to try on jeans, asking Moor if she wanted a pair. I was about to choke. Moor? Wearing a pair of jeans? Ha! I think Moor did realize, though, how ridiculous it would be for an older Afghan woman to wear jeans when I couldn't. I got Spoozhmai to suggest that I try on a pair, and I walked out of the department store with brand-new jeans. I loved putting on the jeans that had a bow in the back, and below that a zipper that reached to the very bottom. I thought I was the coolest girl in town when I wore those jeans. I felt unstoppable.

When I finally made it to the headquarters of American teenage fashion, the Gap, I was thrilled. In junior high school, almost everyone looked the same, and they all shopped at the Gap—except me. I never wore anything resembling trendy. One time we got close to buying something there, when I managed to get my parents to walk into the store in the Kings Plaza Mall in Brooklyn. They walked out promptly, gasping at the prices. It wasn't until my first year of high school, when we moved to Flushing and found discounted Gapwear, that I was able to buy my first shirt there.

Nothing I would ever buy again, no matter how expensive, or how cool, will ever make me feel as good as my first pair of blue jeans and my first shirt from the Gap. They were recognized entry points into American society, and acceptance. It wasn't that I grew up wanting to be American. I just wanted to look American, to be accepted by Americans.

Many Afghans thought that I already looked pretty American. Unlike the typical image people have of an Afghan woman, I am very fair and have brown hair, which in my high school photos had natural light highlights in the front. My hair is not as thick as most Afghan women, and I don't have as thick eyebrows or as much facial hair. In short, I don't have the dark glamorous look that so many Afghan women have, the image I always perceived as gorgeous. When I was young, Afghan women would tell Moor I looked like a little American girl, which made me feel special and proud. When I was in Flushing High School, for the first meeting of the Afghan Students Association, the other students didn't know what to make of me joining. Sensing their discomfort, I realized they didn't know I was Afghan, so I told them. They didn't believe it. I told them I could speak Pashto, and they asked me to say a few words. As I spoke, their faces lit up with surprise. Even my own people didn't believe I was one of them.

It wasn't until I traveled to Afghanistan that I saw so many other women that looked like me. Many Pashtuns, mostly from the countryside, have light hair and even green eyes. The ideal woman in Afghan society has large eyes, a "tall" nose, and a small mouth. She is fair-skinned and plump, a sign of good health. Some Afghans have told me that the fair-haired, blue-eyed rural Pashtuns are the descendants of people ranging from the European armies of Alexander the Great to the ancient Aryan invaders of the lands of the dark-haired indigenous Afghans. Most of the Afghans that have made it to the United States come from the cities, where people usually have darker skin and black hair and eyes.

My light skin would be a benefit to me in later years, making it easier for me to weave in and out of American society, without being seen as an outsider. It also opened doors in post-Taliban Afghanistan, where being a foreigner meant I could walk into government ministers' offices without question, while Afghan women, especially those that looked local, were stopped. Soon after 9/11, I learned how my looks could shelter me from the anti-Muslim backlash and make people feel that I was one of them. A few days after 9/11, I was waiting in line at a convenience store behind a pair of white, blue-collar men when one pointed to the cover of *Newsweek*, which read "Why They Hate Us" (referring to Muslims), and said, "Those fuckers. We need to nuke 'em. Just get rid of all of them before the next generation grows up." I was repulsed, and I knew that they didn't know who I was. They wouldn't have guessed who I was if their lives depended on it. I wanted to say something, I wanted to tell them Muslims come in all looks, in all characters, and shock them. But by the time I came out of my thoughts they were already gone.

Islam guided almost every facet of my family life, although as I got older I wondered how much of a role culture played in the way that we lived our lives. In any case, the two appeared to be in collaboration, rather than in confrontation, with each other. As I became older, I questioned cultural practices as being anti-Islamic, and although my points were often acknowledged, little attention was paid to them. I began to feel Islam as a legitimate and acceptable path to counter harmful traditions. When a relative had his marriage arranged to an Afghan woman living in California, I asked the bride if her parents asked her permission. She said she had not been asked, only notified once she had been promised. The *wakil*, her representative, had eventually asked her at the *nikkah* if she agreed, but by then families of both sides had gathered, and the pressure to agree was probably the heaviest any Muslim girl would experience in the course of her life. Some women have been promised to older men at a very young age, beginning as early as birth. It is considered to be a sign of great friendship between men to promise their children to each other. One woman I met in Afghanistan had been promised at birth to a man many years her senior, but had refused to marry him when she became of age, and instead told her parents of her own choice, a man she had met at university in Kabul. She rose to become a deputy minister in Afghanistan in the new administration of President Karzai after the fall of the Taliban. If she had obeyed her parents' wishes, she would likely have been a housewife. Some Afghan women tell me they had either not been consulted or were actually forced into agreeing to their families' choice of a husband. There are many other Afghan women I know, of course, who have married the person of their parents' choosing and are happy with the choice.

Growing up, I did not have anything against arranged marriages. It had worked for my aunts, cousins, and even my mother. Everything about my mother's wedding was traditional—she was a traditional woman. She had never been allowed to attend school, and had worn a *burqa* all her life. The only picture of her before being married was taken when she had snuck into a photographer's studio with the maid and a few other members of the family. She had met my father on their wedding night, an occasion on which no pictures were taken. Moor acknowledges that she got lucky in being given to a well-educated, hardworking family man. My father neither drinks nor smokes and is well respected by his family and members of the community for his involvement in their lives, especially for his recitation of Qur'an at community events. Perhaps the most surprising thing about my father is that he often washes the dishes and sometimes helps my mother cook. The women on Agha's side of the family are quick to point out that these are positive attributes any woman would wish their husband had.

I agree that Moor got lucky. Agha was an unusual man who helped out in the kitchen. He was especially adept at cleaning and preparing raw meat. At the height of his perfectionism, Agha would stand over the kitchen sink for hours cutting every last bit of slimy fat off the chicken breasts he would buy and freeze for our family. This was an unpleasant job, and one no one else volunteered for. As a result, while Agha developed a stiff neck and back performing this task, he also became better at it than anyone else. This was one unusual way Agha showed devotion to our family.

Agha was lucky too. Moor believes it was her fate to end up with Agha. Fate is an important part of life in both Islam and Afghan culture. The Qur'an says that God, who has created and balanced all things, has long ago fixed our destinies and guides us to our fate. Nothing can befall us but what God has planned for us. Muslims often remark that you cannot change what God has destined. While I agree that God's will rules over mine, I also think that Muslim women's resignation to fate has become an excuse for complacency. Perhaps it is a way of coping with being powerless. A less-cited saying of the Prophet goes, "Tie down the leg of your camel and *then* leave the rest to God."

Afghan women often told me that I was fated to be married to Nadir, that he appealed to my parents as the best choice for me, the best choice to fulfill my destiny. Everything, indeed, was fated. I know that I am considered to be more American for my belief in the power of the individual to determine her own fate. I believe this more so since my divorce. Until then, I questioned why God had resigned me to such an unhappy fate. I thought that I might have everything, a doctor husband, bright children, a big house, and a comfortable life, but I would be miserable inside. But I realized that God did not condemn me. He gave me a will. He gave me opportunity. I needed to exercise it. If I didn't, I would be condemning myself. It also helped that I studied existentialism in college, which perhaps overemphasized the role of the individual. But I would later meet a cousin in Afghanistan, Suraya, who had never been to school and was illiterate, but who believed strongly in the will of the individual even in the face of unanimous opposition by the rest of her family.

Chapter 5

A Suitable Match

*If you do not marry a gentle woman, she will not bear
you a gentle son.*

—Pashto proverb

When a Muslim girl in a conservative society reaches puberty, relatives and members of the community begin to take notice of her. An ideal girl is one that is beautiful, shy, polite to her elders, and knows how to cook and sew. Many girls know how to run a household by the time they are fourteen or fifteen, having practically raised their younger siblings and assisted their mother with all the chores. Girls who are especially prized are those who have actually taken over the running of the house, because it shows a willingness to work. Although in the United States these girls also go to school, it is clearly understood that their family life is more important, and that school will end one day but family won't. Girls are expected to be at home when not at school, and generally are not allowed to have a life outside school. Besides the fact that families want their daughters to be "under their watch," there is the additional threat that non-Muslims will expose their innocent daughters to evil influences such as alcohol, drugs, or sex. A girl is taught that a man's goal is to bed them, no matter what it may seem at the time.

Love is not recognized as a valid reason for premarital sexual relations. In some very conservative homes, love is not recognized as a valid reason for marriage either. Young girls may fall in love with a guy because of his handsome looks or charm, but it is seen more as a youthful infatuation. Mature love will come with a husband who will prove himself as a provider and protector. A woman will appreciate the man chosen for her as the years pass and their love grows.

First marriage, then love. Even with my experience, I'm not an opponent of the idea, so long as the girl is familiar with the kind of man she is marrying, and so long as she truly agrees with the idea. That's the hard part, because what constitutes agreement? Many families can claim that their daughter has agreed, but in private she often confides that she didn't want to do it. Part of the problem is that in tribal societies, as most Muslim societies are, a woman hardly ever meets any men outside of her father, brothers, and cousins. Even in America, where there is a lot of exposure to potential mates, a woman is expected to remain loyal to her parents' wishes and not pick from the vast opportunities before her.

Around sixteen years of age, the delegations of families to a girl's home greatly increase, as she has become ripe. Usually, the women in the potential groom's family visit the girl's family. The elder woman has the most prominent role, followed by the sisters of the groom and then his brothers' wives. Children are rarely brought along, and the women take special care of their appearance and clothes. They come for afternoon tea, and their first trip is considered an introduction, even if the families know each other. This is probably one of the most sophisticated sales teams one can witness, as the charm of the elder women becomes the grease for the conversation. The groom's family praise the daughter they are coming to ask for in the highest terms, and exaggerate the greatness of their son. The visits continue, and depending on the reception by the girl's family, they may be frequent. If the groom's side senses there is interest, they continue to lobby hard and get family and friends to vouch for them. Sometimes the girl's family expects the man's family to make repeated visits over many months before they will give her away. A girl whose in-laws have spent much time and energy to win her is seen as valuable, while a girl who is given away quickly is reminded of her low status in her own family by her in-laws if she misbehaves.

Once the girl's family is satisfied with the choice, they usually ask the girl. This is when it gets interesting. If she says yes, or that it's up to her parents, or that she doesn't have an opinion, she will be considered in agreement with the idea. If a girl says no, she is subject to questioning, often intense. She is asked if she has a boyfriend she is considering for marriage, or if she has someone else in her thoughts. If she has a boyfriend, it is up to her family to accept him. If she doesn't, she will be asked to give reasons for denying her parents' choice. She might say he is too old or she simply does not want to marry now. She is told that she will soon become too old for marriage, unwanted, and will become an old maid like other women in the community. She will become dependent on others, and when her parents leave the earth she will be at the mercy of her brother and brother's wife, who will treat her badly. She is told that all the other known choices have already been evaluated by the family as unsuitable, whether because of the tribal background, family background, or the man's own shortcomings. They may go through a list of available choices with the girl, and eliminate one after another. All of these choices are, of course, men who are Muslim and share similar ethnicity and language. Eventually the girl gives in under the pressure that her parents will not accept anyone else she chooses, or she will risk being disowned. Unless she feels strongly for someone else, this is the point at which she breaks.

I've often thought of the process of getting a Muslim girl to agree to an arranged marriage as an interrogation. The goal of the interrogators is to get a confession, at almost any cost. They will use persuasion, fear, intimidation, gifts, or negotiation to get the girl to agree. The girl, under pressure from the people whose role has always been to protect her, agrees to be married. Turning back after the ensuing momentum is highly unlikely. The man's family is notified, and yet another trip is made to the girl's family, which makes the acceptance official. On that occasion, the girl's family presents large trays of candies, chocolates and sugar-coated almonds, decorated festively with green and glitter. The girl usually stays hidden from the man's family, sitting in a separate room and accepting visitors only from her own family.

The next time the families celebrate together is at the *nikkah*, the ceremony I experienced in Flushing. A local *mullah* often marries them, though in Islam a couple can be married by anyone. After that, according to Islam the couple can live together, have children, whatever. According to many cultures, though, there must be a wedding ceremony before that occurs, and the period between the *nikkah* and that ceremony is one in which the families can get to know one another better. Gifts, fruit, and sweets are sent to the bride and her family on the Muslim holiday happening twice a year, Eid. After the wedding the bride is taken to her new home, which is likely with her in-laws, and many days of visits to her new home by her relatives follow. A few days after her wedding, sometimes on the seventh day, she is brought to the kitchen to carry out a few symbolic chores. She raises cups of rice out of the large burlap sack full of basmati rice and pours them into a bowl, she cuts Afghan bread into pieces for lunch, and she garnishes a dish with salt. This marks the beginning of her life as a woman, the first of thousands of times that she will lift the rice from the sack, preparing meals for a growing family until she has daughters old enough to help her. The tired, aging woman is ultimately relieved on the seventh day of her son's wedding, when the same process occurs with her new daughter-in-law, and she will finally be able to claim a role of authority in her house.

Arranged marriages are especially unpredictable because the girl has to live not only with a man she doesn't know very well, but usually with his entire family too. Mothers-in-law expect their new daughters-in-law to act like servants for their son and his parents. The role of the elder woman is elevated when her children marry and again when her grandchildren are born. Rather than doing more, elders are expected to do less. This is when a woman finally attains some power in the household, and her husband has either died or is past the heyday of his youth. Too many new brides bear the burden of liberating their husband's mother, rather than enjoying their own youth.

Arranged marriages compete with love marriages for young girls in probably every country in the world. Today they are more common in Africa and Asia, but thousands still occur every year in Europe and the United States. The British government even set up a task force to investigate the problem after receiving hundreds of reports of domestic violence against young women from India, Pakistan, and other countries, women who resisted their parents' attempts to force them to marry strangers. Islam dealt with the problem of forced marriage by declaring a marriage without a woman's consent to be invalid. But the tradition and cultural importance of arranged marriages, and young people's desire for love marriages, mean that girls continue to be pressured into them.

For Muslims in America, everything is changing. For some people, like my parents' generation, it's too much change, too fast. They see their children's desire to assimilate as a repudiation of their culture, and of Islam. What they fail to acknowledge, however, is the change even within themselves, regardless of how slow. Perhaps they sense it, which is why they begin to cling to their culture and religion more strongly. For my parents, some of the resistance to assimilating exists because they are so much more valued in the old way of life. The Afghan community recognizes and respects my father and others like him as pious men, and leaders. In American society they are anonymous and, at worst, strange people from backward lands.

Islam has a greater role today in my family and others' than it ever did before. It has become the most comfortable way to maintain a sense of community. Muslims are afraid of being ignored, not mattering, but they are also afraid of standing out.

For younger Muslims, the change is often not fast enough. America has been good to us, and the quality of life here, sustained by the values of freedom and democracy (which of course are not always respected), is far better than the options back home. My generation sees our parents' homes as effectively failed states. Our parents wouldn't be here if they had not been failed in some way in their homelands—whether by the lack of economic opportunity, political tyranny, or the devastation of war. Many Muslim refugees in the United States have fled war, revolution, and poverty—whether in Iran, Iraq, Lebanon, Palestine, Pakistan, or Afghanistan. We also know that the Islam our parents learned in their home country is not the only and final version, that in America we can debate so many of the accepted truths of the mainstream Islamic world. But in doing so we are called disrespectful, we are accused of disgracing our people, and, worse, of angering God. When we say there are other interpretations of the Qur'an, we are reminded of the lack of understanding of Westerners of Islam, and of the deliberate attempts by Westerners and heretic Muslims to distort the word of God. When fathers—not scholars who have debated and pored through texts, questioning and learning as they go— are the teachers of religion, passing on an oral tradition of Islam in most cases, we know there will be trouble. The very idea of questioning is often considered to be unacceptable in this situation, even though sometimes lip service is paid to it.

"Islam is simple, it's a way of life," my *madrassa* teacher used to say. It was so simple that I just had to do what he instructed and I would have a real shot at Heaven. It seemed that he considered *mullahs* who taught in villages to be the highest authorities of religious thought. Memorizing the Qur'an in Arabic has far more value than reading it in English, we were told. "Authorities" know and you don't. You don't know anything. You are a silly young girl. You better watch out that no one tricks you into having sex. That is what Muslim girls are taught to believe. Protect your chastity, your honor, your family. But do not expect them to protect you unless you follow their rules.

Following rules was something I began to get tired of after my divorce. I had done that my whole life, and following the rules was precisely what had gotten me to my misery in the first place. I began to explore how girls who weren't following the rules were living their lives. What I learned is that Muslim parents have forced their children to wallow in lies; feel awful, guilty, confused; and live a double life. The stories of some of my friends that follow are not limited to the people that experienced them; they are repeated over and over again in Islamic communities in America, and perhaps all over the world.

An Arab man, we'll call him Hussein, was dating a Colombian woman, unbeknownst to his family. I met Hussein's girlfriend, and when she learned I was Muslim, she cornered me at a party, eager to discuss his dilemma. Like many Muslim men, he dated her to experience life on the "outside," thinking he may have an arranged marriage later in life, but this was fun for now. He would never have approved of his sisters dating at all, let alone being with an infidel Colombian. Hussein fell in love with the woman, accidentally impregnated her, but feared telling his family. Even though in Islam he is allowed to marry this woman, he feared the judgment of his tribal family, who will disapprove of his affair with a woman outside of marriage. But he knew that he must tell them, because he wanted them to be present at the union with his lover. Hussein continued to delay telling them the truth, while the Colombian's belly grew larger and larger. Finally, she gave birth to a baby boy and they are neither married nor living together, nor does his mother know she is a grand-mother. Hussein has not told his mother to this day, even though he has moved out of the house and claims to be living with friends.

Doonya is eighteen years old, in her first year of college, and living with her parents. Although arranged marriage is not out of the question, she has the option of meeting a nice Muslim boy during college and marrying upon graduation. She is expected to live with her family until marriage, and be present for family and religious events. She is expected to pray five times a day, dress modestly, but not to wear *hijab*. Doonya is a member of the Muslim Students Association at her university. But Doonya has another life. When she tells her parents she is staying over her friend's dorm to study, she spends the evening with a new boyfriend. She begins to go to parties on campus, drink alcohol, and enjoy a typical American college experience. Doonya tells me she "wants to change," but that she's not sure she even wants to be Muslim. It has always felt oppressive, and rather than leaving the religion she has chosen to remain Muslim for the sake of her family. Besides, she doesn't want to convert to anything else. She used to believe in Islam and there may be a day that she practices it again.

Tribal Muslim men may be right to see college, or any educa-tion for that matter, as a threat to their power. Some girls are taken out of school when they hit puberty, even in the United States, where it is illegal to do so. I know of a few cases where the girls who were taken out of school were later married to men that their parents imported from the home country. I call these men "cheap imports." The men were considered more pure, not having had American experiences with women. It used to be that women were imported for their purity, but now that Afghan women in the States are having a hard time finding husbands because they are considered too "open-eyed," they find they can import husbands from abroad, who are desperate not only for a wife but also for life in America.

Parents believe that in school, their daughters will have "too much freedom" and be enticed by boys to do bad things. Just speaking to boys is bad enough. In high school, Afghan girls would disassociate themselves from the boys once they left the school grounds. I became a nervous wreck when one male student who also lived in my building wanted to speak with me while waiting for the elevator. When an Afghan guy walked by, I had to pretend I wasn't feeling well and held my arms around my stomach, hoping the shock would silence the student until the Afghan guy left. Just being seen with him would have made my Afghan neighbors suspicious, thinking he was a boyfriend. It was while in that building, as a young teen, that my mother advised me to untuck my shirt from my pants, so that the fabric could drape over my behind. Sometimes I would try to tuck it in by the time I walked to school, just a few blocks away, sneaking into the stairwell of our building and hoping to avoid the occasional man flying down the stairs. Then I'd make a dash for the exit and around the block, out of sight from the main street.

I was also expected not to wear any makeup, a duty that I obeyed until I had my *nikkah*. I was encouraged by girls who already wore makeup to do so. I was technically married, after all, an adult. So I began to sneak my lip liner into class and make myself up every morning in the gym locker room. Drawing around the outline of my lips and filling in with the brown creamy pencil made me feel so beautiful.

But Moor objected when I painted my lips in front of her. She said girls should not wear makeup until they are living with their husbands. At the end of the school day, I would go to the bathroom and wipe it off with wet tissue.

All these things, secret makeup, changing my appearance on

the way to school, and hiding my conversations with boys, no matter how innocent, fed into the myth of "little, little Masuda." Sometimes I would stop and think how absurd it was that there were so many "little lies," but I got used to them as a way of life. When I tried to be honest, explaining to my mother that I needed to wear makeup because girls my age just had to or they would look pale, she didn't buy it. There was little room for persuasion, so I learned not to ask for permission, but rather for forgiveness if I was caught.

I grew up thinking love was the worst thing that could happen to me. It would make me settle down and therefore slow down, and it would ruin my opportunity to chase my dreams. Love was what caused normally good girls to give up their virginity. Virginity is much praised in the Qur'an as in the Bible. The Qur'an says that Mary, mother of Jesus, was "chosen above the women of all nations" because she "guarded her chastity." Because she was modest, God "made her and her son a Sign for all peoples." Growing up, protecting my virginity, and therefore purity, was perhaps the single most important goal for me. Getting good grades, doing chores, praying, obeying my parents' wishes— these were all worthy goals, but would mean little if I wasn't pure. Still, sometimes I would think that I might still get pregnant, being a virgin. I mean, it happened once, why wouldn't it happen again? It was entirely possible.

Living in Brooklyn and Queens, the threat of rape haunted me. I would rather die than be raped. And if I should ever be raped, I felt that I should commit suicide. The idea of losing my virginity to a lover before marriage was completely out of the question. I would never allow that. In fact, I could never imagine a situation where I loved someone so much that I would allow them to do that to me. The idea of a girl consenting to premarital sex meant that she was duped. That she allowed herself to be duped meant that she was stupid. According to the stereotype among Afghans, "their" girls usually didn't get duped, but "white" girls often did. This was because their family structure often wasn't strong enough to teach them how to be "smart." In effect, their families were also "stupid" when it came to this issue.

For the most part, the idea of sex was quite repulsive to me, even into my midteens. It seemed so primal and animalistic. I first learned of sex from a scientific point of view. From pictures and video they showed at school and on PBS, which I secretly watched while no one was home, I knew about—and had seen—sperm, eggs, and the whole process of reproduction, from the ovaries and scrotum to embryonic development.

Once, in health class in ninth grade, they showed us a video from inside the vaginal canal, and in slow motion I saw male ejaculation inside a woman. It was scientific porno. I remember every detail of it. It was over in four seconds in slow motion, and I was changed for life. I had witnessed intercourse from a most intimate perspective. From inside a woman's vagina! I had been mesmerized. I was thinking how I wished I could see it again when the health teacher said, "Bam! Let's see that again!" He rewound the video, and again I watched, this time recording it all in my mind so that I could play it over and over again. She was being pierced. The thought of it gave me chills. From then on, I would replay those four seconds in my head when I was bored, when I was at a wedding, or doing chores.

While I don't necessarily agree with many Afghan parents' black-and-white distinction between youthful lust and married love, I do believe infatuation and desire are quite often confused with love among young Muslim men, because they have very little experience to draw upon. I have, on more occasions than I think anyone will believe, had Muslim men proclaim their "love" for me, even when they have known me for only a few minutes.

It happened to me in Paris. I was surprised to see bright

orange-colored *jalebi*, syrup-glazed swirls, in the window when passing by a corner shop near my hotel that also served *panini* and Greek food. Drawn inside by the familiar glossy orange treat that I often enjoyed in Indian and Pakistani stores in New York, I went in to buy some. I asked the man behind the counter if he was Muslim, and when he confirmed that he was, I shared that I was too. "Muslim from America!" he declared. "First time I meet," he said. He immediately went into the back room and fetched a brand-new scarf for me, asking me to come by the next day so that he could provide me with a Qur'an in English. Honored by his kindness, I sat down to have a meal when his Egyptian friend spotted his prey. The friend sat across from me, a fortysomething with a sizable belly. He asked about me as I ate—where was I from, where was my family? "What about if we get married?" he asked, with a smile sweeping across his face to reveal his cigarette tar–stained teeth. "Oh, I don't think so," I said nervously. "Why not, I love you," he said, indicating that his affection for me would mean our marriage would be considered a love marriage.

"I'm sorry, I can't. I don't even know you."

"But you can get to know me, you can spend some time with me. I will show you Paris, then we will get married."

"No, I have to go back to my parents."

"We can visit your parents. It's no problem."

"I don't think I'm really right for you."

"Why not, you are beautiful! Afghan women are so beautiful . . ."

"You wouldn't be happy with me. I'm not such a good girl."

"Why, why?" he asked, upset that I had such low self-esteem.

"I like to party."

"I love to party!"

There was no way out. Nothing I said to this man would make him get the point. I insisted that I was not a good person, not a good Muslim, and that I worried I might shame him. I finished my sandwich, and he insisted I take his number as I walked out. I would have similar experiences with many Afghan and Pakistani men.

Oddly, even though I fantasized about marrying an Afghan man, I never could find one that suited me. There was always some underlying strain of conservatism.

Sitting with some Afghan girlfriends in an Iranian restaurant, sipping black tea with cardamom, we reminisced about our past run-ins with Afghan boys. "I dated one for four years," said Farishta, turning to Meena, who was looking at my face to see how I reacted. "Well, at least you dated one." I smiled at Farishta reassuringly. I never dated an Afghan, even though I was married to one for almost three years. Everyone at the table held their breath for a second and then let go in tandem, after I smiled again as I pressed the teacup to my lips. Farishta went on to say that she had many Afghan male friends who were well educated, modern, and handsome. "But I no longer see myself dating them."

I thought back to the Afghan boys I had met at various community events, weddings, dinners, and high school. Some of them were indeed very cute. But I had not dared to be too open around them. We knew each other's faces, but there was an invisible barrier of respect that none of us ever crossed.

Once, in high school, I knew a pair of twin brothers who were sons of an important Afghan diplomat whose plane was shot down over Afghanistan on a visit during Taliban times. My Colombian friend Carmen told me she had a crush on a boy. At lunchtime, she pointed across our table at the cafeteria and I followed the imaginary line to one of the brothers.

Instantly I was jealous. I felt as if I owned any chance at an opportunity with one of these boys because they were Afghan. I never told Carmen, but I firmly believed she had no right to these men. No, they were reserved only for good Afghan women.

I never pursued any of the Afghan boys I knew in school. I was quite shy about the subject, and was also very afraid of being caught. Once, I saw one of the brothers in the hallway carrying a blue math textbook. I was in the higher red level, and I told myself that neither of them was suited for me because of their inferior intelligence. I wanted a smart, worldly guy who was way beyond my math level. I still remained insatiably curious about the twins. I wanted to know where they lived, how fashionable and educated their mother was, and if they ever really knew who I was. But we never said two words to each other in high school. I would only meet them again in the airport in Kabul, seven years later, when we were all drawn back by the power of our roots.

Meena, deceptively quiet, finally chimed in. "Yeah, I dated a guy for a few years too. It just didn't work out. He was so possessive." We all agreed that there was a certain something about every Afghan man we had met that made a romantic relationship almost impossible. "Are they all so possessive?" I wondered out loud. Although many may have been, we could not figure out what made them "unmateable." Even the young, educated Muslim men who would otherwise fit my lifestyle always seemed to raise red flags.

I used to believe I had become narrow-minded and prone to the Afghan proverb that says, "Once burned with [hot] milk, you blow air on yogurt." But I learned that many Muslim women had problems with the Muslim men they dated. Indeed, even non-Muslim women who dated Muslim men have had possessiveness or control issues in their relationships. Of course there are exceptions, but what was it that made men this way? This is a question I still have been unable to answer. Perhaps it was a characteristic of certain personalities in general. Still, I found this trait to be more common among Muslim men.

One explanation is that the Muslim men I have met come from cultures where women are still considered to have a particular and limited role at home, where honor is esteemed very highly by the family and community, and where little diversity exists, leaving the majority fairly uniform in their thought. Shame and honor are perhaps the two values that have practically destroyed the ability of women to perform as full citizens of many Muslim communities. In small doses, these values promote morality and order, but taken to extremes, as they too often are, they ruin women's lives. Everything from her appearance and dress to her contact with others becomes the center of identity for a family. Perhaps the greatest fear of a Muslim parent is that men will "trick" their daughter into giving up her virginity, something that will not only shame the family's honor but also render her defective property that they will have a hard time marrying off. Girls are often seen as a liability, or a potential liability. So like a time bomb, ready to explode shame on their families, girls are married off quickly.

Attending Islamic funerals was another important rite of passage for my sisters and me growing up. The first time I remember my father crying was when he received the letter notifying him of his mother's death, the third most important day of her life. He burst out like a child, and I wished *I* could be his mother. While he had hoped he could have brought her to the United States to live with us and to receive medical care, he was relieved that she had died in an Islamic country and was buried on Islamic soil. Muslims believe greatly in the importance of being buried in an Islamic land, preferably the one of their birth. If they couldn't die in those places, they would hope to be buried there. I always found it fascinating that people struggle so much to be buried in a particular place. Once you're dead, what difference does it make? Besides, it makes it harder for your loved ones to visit your grave when you're buried far away from them. I would like my family to remember me by visiting my grave.

The best way to go is in Mecca, on the pilgrimage. One old Afghan woman, who lived in New York with her mentally ill son, died the day she got to Mecca. She was considered to be lucky, rewarded for her pains in this life, and well on her way to Heaven. The death of a person often invokes a strong emotional reaction, particularly from women who are close relatives. Even in a culture that prides itself on the honor and shame of its women, women are allowed (and even expected) to do such frowned-upon things as yelling, screaming, hitting themselves, and tearing their clothes. It is a sign of extreme anguish, and a strong emotional reaction indicates a high degree of love and hurt. It also perpetuates the idea of being victimized. That being said, the most quiet and reserved women are still considered very strong.

Word quickly spreads of the death, and all the elders are expected to visit. Funerals are known for their high cost, not for the actual burial costs as in the West, but rather for the cost of hosting a large number of people over the course of three days of mourning. When Moor's mother died, or "other mother" as I used to call her, the young women of the extended family were expected to cook and serve the guests. Sometimes guests would also help out, and even after the three days of mourning, friends and relatives sent meals to our home, to spare Moor from having to cook. Most of our relatives died in Afghanistan or Pakistan, which meant that we observed the funeral by reading Qur'an and mourning with the family in the United States, but it wasn't until my uncle's wife, Khanum Jana, died that we were responsible for carrying out all the arrangements for a Muslim funeral in America.

Khanum Jana was devoutly Muslim. She had seen hard times in her life, and Islam had kept her strong. Her life had been torn apart as an adult during the Afghan Soviet war. She lost two sons in the war for Afghan independence; leaving only one remaining son, who fled to America. One of her daughters had been widowed at a young age and had come to live with her mother along with her children, a boy and two girls. The two girls were young budding teenagers who had helped me prepare for my wedding in Pakistan. They would tell me how sweet my perfume smelled, how lucky they were to have a cousin like me, and I would secretly give them nail polish and hair clips from the collection my in-laws meant for me. One of the sisters often complained of a headache, sitting in the bedroom and holding her head in her hands. I thought they were migraines, but they must have been symptoms of something even worse, because I learned that she died soon after we left Pakistan. At first Moor hid the news from me, as family often does if telling can be avoided. But she couldn't hide it for long because I wanted to speak with my cousins on the phone. Khanum Jana had seen her granddaughter die in front of her eyes. The doctors they took her to said they could do nothing for her extreme pain.

Khanum Jana had come to the United States from Pakistan only two years before her own death, refusing for many years to live in the land of infidels. She stayed as long as she could in Afghanistan, her homeland for which her two sons had died. But she could not bear the cruel conditions in Afghanistan, and had no remaining male family in Pakistan, because America was where her last remaining son had begun his life, marrying a wife Moor arranged for him, who bore him four sons. Khanum Jana prayed five times a day, refusing to watch TV and looking away when her grandchildren were being entertained by the "infidels in the box." She had an obsession with infidels, whom she barely came into contact with because she was always home. She told her grandchildren to stay away from them, as if they were dirty. This often angered me, but Khanum Jana was beyond the age of reason. Her grandchildren already secretly rolled their eyes while they nodded their heads.

Khanum Jana's husband, Gran Agha, who was my father's much older brother, was also very conservative. Because of a large age difference and the bond of having come from the same mother (my grandfather had two wives), Gran Agha was a father to my father. My father tells the story of Gran Agha chastising him harshly while teaching him how to read the Qur'an, so harshly that their father would scold Gran Agha and begin to teach my father himself. We lived with Khanum Jana and Gran Agha in Kandahar when I was young. Moor tells how strict he was and how much she and Khanum Jana were afraid of him. I still wear *hijab* in Gran Agha's presence, even though he knows I don't usually cover. I think he appreciates that I wear it around him, as if he still has some influence over his sphere, one that shrank greatly the day Khanum Jana died.

My parents felt Gran Agha had already become soft, but the death of Khanum Jana would make him very humble. Gran Agha became quite fragile after he was beaten up on the way to an Afghan mosque in Flushing early one morning before the sun had come up. He came back home with his perfectly white long shirt bloodied from a punch to the nose. He hadn't been carrying any money, and since he didn't speak English, it was unclear what motivated the cowards who had struck him. The police were unable to locate the culprits, but to Gran Agha it was a message that his kind weren't welcome in the neighborhood, and he stopped going to the mosque for many months. It was one of the few times in my life I considered joining the NYPD. I wished I could protect the people I loved somehow.

Khanum Jana died after a sudden heart attack, and though she was taken to a funeral home, it would act only as a holding place, and the family would carry out the preparation of her body for burial. Moor made phone calls to elderly women in the community, who would be able to guide the process and help. For them, the assistance was seen as a duty, work that would be rewarded by God. Although Khanum Jana's daughter-in-law fainted at the sight of the body, Moor thought I should learn what to do in preparation for Muslim burial, so she took me into the room where the body lay on a flat table. She said every person should wash three bodies in their lifetime to fulfill their duty. I wondered if Moor wanted me to be prepared for the day that I would be caring for her in the same way. Moor thought this way. She even told Sara to come, though she was only sixteen at the time. There were two elder Afghan women in the room, and Khanum Jana was lying there, uncovered, her skin somewhat yellow, her body stiff. I didn't feel any emotion toward the body. Perhaps I was able to deal with it because I imagined it to be a Hollywood-like creation for the set of a movie. We discussed the washing strategy for a minute, then poured water from the little white opaque hose in the sink onto her body, rubbing her skin. She had such smooth skin, so young-looking even though she was in her late seventies. I made a mental note to myself never to get a tattoo, because as fun as it may be, no matter how hidden, in death my closest loved ones would see it.

As the young, strong one, I was given the job of holding her up on her side as the elder women washed her back. I wrapped my arms around her hardened cadaver as they mishandled the hose, the water splashing from her body onto mine. The plastic garbage bag I was wearing didn't cover my whole body. I wanted to shower immediately, the water of death lying on my skin. One down, two bodies to go before death lay permanently on my skin.

Chapter 6

A Pure Kandahari Girl

Fortune is like a potter—it fashions and it breaks;
Many, like you and me, it has created and destroyed.

—Abdur Rahman, Afghan poet

Under the heavy *burqa*, it was incredibly hot in the back of the rickety taxi. I didn't know whether I liked the wind rushing into the car, because it brought with it particles of dust that smelled and tasted like cement. It was the first time I thought of dust as clean. It was sterile, yet part of the natural landscape. The traditional Afghan music playing in the back of the taxi made me excited, however. It sounded like a festive mix of the stationary accordion and *tablas*—or skin drums—which are beaten by men with the heel of the palm and fingertips.

Our journey from Quetta, Pakistan, toward the Afghanistan border had begun at the break of dawn. It was late July 2001, just weeks before al Qaeda's terrorist attack on the United States. Afghanistan was still a forgotten country. Hidden under the obscuring garments that would make me indistinguishable from other Afghan women, I was stealing into my birth city, Kandahar, for the first time since my family fled from the Soviet invasion when I was four years old.

A few months before, my uncle Jan Agha had decided to take

his wife, Lailuma, and their three sons to visit his brother and other family in Kandahar. Aunt Lailuma was Moor's youngest sister, the closest thing I had to a mother outside of my own. Because my father's side of the family was so pleased with my mother, they decided to pick from the same tree when they arranged a marriage for Jan Agha. In Pashto, Jan Agha means "dear father." That was not his real name. Older Afghan men are often called "father" even by other men's children, usually combined with a term of affection such as "dear," "flower," "sweet," or "little."

Lailuma had been present at my wedding in Karachi, spending days and nights with us in our rented apartment. At the time, she was living in Pakistan with Jan Agha's parents. Of all the relatives that would stay with us over that time, she was the most giving, the most loving. She cooked and cleaned and served the rest of the family, even when they would get tired and sneak out when chores needed to be done. Moor and I had spent most of those days shopping in preparation for the wedding, while Aunt Lailuma watched my younger sisters and ran the apartment. On the day of the wedding, everyone went to the salon to get their hair done, but Aunt Lailuma stayed behind to make sure I had everything I needed for the day. Moor said when we were finally leaving Karachi, Aunt Lailuma's eyes had large dark circles around them from the exhaustion and sleep deprivation. I would be comfortable traveling with Aunt Lailuma and Jan Agha. Like a mother, Lailuma would protect me.

The decision to visit Taliban-controlled Afghanistan, even with Lailuma and Jan Agha, had not been easy. Just a few weeks before, I found myself on the far more inviting sands of Malibu Beach, contemplating a very different path. I had applied to law schools the previous winter and had been accepted to Pepperdine Law School. I visited its mountaintop campus in Malibu, which looked out over a stunning view of Southern California sun, sand, and sparkling crystal-blue water. Pepperdine was a gateway in my mind to a glamorous career in entertainment and corporate law. But when I learned of Jan Agha's trip to see family in Kandahar, I kept thinking what it would be like to confront my roots and even explore living in Kandahar and finding some way, any way, to help the people there, whose continuing agony I had learned more about through my family and in the newspapers. Ultimately I could not shake the idea, and I turned down Los Angeles for Afghanistan.

As far back as I could remember, my parents spoke of Kandahar as a peaceful place, with lush springs and few worries—a simple utopia. Kandahar is known for its succulent apricots, melons, figs, and pomegranates. Afghans from other cities often remark on the spectacular pomegranates they tasted while in Kandahar, like cracking into a ball of rubies. In Kandahar, I would watch mothers feed their children the pomegranate rubies by squeezing them until they burst into the children's mouths, spraying the deep red juice all over their taste buds. To me, pomegranates are the symbol of the good life in Kandahar. They were hard to find in the early years in Brooklyn, but when my father once found them in Chinatown, it was like discovering lost treasure. I was surprised to see pomegranate juice become popular in Manhattan in 2004, as local delis and grocery stores stocked up on the POM Wonderful brand of the juice.

My parents spoke of family trips to a fruit farm owned by my grandfather. There they'd pick apples and oranges with an aroma so rich and a color so bright that they overcame a person like a drug. They would talk of how tangy each orange was when you put a slice in your mouth, and how the sweet nectar dripped down through the valleys between your fingers and over the space between your knuckles and down the backs of your hands.

In the heat of the Kandahar summer, my father would come home for lunch from teaching chemistry at the local girls' high school. Moor would prepare a big meal, complete with an Afghan drink made of liquefied yogurt, mint, and diced cucumbers. This sour-tasting drink is a favorite for bringing relief from the heat, but is also legendary for putting whoever drinks it to sleep. So after lunch, we would all fall asleep, right there in the room, with the dishes from our lunch still lying about. Now, that was satisfaction. Americans sometimes balk at the idea of eating a big meal and then sleeping, but in Afghanistan it is a way of life.

In our family's mythology, life there was perfect. Now, almost twenty years later, I would see for myself. I was looking forward to having lunch Afghan style.

As I breathed in the dust swirling up from the bumpy road, I tried to picture our family home in the old city of Kandahar. I had a clear memory of riding in circles in the courtyard on the back of my brother's tricycle. I was anxious to visit the house again. This is where I could gain the greatest taste of what physical life was for my parents. I wanted to see the kitchen again, so that I could imagine my mother as a young twentysomething, just as I now was. The lids of her eyes would have been smooth, and the light coffee eye shadow would not have gotten stuck in the creases as it did now.

I recall waking up early one morning—I am told I was two or three—to find that Moor was no longer sleeping next to me. I stood in the doorway of our bedroom and looked across the courtyard to see smoke rising from the kitchen. Our kitchen was shaped like an upside-down ice cream cone, with the top sliced off to allow smoke to waft up and wander over the earth. Its walls looked like kneaded dough that had been dipped in flour. I could smell the bread. Moor was in the kitchen making bread at dawn, as she often did. She would flap the dough over one palm, then the other. The dough would turn into a larger and thinner circle. When it was the right thickness she would slap it onto the *tandoor*, a black coal-fire heated iron dome.

My pajamas were the same style as the clothes that I lived in.

Like all women, under my dress I wore a *kootana*, an almost titanium white–colored loose pant. On top of that I had on a full skirt reaching down to my knees, like a princess. The fabric was the color of the powdered milk Moor made for me. Flowers were scattered across the ocean of milk fabric that made my dress, some small frowning yellow flowers the size of my toenails, and some colored brown, which made me look wise. Women older than my mother, who had grown old enough to give up makeup and stop wearing bras, would wear dresses only of particular colors suitable to them. Nothing bright like red, green, or pink. Just navy blues, black and white, or brown, like my flowers. These were the wise women. Everyone listened to them. Moor told me to be quiet when they spoke.

As I moved forward to find my mother, the heel of my foot landed on the edge of the rug, and I felt the rudely cold floor against the ball of my foot. The balls of my mother's feet were dry and cracked. As a child in the United States, I'd stare at the dry cracks in the heels and balls of her feet and wonder what they must have been through. Moor had lived. She had walked far. That's why she had the cracks in her feet. When the ball of my foot hit the floor, I felt a sharp burn from the floor's cold, which sent a jolt through my body. Moor had always said "oof" when I wasn't supposed to touch something. I had once touched the hot iron with my index finger and a small painful balloon had grown from it. Now I said "oof" and screamed out "Moooor!" In my memory I waited a long time before she came to answer my wail for attention.

As we rode on the right side of the only road leading through Pakistan's legendary Khojak Pass, which winds through a range of mountains soaring a mile and a half into the sky, I remembered driving through this pass in the other direction as we fled Kandahar on our way to Pakistan, when I was four. Afghans translate the word *khojak* to mean "crooked" in Pashto. Millions of Afghans like us, including many family members, had traveled this dangerous route to Pakistan in order to escape the Red Army. The month I was born, in April 1978, there was a revolution that killed about two thousand people, carried out by Afghan Communists using Soviet-made tanks and bombers. After Afghan rebels based in Pakistan began to retake the land from the Communists, the Soviet Union sent thousands of men, tanks, and bombers to prop them up. The Soviet invaders and the Afghan Communist air force bombed Kandahar heavily before we left, as *mujahideen*, or "holy warriors," took control of the city several times. Two-thirds of the city's population had fled or been killed by 1983, the year that we came to America.[1] Many of its buildings had been made unlivable.[2]

In the months before we left, I often woke up to find new dents from gunshots in the clay courtyard wall. Every house in Kandahar, indeed probably in all of Afghanistan, has bullet holes in its walls. I remember hearing the shooting in the night and feeling like our house was going to cave in on us under the fear of the bullets. Once, I arrived home with Moor to find Soviet troops banging on our door. They had come to search the house, looking for men to induct into the Communist Afghan government army. My grandmother, who was sitting on a mat in the courtyard when the soldiers came out, told them she couldn't get up to help them because of her arthritic legs. They searched our house, then left. This became a legendary family story of how Grandmother drove away the troops with her old woman's wiles. Another time, Moor was bathing my older brother in a tub in the middle of the courtyard, when suddenly she heard a loud swooshing sound and felt the rumble of Soviet jets approaching. She darted across the courtyard and into the house. She was so startled that it was only once she caught her breath that she realized she had forgotten my brother in the tub in the middle of the courtyard! By then the jets were gone, but Agha still likes to tease her about the incident.

I felt anxious. My parents had no plans to return because they felt the country was still too dangerous. Afghanistan was actually the safest it had been since I was born. After the *mujahideen* drove the Soviets out, they began to wage war against one another, killing hundreds of thousands of people. The arrival of the Taliban, though regrettable because of their atrocities, and their support of terrorism, had made the country relatively safer by ending much of the fighting and imposing strict laws. This was the first time I had heard of Afghans in the diaspora going back to visit family, and although my parents weren't going back themselves, they felt the risk was measured for me. As long as I obeyed the rules, I should escape unscathed. They also hoped that by visiting our family, I would become humble and less interested in American culture, and in the end a better Muslim. They worried that my negative experience with arranged marriage would cause me to distance myself from Afghan culture, and welcomed any connection to it.

Although the winding narrow road through the Pass flowed both ways, it was at places so narrow that only one vehicle could pass. I still remembered the moment when I looked out the window of our taxi as a child and saw the vast earth off in the distance beneath us. It was the first time I had looked out from a mountain. The whole time I thought we would fall over the edge. I later learned my fears were not misplaced. Every year, people are killed when their car falls off the edge of the mountain pass—nobody keeps count. But I learned that winter snows made the roads slippery, turning travel on a snowy night into a suicidal journey.

Now, driving through the Pass, I felt again like a little child. I knew that Afghanistan was the part of me that I hadn't quite figured out yet. I was like a floating piece of a puzzle, and if I connected to the larger pieces, I might have a better sense of where I belonged.

When a cousin first pulled the hood of the *burqa* down over my face, the shiny polyester fabric made a sound like fingernails across an open umbrella. Its sky blue folds covered my body from head to toe. The headpiece of my *burqa* was a thin blue mesh screen from which I could, in a stifled way, discern the world around me. Putting on this piece of my identity, of this history that I had escaped, I suddenly felt very much connected to my mother, and her mother, and her mother. Although the *burqa* sometimes symbolizes restrictions on women, I wanted to see it the way Moor would have seen it—as a protective garment, as one that creates comfort for the woman because she doesn't have to worry about men looking at her body. Putting on the *burqa* also represented my leaving behind the New York woman who had just graduated summa cum laude with an economics degree, and becoming a native, organic Afghan, the person I would have been.

I peered out intently from the ledge of Khojak Pass, looking for that same vantage point I'd seen as a child, hoping to capture it forever with my concealed video camera. I wanted to feel four years old again. Suddenly I let out a high-pitched scream. As we turned a blind curve on the narrow mountain road, a huge speeding truck confronted us head-on. Our driver immediately hit his brakes and swerved, taking us to the edge of the cliff. Almost as soon as we stopped, he hit the accelerator again and lurched back onto the path. Getting to Afghanistan might be just as perilous as being there.

This was the same type of truck that I had seen in Pakistan. Unlike American trucks, it was shaped like one long rectangular box, with no discernible difference between the cab and the trailer. It was about fourteen feet long and painted in colorful designs, with red, yellow, and green. It looked like it came from a circus. It was also decorated with interlocking metal chains that hung from the bumperless front of the vehicle and made it sound like Santa's sleigh bells as it drove. When people heard the rhythmic clanging of the metal chains, they knew that a truck was approaching and they should get out of the way.

A few days before, I was almost run over by one of these trucks. I had been shopping in the bazaar, browsing the counterfeit CDs of Christina Aguilera and Microsoft Office, trying to cross a busy street in Quetta with no stoplights and no crosswalk. My cousins ran across, but the traffic never seemed to slow down enough for me to follow. Finally I got tired of waiting and decided to make a run for it. I heard the honking of a monster horn and when I looked up I was facing the bumper of a Pakistani truck closing in on me. I screamed, jumped up in the air, and ran to the other side. When I got across and looked back, the truck driver was laughing. So were my cousins. They were getting a kick out of watching an American girl adapt to the mean streets of Quetta.

And what was awaiting me in Kandahar? I was afraid to come face-to-face with those who had stayed behind in Afghanistan through all these years. I had met our relatives living in Pakistan when I came for my wedding, but had not yet met my mother's sister Khala Sherina or her children in Kandahar. I knew they were going to be happy to see me because to them Kandahar was where I belonged, with family. To Muslims, the most important thing is that families remain together. Even in America, if one of my relatives found a good job opportunity away from her parents and relatives, she didn't pursue it. A person only left her family out of complete desperation. I worried about how they really felt about my family leaving them alone during the Russian war. I felt guilty for that. Was my father a coward for leaving? Should we have stayed?

Just because my immediate family made it out didn't mean I belonged in the United States. Maybe I was supposed to be living in Afghanistan all along—fulfilling the purpose that was meant for me. Coming to Afghanistan, I might learn what that purpose was.

My parents once explained to me what a difficult decision it was to leave our country. We were living with my grandmother at the time, my father's mother. The original plan was that my father would leave, and if he could get to America, he would work hard for a few years and then apply to bring the rest of us there as asylum seekers. But Moor wouldn't do it. She later told me she did not want to split up our nuclear family, fearing that many years might pass before we were joined together with my father again, years of war in which anything could happen to us. My father always reminded me that the Prophet Muhammad taught that a man should consult his wife before making decisions for the family. Insisting that we all stay together was one of the best decisions Moor ever made. Moor later said she did so for the sake of her family, not herself. It was either all of us or none of us.

My father's mother was too frail to make the journey, however, and she had other children to live with in Afghanistan. We would come back once there was peace again at home, or she could join us later in America. We didn't know how long we would be away, but everyone knew there was a good chance we might not see one another for a long time, or ever again. Moor tells me of how her mother, who my brother and I used to call our "other mother," would cry and cry the last time she saw us, patting me on the head, then kissing me and telling me how she would miss me. She hoped to join us in America, but couldn't do so until almost ten years later, because two of her sons were drafted to fight in the war between the Communists and the *mujahideen*. For more than three years my mother and grandmother did not have contact with each other, and neither of them were in touch with my uncles who had been forced into the war. My grandmother was eventually granted political asylum, enabling her to be reunited with her daughter in the United States. I couldn't sleep the night I found out she would join us soon. I was looking forward to having someone around to counter the pressure my mother placed on me to be good at cooking, cleaning, and embroidery. I knew that my grand-mother would love me and defend me, and Moor would have to listen to her. I decided I would take care of her as well. Older women wore white chiffon scarves, which constantly needed to be ironed. I would iron it for my new grandma so that she could have the crispest chiffon scarf anyone had ever seen. I wondered what she looked like, what she smelled like, and whether she would spark any old memories. More than a year later, we pre-pared for her arrival in New York, making her a new red vel-vet–covered mattress, counting down the hours to the moment when I would have a grandmother again. Hours before her plane was to take off, however, she suddenly had a heart attack in Pak-istan. She never set foot on her scheduled flight and died right there. People said she was lucky to have said good-bye to all of our relatives before she died, something most Afghans killed in the war never had a chance to do.

Although she regularly went to the doctor, nobody knew that she had heart trouble. We sometimes think that if she had only made it on the flight to the United States and gotten to a doctor here, she might still be alive today. I wondered to myself: If only she could have gotten on the plane a day before, if only she could have been given asylum just a few days before, I might have a grandma. I decided that I would find a grandma in the United States, and I would search for a few years before I would find her.

After the Khojak Pass, we drove through many small villages, which were built around the main road. The same type of shops appeared in every village. There were vehicle parts shops with rubber tires hanging inside, fabric shops, fruit and vegetable vendors, and shops that sold essentials like rice, oil, and sugar. We were coming up to a mountain of large yellow-green indige-nous cantaloupes piled in front of a shop, the kind that made the back of your jaw twinge when you took your first bite. They were the size of watermelons and shaped like huge footballs. My mouth watered. I didn't have a knife, so I kept thinking of smashing one against the ground and eating the fleshy insides with my bare hands.

The closer we got to Afghanistan, the more the roadside shacks appeared forlorn. Everything for sale looked less appealing. The packages of goods were dustier. The items looked older and there was less of a selection. The only thing that improved was the quality of the cantaloupes and other fruit.

Finally we were approaching the border. I knew this because the driver pulled out the cassette tape of music that had been playing over and over again all through the ride. He then pulled at a knob in the middle of the dashboard between the passenger and the driver to reveal a secret compartment into which he slid the cassette. He quickly pushed the plastic cover back over the compartment. The Taliban banned all types of music except religious chanting without instruments. The songs our driver was playing, about land, love, and pretty women, were all certainly criminal.

I clutched the leather purse that contained my video camera under my *burqa*. It was also a crime to travel into the country with a video camera, but I needed to capture my relatives on tape. These tapes could be the only memory I would ever keep of them. Their lives could not be forgotten, even if they were only remembered by my family and me.

This would also be my first encounter with the Taliban. The grip of the Taliban regime was strong. The Revolutionary Association of the Women of Afghanistan (RAWA) had a video of a woman accused of adultery being shot in Kabul stadium. A woman going without a *burqa*, or found wearing nail polish and lipstick, could be beaten unconscious by the Taliban's religious police, the infamous Department for Prevention of Vice and Promotion of Virtue. A year earlier, a cousin who was visiting Kandahar from Pakistan put on the Saudi-style veil she wore in Pakistan, which was black and covered her face, but revealed her eyes. Because she was only walking next door, she felt like she didn't need to put on the traditional Afghan *burqa* with a hood covering the eyes. At that moment, however, the Taliban's religious police had been cruising by in one of their notorious black pickup trucks with black tinted windows.

A Talib stepped out of the vehicle and began to lash at her ankles and her legs with a whip, all the while yelling, "Why are you wearing this?"

My cousin cried out, "Aren't you ashamed that you're beating a woman?"

She paid the price for her remarks with even more lashings.

Under the Taliban's rules, a woman would be imprisoned for wearing shoes that made the slightest noise. Even women's footsteps have to be silenced. Could I, an outspoken American, stay silent? Since our departure from Quetta, I had to keep reminding myself not to utter any words in English. I felt that as long as I played by the rules and denied my American identity, I'd be safe. I was going to be a pure Kandahari girl.

My strongest fear was that a Talib would discover I was American, find my hidden video camera, decide that I must be an American spy, and try to detain me and interrogate me—or worse. I had to pass as a local.

Although my family was not ready for the possibility and I hadn't wanted to alarm them, I had come to Afghanistan with the secret idea that I would work for women in an aid agency in Kandahar City for a year. I had come thinking I might be so enthralled I would stay, living with Afghan relatives as an American woman; I'd find a nonthreatening way to repackage myself as something acceptable and let them see that Western women aren't dangerous to society. I would be the emissary and the bridge between my two countries.

I fantasized that I would marry the leader of Taliban-controlled Afghanistan, Mullah Omar, becoming his fourth wife, and convince him, by showing him who I was, that women should be given more rights in this society. I believed I could make anyone like me if I tried hard enough, including Mullah Omar, and that would translate into better conditions for the women of my country. I dared never to express the idea to anyone, because they would think I was either crazy or an American spy. The latter worried me more.

On the other hand, one part of me secretly felt drawn to taking risks. A part of me wanted to get captured, to have an adventure. I'd heard that the Taliban treated women respectfully in prison. I thought if worse came to worst, and I was imprisoned, they would feed me and treat me well.

But for now I was safe. By law I had to travel accompanied by a male relative in Taliban-controlled Afghanistan, and I was traveling with Jan Agha as my *mahram*, the Arabic word used in Islam to refer to a woman's male guardian.

At the border, I saw three men in traditional Afghan clothes, in pale blue, with thick black beards. Jan Agha had also grown his beard to prepare for the journey, as did any male that wanted to go into the country. Later, I wondered if there was a business opportunity near the border—selling synthetic beards. The Taliban also had thick black turbans twisted around their heads, and Kalashnikovs slung over their shoulders, fingers on the triggers. I thought their loose-fitting pants and black turbans made them look like ancient assassins, groomed from birth to fight the Crusaders. Our driver turned to Jan Agha and said, "You know I've got to pay a fee here." He spoke in Pashto. Even our driver must not know where we came from. When, a couple of hours into the trip, he asked if we were from America, Jan Agha responded that we were from Karachi in Pakistan. No one could be trusted.

After paying the bribe, we switched drivers and pulled onto the dusty path to Kandahar. I tried to settle into my seat on some luggage that rested right in the cargo area between the front passenger and the driver. This leg of the trip was especially bumpy. The unpaved road was merely a path of light gray and sand-colored rocks guiding us through the hard-baked, sun-bleached earth around us. From where I sat, I tried to make out the driver's face in the rearview mirror. I wondered what his life was like. How long had he been driving? Who had he transported? Criminals? Taliban? Drugs? All sorts of things traveled across the border.

The replacement driver asked where we were from. This time, Jan Agha admitted we were from the United States. I sensed he trusted this driver. This made me calmer.

"So, can you make a good living there?" the driver asked.

"Yes, but the work of fried chicken is hard."

Jan Agha worked in a Kennedy Fried Chicken—one of many by that name. Like the Korean immigrants who had seemingly monopolized the corner grocery stores in Manhattan, Afghans thought of success in terms of ownership in proprietary fast-food establishments whose main product was fried chicken. These chicken stores were often located in low-income neighborhoods and were prone to armed robbery. The order taker stood behind a thick slab of bulletproof glass. He was always the one who spoke better English. This meant that he could take orders for food just as well as orders from robbers. They would understand things like "lay down on the floor," or "I'm going to lock you in the large meat freezer." Bad communication due to a lack of basic English made for greater danger in a time of panic. He'd speak through the pattern of small holes drilled through the glass above the security carousel, into which the person would place the money in exchange for the white-colored paper bags filled with fried chicken. The money would come first. The carousel would rotate, delivering fried chicken and change to the customer. When you came to America, you were placed in training at one of these restaurants for about two weeks before you were allowed to work the back, where you prepared the food. A promotion meant you could speak enough English to work the front. My father had worked his way through the fried chicken business, starting in the back, working his way to the front, and eventually owning larger and larger stakes in the stores he worked in. My father once worked at Texas Fried Chicken in Brooklyn. It was located near the subway stop, which meant it was a high-volume site. Once, late at night, he had to step outside of the bulletproof encasing in order to mop the sitting area, the most dangerous task. As he was doing this, a largeman walked into the store and immediately lunged at my father. The story was that my father had managed to pull out a knife that he kept in his pocket and held it toward the man. I could imagine the look of my father's small, fear-struck eyes, likely made beady to scare the man away. It worked.

The driver glanced toward Jan Agha. "Yes, but you can do well in fried chicken. Work here does not make us any money."

Driving over the rocks caused the dust on the ground to rise and fill our van. We did not drive straight ahead on the path but snaked our way through, sometimes climbing to the edge of the rocks and back down. Sometimes the dust of a passing vehicle would kick up ahead of us, making it impossible to see where we were going. It was in these moments that I was most afraid the same would be happening to the car coming toward us and we would hit each other head-on. The driver never flinched.

By noon, the sun created an invisible blanket of heat so intense it was angry.

I missed the cool air in Pakistan, and I sat quietly in the car reflecting on my cousin Suraya's life. She had just been married and was pregnant with her first child, but had just left her hus-band and returned to her family after unsuccessful attempts at both suicide and a crude abortion. Suraya refused to slave away in service of her in-laws, but her family was still hoping she could be convinced to return to her husband. She was only in her fourth month of pregnancy and was already having unusual pains. I wondered if she would share her mother's fate. My mother's eldest sister had died suddenly while pregnant with her fifth child. It was never clear what exactly went wrong, but death during pregnancy and childbirth was not an uncommon end to a woman's life.

Afghanistan had the highest maternal death rate in the world, with only one clinic for every forty thousand people. That statistic, combined with one in four children dying before the age of five, meant that my family's survival alone was no small feat. When I was born, the rate was even worse, with one in two children dying by the time they reached the age at which I left Afghanistan.[3] I must have survived because I was meant to do something about it. But I couldn't even help my own cousin. What would I, a young American woman, be able to do?

Back on the road to Kandahar, I looked out at the desert landscape. We drove along on a barren path, encountering nothing save for an occasional man or youngster squatting by the side of the road. We drove past no villages. We encountered no shacks. Where had the squatters come from? It was even more of a curiosity because it was so hot that the idea of traveling a long distance on foot seemed impossible. These people were tough.

So was Jan Agha. He did not complain about the heat or the dust or being hungry or thirsty. He seemed to be an object without any needs. He had been hardened in some way, though I was never sure what caused it. Moor used to say that it was the way my father's side of the family was; they would never admit personal pain. It was a trait she attributed to the Popalzai tribe, one that I reflected on during my own pain in my marriage. I wanted to be a tough Popalzai. Once, Jan Agha told me that he didn't feel cold, not even in the freezing temperatures of the record-breaking blizzards in New York in 1996.

A few times, we passed men hard at work shoveling rocks from the edge of the road closer to the center. It looked like dangerous work. As we'd drive closer, they'd slow their work and try to make eye contact with us.

"What are they doing?" I asked as I looked toward Jan Agha.

After a pause, the driver turned toward him and answered. "They're not doing anything useful. They're just hoping we'll tip them for seeming to be maintaining the roads."

The level of desperation was stark. I hated that the Afghans had to beg, that they were turning into a nation of beggars. Still, one of my fantasies was to return home and hand people money. My long-standing dream was of going into my families' homes and villages of people I didn't know and giving them everything they wanted—like a showering from Heaven of good things. And since I'd arrived, I couldn't stop myself. I just kept giving people money. I wanted to feel like I personally could bring them relief and that they would benefit and feel good. They would feel loved. And I would feel less guilty for having so much.

Finally we drove up to a large rusted piece of metal gate with an opening big enough for two vehicles to pass through. It was misshapen, incomplete, as if it were torn off of something larger. I sighed. When would we arrive?

My aunt leaned over to me. "That's the gate to Kandahar."

We slowly edged through and soon came upon what I thought were the outskirts of the city. We were greeted by a row of yellow lights hanging from the connected shacks. Here men rode by on motorbikes. Some men were on foot, others on bicycles, others perched on top of horse-drawn carriages. There was no order, just chaos flowing in the same direction on one side of the path.

I saw shacks that looked ready to fall apart and crumble. I wondered if they would dissolve when it rained. They looked like toys.

My aunt pointed to a shack situated in between a fork. "That's the general store. That's where all the rich people come to shop."

I stared. Not only was it deserted, but I could only make out a few dusty green slabs of Wrigley's Doublemint gum in the window.

We drove past a few more shacks and turned a corner where a motorcycle whizzed by us and kicked up the dust. The honking of car horns mixed with the squeaks of bike tires against fenders. A moped roared by—a bolt of energy, an independent random streak leaving the sound behind.

We drove straight and took a sharp right turn and stopped. I could see blue traditional men's long shirts hanging from a clothesline over a wall that had been beaten down. I was sure it was a mistake. We must have stopped here to get directions. The entire house seemed to be made of crumbling khaki-colored adobe-like clay walls. But no, this was the house of Jan Agha's older brother, also my first cousin.

So this was the legendary place my parents had talked about endlessly? Had we gone through all that traveling and risked danger to come to this decaying place in a little town in the middle of the desert? Driving through the streets of Kandahar City, I felt like we had been in a maze, and now I had reached the end, and it was as if we had suddenly come to the end of the earth.

Then I smelled the same aroma as when Moor made Afghan bread from scratch in Brooklyn. I also remembered the smell from when I had been a child. It smelled like home.

Growing up, I wondered where earth ended. Surely there must be a place where it stopped. This felt like the farthest place one could travel to from America. This was the far corner of the world no one had ventured to. This was the place I was born and where most of my family lived. This was the place I had come to find myself.

This was Kandahar.

Chapter 7

A Visitor from Hollywood

Even God is a refugee from Afghanistan.

—Afghan refugee living in America

At first, Mamoon reminded me of a mouse. His head was a little big for his tiny six-year-old frame, and his eyes always seemed to be looking for something to play with, scuttling and darting from one object to another, like a mouse scampering to and fro. The youngest of six siblings, he ran about my aunt's house poking the other children, peering back at me as he did, apparently waiting for me to notice and stop him from acting the provocateur. Playfully, I gave him a poke instead of a scold, and his intense dark brown eyes froze in shock for just a moment, then lit up again as he burst out in laughter, revealing a huge smile of tiny little teeth. He realized that I was willing to play his game.

It was late July 2001, and I was nearly two weeks into my journey. I had left Kandahar when I was nearly Mamoon's age. I was twenty-three now, the same age as the war.

It was several weeks before the Towers were to fall, during the time when Kandahar and Afghanistan were still forgotten by the world. Kandahar got its name long ago, but no one seems to know where it came from. The name Kandahar is supposed to be a corruption of Iskandar, the Persian name for Alexander the

Great, who some believe built the city more than two thousand years ago. History records that Alexander's successor sold the "oasis" of Kandahar to the emperor of India for five hundred war elephants.[1] Others trace the name to the ancient Indian city of Gandhara. Some even claim that the Indian settlers of the Kandahar area brought with them a large stone vessel now kept in a mosque in Kandahar, said to be the begging pot used by Buddha. Everyone agrees that Kandahar has stood through history as a gateway to Greece and Persia in the west, India in the east, and Russia and central Asia to the north. As a result, Kandahar has been the frontier of great religions, where Buddhism mingled with Greek mythology and Zoroastrianism. A Chinese visitor in about AD 630 found Hindu temples, but also gods worshiped on mountaintops by horsemen who would offer up gold and livestock in sacrifice. I found it tragic that a city with a history of such great religious and cultural diversity could be reduced by a small group of narrow-minded men into their own pet theology project.

An Arab historian described Kandahar in the fourteenth century as a large city near the sea. A sixteenth-century writer even called it a "seaport," although every time we drove through a canal, it looked more like a large dried-up ditch. The whole city was dehydrated, and Afghans who could afford it were drilling into the water table to pump the water up. Afghans in the diaspora were paying for wells to be drilled for their families in Afghanistan, and the *mullah* at the mosque in New York even encouraged people to pool their money for well drilling as their charitable work. By July of 2001 Afghanistan had suffered three years of the worst drought anyone could remember in his or her lifetime. Kandahar's drought was the longest, and experts now say it is turning into a desert. The United Nations long ago declared the water in Kandahar City to be unfit for drinking. Only one out of four Afghans had access to safe drinking water. People were desperate for water, but as more of them drilled for wells, the water table receded farther into the earth, making it necessary to drill deeper and deeper. Afghans say they can drill a hundred meters into the ground without finding any water; in the past, they found water at five meters.

Mamoon's mother was Khala Sherina, my mother's sister. Khala Sherina means "sweet aunt" in Pashto. Her given name was Spoozhmai, a dreamy Pashto word which means "moon." Twenty-five years ago, Khala Sherina married and moved into the same home I was now visiting in Kandahar. Since then, her only travel outside the city had been a recent visit to her nieces and nephews in Pakistan, after her sister, my other aunt, passed away suddenly while carrying her fifth child. It was a simple household fall while cleaning; had she not been living as an impoverished refugee in Pakistan, she would likely have survived. At Pakistani hospitals, crowds of Afghans seeking medical attention are beaten back with batons. Death during pregnancy and childbirth was not an uncommon end to an Afghan woman's life as a refugee.

After finding me a willing playmate, Mamoon poked me back, only to have Khala Sherina shoot him a stern look of motherly discipline. Mamoon froze and dropped his arms. Innocence quickly replaced the mischief in his small dark eyes, which also began to fill with an imploring look of apology. A naughty glint, however, returned when Mamoon glanced at me to see if I would defend him and continue the game.

Khala Sherina embraced me, and then turned to Mamoon. "Do you know what a valuable guest this is?"

I looked at Khala Sherina and her warm smile. In her youth, she must have been stunning. Even now, in her off-white dress with autumn-colored flowers, she looked almost like a little girl. Only the wrinkles surrounding her eyes and lips betrayed her age. Her jet black hair, adorned with a single pin, had recently been dyed in anticipation of her guests. She wore it short, in what would be referred to in America as a trendy "bob cut." For Khala Sherina, it was the haircut she had had all her life. My arrival had surprised her. She had only been expecting her youngest sister, Lailuma, to visit, and not me, the daughter of Runa, her second-youngest sister.

As Khala Sherina explained who I was, Mamoon sat on one of the red velvet mattresses on the floor. He flopped around on the mattress, bored. Khala Sherina explained how important I was to her as her niece, that she hadn't seen me since I was almost five, and that I had traveled very far to make this visit. Mamoon knew that I had come from America, but he was more interested in the fact that there was someone new for him on which to focus his apparently insatiable curiosity. It was the young adults and older people who were more fascinated by my having become an American.

To Khala Sherina my first return meant everything. I was regarded with such respect—almost with awe—that I actually felt embarrassed. Just because I had come from America did not mean I was better than my relatives, although this is how they treated me. They insisted that I have the best seat on the floor during meals. They insisted that I take my food before the children. I was not allowed to wash the dishes or to help with any other housework. They even wanted to wash my clothes for me.

At Khala Sherina's house, I had gifts to give out. We were all seated in the guest room on the red velvet mattresses. By the time we started opening up gifts, Mamoon and I had developed a friendship and I felt close to this little boy with the big smile, tiny little teeth, and intense dark eyes. Mamoon sat close to me so that he could help pass the gifts. He waited very patiently and politely for his gift as the others were passed out. I looked at him, the ever-present cowlick in his hair waving back and forth as he moved his head. I felt like I wanted to sink into the earth and fall through. I had brought no gift for Mamoon.

When the gifts were all passed out and he realized there was nothing for him, he looked at me not with anger, but with an expression of sadness and puzzled disappointment. Here I was, this person who could have brought something from my world for him—and I had failed. I only learned of Mamoon's existence upon my arrival, so I had brought no gift for this six-year-old first cousin of mine. I thought about how one can't do anything for a person whose existence is not known. To most of the world, I thought, this overlooked country of Afghanistan didn't really exist either. Mamoon was an unknown child in a forgotten land. It took my traveling thousands of miles, not knowing what to expect, to find this little kid, who was family and with whom I fell in love.

The next morning I promised him I would take him to the market and buy him whatever he wanted, regardless of price. Khala Sherina thought I was being silly. Worried about my own protection, she did not want me to go out alone with a small child into the marketplace. But I was determined to make this special trip with Mamoon.

The marketplace was a bazaar like something out of *The Arabian Nights*. There were street vendors on all sides hawking their goods, yelling at people to come look at their wares, and then haggling with those who ventured over. People were pushing into us in the bustle, and shouting at us from every direction. I was wearing my *burqa*, which greatly obscured my vision. I told Mamoon that he had to hold my hand because I didn't know where I was going. He kept running ahead of me in his excitement and I was afraid that he would abandon me in this world I didn't fully understand. I was now very dependent on this mouse of a six-year-old.

Soon I stopped and shouted to him, "Mamoon, you have got to come back and hold my hand!"

I told him that I was not going to continue unless he led me. He turned back and shook his head, his little skyward cowlick hairs rocking back and forth. He walked toward me, took my hand, and said, "Don't worry. Don't pay attention to the people yelling. Just follow me."

I began to see the more grown-up side of this little child. He knew exactly where he wanted to go and we soon arrived at one particular vendor who sold plastic toy trucks and other vehicles. The toy trucks were probably the cheapest, most badly made toys I had ever seen. Mamoon picked a tiny little toy car. I thought, That's it? I had told this kid that he could have anything he wanted, and he picked a very modest item from a very modest selection. I was disappointed in his choice, as I hoped he would have wanted something a bit grander. The item cost only pennies.

I asked him if that was really what he wanted. Reluctantly, almost embarrassingly, he pointed to the biggest truck the vendor had and said, "That is really what I want."

I told him to take that and to pick some other items for his brothers. We ended up buying a whole bag of toy vehicles. When it came to paying, Mamoon became very protective of me, as he was afraid I could not handle the payment. I pulled out my money, not really knowing how much I had, and gave it to him. After he talked with the vendor, Mamoon carefully counted the money out.

My family was curious when I got back. They thought that the vendor probably exploited us. I intentionally didn't haggle with him. I expected to be a little exploited. This was the first time in my life that I didn't care if I was exploited for some money. It was the first time I had dealt with a merchant in my native country and there was something deeply beautiful in that for me—to be able to talk to him in my own Pashto, to be buying these items in the bazaar. If he wanted to rip me off for a few pennies, then that was my gift to him for the experience. I explained this to my family and they laughed at me.

I loved watching Mamoon's delight as he played with his new trucks. I later realized that he didn't have much else to do. There were no schools to attend, and only his siblings and occasional pest cousins to play with. He was confined to the house—which was probably fine for now. He was still young enough that the house appeared huge and there was enough he could explore and find to amuse himself with. However, I knew he would soon outgrow this and become restless.

While Mamoon was still curious about the things he could find in the family's courtyard, his older siblings were listless from the boredom and confinement inflicted on them by the heartless rulers of this torn and barren country. I recalled the times that I had to stay home—when I was just a bit older than he was. With nothing to do the day becomes endless. I remember how the hours crawled by, how the days stretched and became eternal. What if every day was that long, all 365 days of the year? This is what life was for Mamoon's older siblings. It would soon be this way for Mamoon too.

There was a whole world for Mamoon to discover, but there were no schools to teach him this. He could attend a *madrassa*, but his family refused to send him there because the Taliban would teach him violence and he might be trained to fight holy wars for the movement. While there was so much to see and learn about, he would probably spend his whole life in and about this house. His little mind could be touched and stimulated and expanded in so many different ways, yet here, that would probably never happen.

Mamoon's older brother Qais was twelve, and lucky enough to attend a Turkish-run school for gifted children. The quality of his education was poor, because his school was repeatedly shut down by the Taliban, but his dedication did not waver one bit. Every night at Khala Sherina's, the light in his room stayed lit long after we had fallen asleep in the courtyard. Qais was the last one to sleep, and the first one to rise, soon hopping on his bike to ride the potholed streets to school. He had a workbook to learn English, his only tool for accessing the language that would one day connect him to the rest of the world. He would soon finish the workbook, and I hoped I could smuggle in more English-language books through relatives so he could continue his studies. Qais's older brothers, while not quite as studious, were learning Microsoft Windows 98, Word, and even Excel, but there was little prospect of putting their knowledge to use under the iron-fisted Taliban regime.

Khala Sherina's home was older than they could remember. Like most homes in Kandahar, it was "Muslim appropriate" because it had high walls on the outside so that no one could see the women inside, and a large courtyard around which the foundation of the house was built. By American standards, the house was cramped. Four families lived there, including Khala Sherina's mother-in-law, her still unmarried sister-in-law, and her two married brothers-in-law and their wives and children. Each family had one room, and there was also a guest room, and a basement that the family shared on the hottest summer days.

Although all the families slept outside in the courtyard at night, we had almost no contact, and I never spoke to Khala Sherina's brothers-in-law, even though I was staying in the same house. It was considered inappropriate for us to mingle, and I didn't want to disturb the family's relationship. At the crack of dawn, the pet roosters cock-a-doodle-dooed, like nature's alarm clocks that come alive and keep going. The families in the house had already observed their prayers, and as the sun washed the earth with its light, they moved the mats into the house and began the day. I usually slept through all this.

Almost half of the house, the entire left side, was unusable, decayed so badly it was beyond repair. Looking across the courtyard, through the arches, I could see spiderwebs and pieces of decayed wood. The bathroom was located on this side of the house. To get there, you had to walk through a covered passageway where there lay an old rusted wheelchair and go up a few uneven stairs, to a man-made, uneven hole in the adobe ground, which looked like someone had cracked it with a pick. Since the bathroom didn't have a door, you had to cough as you were approaching the bathroom, to make sure no one else was in it. If someone coughed back, that was your cue to wait.

I was most afraid to go to the bathroom at night, where I would often imagine skeletons sitting in the wheelchair and bats on the ceiling of the covered passageway. Luckily I had brought a flashlight, which everyone made fun of me for doing. I was the prepared American, with a gadget for everything, as if I were coming to the wild outback. To much of my family, I was a Kandahari girl coming back home. I should not be afraid of the bathroom in the dark, and I should drink the water they drink, they said, because I was born there and raised on that water.

With Khala Sherina's home as my base of operations, I made several trips to visit other family members. My journeys between homes were always under the cover of a *burqa*. At all times I was to be accompanied by a male relative, although our usual *mahram*, Mamoon's brother Raoul, was barely nine. Whenever I returned, I often found Mamoon running about the house, engaged in mischief. I would talk and play with him most often in the guest room, or what would be the equivalent of a parlor in the West. Khala Sherina would open this otherwise locked room to accommodate guests. The room was constructed, as the rest of the house was, of baked adobe-like clay. There were no windows and the walls were covered in a thinning white paint. Several red velvet mattresses made of a combination of sponge and feathers were spread on the floor for sitting.

The guest room held the family's most valuable possessions. There was the refrigerator, locked in the guest room across the courtyard, and quite far from the kitchen. There was no furniture beyond the mattresses, though the walls had recessed shelves that held family treasures. Each recess, or *tagcha*, pointed skyward, as it was square on the bottom and finished at the top in the form of a peaked arch. In one *tagcha*, matching cups surrounded a liter-sized lime-green glass pitcher. Mounted in a gold frame above it, in elegant red and black writing, was a transcribed prayer. The prayer had been beautifully penned by Mamoon's older brother Homayoon, who was apprenticed to a calligrapher.

Clearly, one of the most exalted treasures in the room was a common plastic soccer trophy. The trophy itself was ordinary and not in itself special. The base was plastic but made to look like wood. The plastic figurine at the top was colored so that it reflected light in a dull gold. Looking at the trophy, I felt for a moment as if I could have been standing in any living room in suburban America. Since sports were discouraged, if not occasionally outlawed by the Taliban, this single item intrigued me.

The trophy had been awarded to Najib, Mamoon's brother. Najib looked like an older version of Mamoon, except that his head was the right size for his body. He was slight at five feet four, polite and soft-spoken, although his big nostrils would flare when he talked to me.

A few days later, Najib told me about his soccer trophy. We were traveling across rock-strewn roads in the hundred-degree heat to visit relatives. Najib was my *mahram*, or male guardian, that day. Though cousins could not serve as escorts under Taliban law, we were both prepared to lie and claim a brother-sister relationship in the event we were caught. He seemed ready to open up as we sat in the back of a shaky motorized rickshaw. He began to talk in his quiet voice. I watched the rocky land pass by; its various tan shades of sun-bleached earth and rock were tinted blue through the fabric screen of my *burqa*. I steadied myself on a metal stabilizer bar and listened.

Najib seemed nervous as he spoke, taking short, fast breaths between sentences. He told me he was a good soccer player. He believed that if he only had the chance to prove himself, his soccer ability would be his ticket to success. He was not unlike thousands of American boys who dreamed of playing professional baseball or basketball. Najib's aspirations were considerably more modest. For him, it wasn't about making it to the big leagues—it was about making it to America. In Afghanistan, America was the big league.

Najib knew that at one time I had worked for CONCACAF, the international body under FIFA (Fédération Internationale de Football Association) that organizes professional soccer in North and Central America and the Caribbean. Najib wanted me to use my soccer contacts to bring him to America. I watched his pride thin for a moment in the glaring sun. The semisteady rickshaw rattled us across the craggy roads. I was being pitched.

He offered to play soccer on a trial basis, happily without pay. If only he could show his talent to the right people, he believed he could make it in soccer and stay in the United States. The rickshaw hit an especially large bump and I held tighter to the stabilizer bar. In my stomach I felt a silent dropping emptiness as he poured his hope into me. It was an uneasy responsibility. He was asking *me* to believe in him. I knew that his dream was one I could not make happen. The reality was as harsh as the landscape passing by with every bump and jerk of the rickshaw.

To Afghans, America was an almost mythical place, reached only by people with strong initiative and great luck. Somehow, people who made it to America suddenly became a different class. This was especially true for women. For women who visited Afghanistan after moving to America, going back was an opportunity to be a star. They were fawned over. They were envied for the fact they were able to drive automobiles, for the jewelry they could afford and the clothes they could wear. They had the American dream lifestyle of washing machines and microwave ovens. Americans were the stars of the world and to walk among them made their Afghan relatives like stars. To an Afghan, reaching American shores holds the same allure and mystique as the concept of going to Hollywood and becoming a celebrity does for an American.

I did my best to downplay my American privilege. I followed my mother's advice and wore nothing nicer than my hosts. I didn't bring my best clothes, and I certainly did not bring any American clothes. I wore no jewelry. Apparently I disappointed my relatives, who expected nothing short of grandeur. They poked fun at my plain shoes, the black Aerosoles flats I had bought in Queens en route to the airport. Ironically, my Afghan relatives looked much more fashionable than I did, and were a little bit confused when the American had not swept into their homes clad in all her regalia.

When I visited Janaraa, one of my mother's cousins, she picked up my shoes and looked at them with obvious distaste. "I would never be caught wearing these," she quipped.

Janaraa was in her forties, with a weathered face, droopy eyelids, and a substantial gap between her front two teeth. The gap in her teeth was aligned with the part in her graying hair, pulled back strictly in a ponytail. She had no qualms about telling you how she felt. She was one of the most outgoing women I had met in Afghanistan, and she almost always infused her words with humor. She was adept at using her wit to say things that perhaps she would not get away with if said in all seriousness.

Janaraa scoffed at my conservative, even matronly outfit of a brown Afghan-style tunic and baggy pants. "Do you have such low expectations of our understanding of fashion that you would dress this way to visit us? If you send gifts, do not send ones like this," she said as she pointed at my shoes.

My austerity stemmed from something that I felt was more important than humility. I was afraid to show my relatives what they were missing by not being in the United States. Many Afghans I had met cherished an ever-present fantasy of someday making it to America. Even the proudest Afghans, in their private moments, would share with me how they would leave immediately for America if they only had the opportunity. For most Afghans this desire sits quietly beneath their unflinchingly stoic exterior. When this deep internal drive to leave is brought to the edge of their hearts, where they must acknowledge and confront it, their already difficult lives become filled with tortured longing. The intense longing some of them felt reminded me of the kind one feels for a lost love, the kind that could drive you mad. I knew that many of the people I would meet during my trip would believe that I could help them get to America. I would represent the freedom and magic of the West. My visit was a tough reminder of a world that excluded them. I tried to minimize the appearance of the already extreme gap between my privilege and their reality.

Sulaiman, Janaraa's husband, was a handsome man with leathery tanned skin, a button nose, and soft eyes, and he had a jovial way of expressing himself. Soon after I arrived, he hatched his own plan for making it to the United States. With my small video camera, Sulaiman recorded a marriage proposal to a very elderly cousin in California. At first, I thought he did this as a joke. He was serious. He would marry this cousin so that he could come to America and then ultimately send for Janaraa and the rest of his family. Janaraa joked that if Sulaiman really did marry this elderly cousin, she would never divorce him because she would want to keep him all to herself.

One day back at Khala Sherina's house, we had taken our afternoon nap, as usual, but I could not get up. My eyes felt heavy when I tried to open them, my body limp.

Khala Sherina stuck her head in the room and whispered, "Masuda, can you please go sleep in the other room?"

I looked up toward the door wearily, surprised but not wanting to be rude.

"I'm sorry, but we have guests," she insisted.

I was sleeping in the guest room, as it was the only empty room in the house. I knew she was being sweet to me by telling me I could sleep elsewhere, but I knew that I should probably get up and see the guests. As I got up I felt my clothes sticking to me, and sweat sliding down the back of my neck. I filled two buckets of water from the aluminum water container and carried them upstairs. Pouring cold buckets of water on my head was not the way I liked to wake up, but that was what they used, and I felt I would have been offered something better if they had it.

I fixed myself up and walked through the courtyard, wondering where my female cousin Ousi was. Being the young woman in the house, Ousi was expected to be present serving the guests and assisting her mother, Khala Sherina. I greeted the guests, kissing each one of them on the cheek three times, and sat down. Aunt Lailuma told them how our trip was going so far, and about all the relatives we had seen, while I helped Khala Sherina prepare tea and cookies. Ousi had a headache and was sleeping in the basement, so I was the only girl in the house to help make the guests feel at home. I fixed the tea for our guests, who were eerily silent, carefully studying my motions as if there were some important secret to my character to be learned from them.

Finally our guests stated the purpose of their visit. "We are here to ask for Masuda," pronounced the eldest woman as she looked over at me expectantly. I immediately directed my eyes at the floor, not wanting to make contact because I felt I would burst out laughing. She turned to Aunt Lailuma. "We know the Sultan family and we think you are all wonderful people. Good Pashtuns. Good Muslims. I have a good son. What do you think?" It was as if she were delivering a prepared speech. Aunt Lailuma, feeling like she should say something, said, "Yes, you are good people too."

The woman continued, "We know Masuda has grown up in America, and has probably attended school there, but my son is educated too. He has been through ten whole years of school. How many years does it take to complete school in America?"

Aunt Lailuma smiled and said, "Well, Masuda's parents are not here, and I think Masuda is an adult and can speak for herself," looking over at me as if to suggest she couldn't take responsibility for me.

I had been getting formal marriage proposals since I was eleven, and informal ones before that, but I had been taught to be shy. I remember the first time a group of women had come over, I was so nervous. I served tea, sat in the corner, and mostly tried to keep myself busy in the kitchen. My mother usually maintained I was still too young for marriage, so I never had to say much.

This was new. I was an adult and had to speak for myself. At first I was speechless, assuming someone would answer the proposal on my behalf, especially in Afghanistan. A tense silence filled the room, as I internally debated how dismissive I could be without seeming rude. The polite thing to do would have been to raise an excuse, like saying I was too young, or already promised to another man. But neither of these excuses would have been true. Still, I wanted to deflect the proposal in the nicest way possible, so as not to insult the family. I especially didn't want them to think I was looking down on them based on their poverty. But if I did not reject their proposal outright, I would have seemed interested in their son. To preserve their chastity and good morals, Afghan girls are expected to be very shy and devoid of expression when the topic of boys or marriage comes up. Our guests had breached a cultural norm in asking me how I felt about marrying their son. Normally a woman in my situation would never have responded to such a proposal, remaining silent until her female relatives spoke up. Because I was an educated, divorced woman who had lived in America, our guests expected a direct answer. I was even proud that Aunt Lailuma thought I could handle this delicate situation.

I decided to seize on the educational gap between my suitor

and me as a source of incompatibility. Generally speaking, Afghan families avoid finding overly educated wives for their sons, because they will be rebellious and chronically unsatisfied.

I looked up at my suitor's mother, still avoiding eye contact out of shame, and quietly spoke up. "School in America is twelve years, then there is college, which I also went to, which is another four."

"Well, you're better educated than our son. That's okay. Even though he was raised in Afghanistan, his habits are like a boy raised in America."

I was touched and flattered that she thought I would be good enough for her son. I also appreciated her boldness in approaching an educated Afghan-American woman for her son. I wondered if she knew I was divorced. The subject didn't come up at all, but judging from the speed at which Afghan gossip travels, it would have been nearly impossible for her *not* to know.

She proceeded to tell stories about her son, explaining how he was her most handsome child and how sweet he was to the other children. This was common practice during proposals. The level of exaggeration, though, would depend on the family. Sometimes, girls were wedded to men who were not as rich as the asking delegation presented him to be, and sometimes the family would even be "tricked" into giving their daughter away to someone handicapped, or crazy. I wondered how much of her description was accurate.

The part of me that had a hard time saying no to any adventure imagined how much my life could change in a second if I just said yes to this woman. The old Masuda could just vanish, and I could become a typical Afghan woman in Kandahar, doing housework all the time, bearing many children. For all I had accomplished, all I had done not to be that woman, the risk was still imminent. As if driving on a fast road, I could make a sudden turn and be the person I could have been. Or maybe who I supposed to be?

I didn't have to live like the people in Afghanistan. I was rich, I was in good health, and I had access to the best people and places in the world. But there was little to remind me of my day-to-day life in the United States, and I had sunk into the environment and forgotten who I was. I felt as though the person I had been was gone. Had I been that woman stepping into chic places in New York, rubbing elbows with the wealthy and eating pricey steaks? Was I really that Masuda? The one who had an economics degree?

Remembering that was like finding extra money in my pocket. I had put it there but forgotten I had it. But none of the women I knew could really deeply understand what it was like to live as me. They didn't know the complexity of the economics courses I had taken—of regression models and the Black-Scholes model for calculating the value of options. I knew all of those things. And it meant absolutely nothing here. I wasn't even allowed to walk into the street, let alone apply complex economic knowledge.

"So what do you think, Masuda?" the mother of the "groom" asked. All eyes were focusing on me intently, including those of the young women that were accompanying her. I later learned one of the women was the "groom's" sister, and that the other two women were married to his brothers.

I wanted to laugh again. I couldn't hold back. It was so rude, but it was all I wanted to do. I smiled, concealing my laughter, and said that I wanted to continue my education.

"But you're already *so* educated," she objected.

"Yes, but in America that is not considered very educated. In America you can be in school for your whole life. I would like to study more before I get married," I persisted, hoping this would be the least hurtful way out of the situation. I certainly couldn't say that her son and I weren't a match. For a long time, I had resisted the idea that anyone could not be good enough for me, but as I grew more confident in myself, I realized I was allowed to believe it. Yes, there were certain standards I had, and if someone did not meet them, I would acknowledge that.

"My son is very forward-thinking. He would let you continue your education," she reassured me.

"I would like to continue my education, then think about marriage," I insisted, feeling like I was running out of things to say.

"We can speak to your parents in New York . . . ," she offered, thinking that I might need their approval before I could say yes.

"I know, but they will tell you the same thing," I retorted.

They finished their tea quickly, and as the elder woman picked up her *burqa* from the pile resting on my arm, she asked, "Are you a citizen?" referring to American citizenship.

"Yes," I replied, realizing why she had come for me in the first place.

"Well, he has cousins in London that are citizens too and we will ask for them," she volunteered, clearly annoyed by my rejection. While American citizenship was especially prized, citizenship from other countries in the West was valuable too.

Aunt Lailuma and I laughed when they left. "You can't blame them for wanting a better life for their son," she suggested. I agreed. Marriage had become a common route to America, especially since the United States had been admitting fewer Afghan refugees since the end of the Soviet war. Life in Kandahar was a far cry from the life that would have been available to this man had I only said yes.

One afternoon over tea I counted over forty first cousins just from my father's side of the family. My aunts Lailuma and Khala Sherina took me to homes of more cousins than I ever imagined I had. I later learned from another aunt that I have over a hundred cousins. They took me to Nasria's house for afternoon tea, which turned into afternoon tea, cookies, nuts, and fruit. One by one, the women in Nasria's family came out to greet us, kissing each one of us on the cheeks three times, and sat on the mattresses set up in the courtyard. Nasria's lanky sixteen-year-old daughter, Arzu, wrapped her hands around my shoulders and held tightly as she kissed me, saying she had heard much about me growing up. Her long black hair was tied in a low ponytail, with a sliver of her bangs twisted in the shape of a hook on her forehead. She kept smiling at me as if she were eager to talk, but I couldn't pay her much attention because the older women were engaged in conversation with me while Arzu went back and forth between the kitchen and the courtyard. A few young toddlers crawled about the carpets on which the mattresses were resting, grabbing at the cookies neatly placed on little plates. Nasria swept in and picked up two of them like a hawk, before one of them could get near a cup of hot tea. At first I thought they were Nasria's children, but Lailuma looked at me with raised eyebrows and whispered, "Young grandmother!" Nasria's house was one of the busiest I had seen, a young robust extended family of at least thirty women and children, but I knew there were more, since I hadn't yet met the men.

Until I visited Khala Sherina and my other relatives, I had never seen people who had so little give so much. Their generosity overwhelmed and moved me. Although I was in a modest home, I was treated like royalty. Cousins who had never met me treated me like a sister. Everyone, from Mamoon to his mother, protected and took care of me. Ousi tried her best to approximate for me the luxuries she believed I had in America, luxuries she herself went without.

I hadn't known that people who felt so abandoned could be so welcoming. Afghans feel that they have been discarded by the world—especially the United States. And yet, the greatest emotion they feel for the United States is a longing to go there—to have a chance at American privilege. What these people want most from America can be stated in a single word: opportunity. Najib dreamt of playing soccer. Sulaiman was willing to try for citizenship through his video proposal to our elderly relative.

Countless others shared with me or hinted at their yearning for the land that is America.

I saw courage and fearlessness in these people. I saw the courage brewing early in Mamoon, when he realized he was to protect me and guide me through the marketplace. I remember seeing it in the men of my country as they boldly rode their motorcycles across the dusty and rocky unpaved roads. They rode without helmets, the tails of their turbans tossed over their noses and mouths to protect them from dust. I remember looking at their faces when they rode next to our station wagon, seeing the unflinching intensity in their dark eyes. It was the same intensity I saw in Mamoon's eyes, only more seasoned and perhaps a bit more sad.

I would wonder what they were thinking about as they were caught in that moment, intrepidly riding down dangerous roads. The rest of the world seemed not to exist, and the only thing that mattered was the uncertain stretch of path before them. I thought they were most handsome in these moments.

It was from the women that I learned how much the men were hurting. The wound of abandonment ran deep. The lonesome resolve and bravery I saw in the men seemed to resemble the unrealistic independence developed by a teenager who has grown up believing that no one cares about him. They were unwilling to be vulnerable. They looked only to themselves and kept their pain behind a stony facade. This strange strength, a combination of fearlessness, male defiance, and fierce independence, was a way of dealing with unspeakably terrifying pain and vulnerability.

Yet, as I got to know some of them later, I would learn about the emotional soft side of these men under their stony exteriors. So many of the men I would later meet were more in love with flowers than with guns. They loved to listen to music, danced together, and had a wicked sense of humor—often making fun of one another, and making the kinds of self-deprecating jokes that are reminiscent of Mullah Nasrudin, a legendary jester whose name is used to hand down popular jokes and philosophical paradoxes from Sufi scholars. Although he may have lived as long as eight hundred years ago, Afghans quote from his jokes like they know him. His fame has spread to many other countries from the Middle East to China, which frequently claim him as one of their own.

Much of my family's joy at seeing me came from the realization that those who had left for America had not forgotten them. This fed the dream they held in their hearts. If they were remembered, then they could hope that they could one day join their families in America.

Wearing the *burqa* and obeying the Taliban's rules took some getting used to, but seemed like a small price to pay to see my family. My relatives would laugh when I wobbled, trying not to step on the hem of my *burqa*, which was a little too long. I had taken a longer *burqa* because when I wore one that was right for my size, it had exposed my clothes while I walked. The *burqa* had to be wrapped around the woman, though not too tightly, which would reveal the shape of a woman's behind, and held in a crunched-up ball in the front to prevent the shape of her breasts from showing. Once, when I was in the bazaar and unclenched my fists with the *burqa* wrapped inside, the hem of my *shalwar kameez* was revealed from underneath. When Khala Sherina saw this, she scolded me to quickly cover myself, as if the most private part of my body had been revealed. I accepted that Kandahar had a culture of modesty, even though I didn't agree with how it was being forced on everyone. But what I learned in the next few days put this culture in a new light. Sometimes, when walking in the street, I would see men adjusting themselves. Other times, I would see them squatting in front of the narrow open-air sewers, facing the wall. I was never sure what they were doing, refusing to believe it was anything dirty. I gave them too much credit.

One time, I watched intently as we approached a man squatting. A cousin I was traveling with was squirming, telling me not to look. The man was squatting and peeing in the open street! As we got closer to him he finished, reaching underneath his *kameez* to fix his trousers. I was stunned by the extreme double standard. Women were not allowed to show a snippet of fabric from under their *burqas*, while men shamelessly urinated into the open sewers in public. I thought Afghan culture was about respect, shame, and modesty.

This was hypocrisy. This was nothing like my parents had described when they spoke of Kandahar. I would soon see more.

Ousi, Mamoon's only and older sister, wanted me to see what life in Kandahar was really like for women. She took me to have tea at the home of a pharmacist she worked with in the clinic. Raoul escorted us, and I loved the idea of visiting a work friend with Ousi because it allowed us to be young modern girls in Kandahar. We met the pharmacist Mahbooba, and her teenage sister, Zeiba, in the guest room, where we kissed and sat and behaved as elder Afghan women. We drank tea kindly served by Zeiba, a feisty fourteen-year-old who asked me all sorts of questions about America. Did I drive a car? How did I get a license? Was I afraid that I would crash into other cars or run people over? What did I pay for my car and how did I get the money? Mahbooba told her sister to leave me alone. I was a guest and shouldn't be questioned so aggressively. But I enjoyed it all because the Taliban had outlawed female driving and I loved telling her what a regular event it was for women in America.

Zeiba's family was obviously very poor, judging from the house. I learned they were sharing it with another family, and that they did not have close relatives in the United States to help them financially. They had been in danger of losing even this place and becoming beggars on the street, but God "saved" them. When we left, Ousi told me that Zeiba had been promised to the sixty-six-year-old man who owned the house. He lived in the United States, and came back to visit a few times, staying with the family, which welcomed him gladly because they could no longer make the rent.

Everything changed on the day that he threatened to evict them from their home. They pleaded with him, begged him, asked him to have mercy. What could they possibly do to stay? He had a solution. If the family would give Zeiba to him in marriage, he would let them stay. As Ousi was telling me the story, I realized I knew this man. He had a large family in the States. He had many grandchildren, some the same age as Zeiba. He had a wife with rheumatoid arthritis who insisted on doing her own housework with her crooked fingers. I had watched her cook meals for *this man*. I was so angry. I wished he could magically appear before us so I could question him. I wanted to wrestle him down with my bare hands. Perhaps if he was a local Afghan I would be angry, but not so horrified. How could a man who lived in America do this? He knew that in America this was considered rape. How could he face God? How could *God* face this girl?

Ousi told me how often this happened in Afghanistan—how powerless the women were. This had been the practice for a long time in their culture. "Kandahar can be an awful place," she lamented as we passed the mud walls of the city's homes. These walls protected families from the hostile gaze of the world, but confined Zeiba and many girls like her in forced marriages and a life of servitude.

Chapter 8

The Worst Health Care in the World

*I came here for treatment. I had a bit of jewelry that I
sold to get here. Most women in Afghanistan have no
money, so when they get sick like I am, they just die.*

—Young woman living in northern Afghanistan
under the Taliban[1]

My cousin Ousi mothered me tenderly while I stayed with her
family in Kandahar. Ousi was Khala Sherina's only daughter, and
was about my age, with expressive almond eyes and auburn hair
as unruly as she was. Her gestures were very sprightly and her
speech animated; she even did her household chores more
quickly than her mother would.

Ousi washed the dishes in the courtyard, being careful not to
use too much water, as their only source of water had been
through drilling into the water table. As a guest from America, I
wasn't allowed to help. I would be uncomfortable in the squatting position necessary to reach the water, and the soap powder
would be rough on my hands. I had watched her filling up old oil
jugs with water so that it could stay out in the sun to warm up
and be used to wash more dishes.

At night, Ousi and I slept next to each other on mattresses in
the open courtyard of the house, separated only by the mesh of

our mosquito nets. Ousi made sure my net was doubly tucked in and safe from breach before settling in next to me, and was ready to guide me at night if I needed something, as there was no electric lighting. When I needed to bathe, she filled buckets from the artesian well and carried them upstairs for me. It was clear that she did not want me to have too hard of a time adjusting to the way they lived.

During some moments, Ousi's enthusiasm to be my guide and protector was both sweet and funny. One night she asked me if I was scared of the dark. I shot her a look of reassurance and told her about how tough I was. I had grown up in Brooklyn and Queens, after all. America had not softened me *that* much. That night, we laughed together as sisters.

I was surprised to learn that Ousi was one of the few women who were still working in Kandahar. Despite the Taliban's prohibition of women's employment, they allowed some women to work. After initially banning all employment by female doctors and nurses, the Taliban relented and allowed limited numbers to return to work in women's and children's wards. I was surprised by Ousi's employment because her family seemed very conservative, but I later learned that her income was the only real means of support they had. Her brothers, also in their early twenties, barely worked at all. Both were apprentices, one at a calligraphy shop and the other at a pharmacy, and both were sometimes paid, but often not.

Ousi worked at a private clinic on the outskirts of the city, which served mostly the Kuchis, or the nomadic tribes of Afghan gypsies, as well as refugees from other areas of Afghanistan, what the United Nations calls internally displaced people. Every morning she would be driven to work in a van furnished by her employer and would return home before lunchtime. I decided to see the clinic for myself and went to work with her one day. As usual, Ousi was the first to be picked up by the van. The driver had a white beard and an even whiter skullcap, the kind that Muslims all over the world wear. We drove a few minutes and pulled up into a narrow path, where khaki walls surrounded us, appearing as fragile as if they had been made with Play-Doh.

A woman covered head to toe in a blue *burqa* appeared, got into the van, and greeted Ousi and me. I asked about her and her family in the Afghan tradition, as she did of mine, but the whole time we had no idea what each other looked like, even though we were sitting across from each other. As she spoke to Ousi about work, I tried to imagine what she looked like, wishing I could watch her lips as she spoke. We made a few more stops until the van was completely full, and I now had many more *burqas* to pay attention to. I found it hard to follow the conversation, trying to remember which woman had made which comment, because they almost all looked the same. I could not even see their shoes in the car, or a piece of their clothes underneath to distinguish among them. I felt blind, riding to the outskirts of Kandahar with a van full of *burqa*-clad women.

We came to a forlorn concrete building on the outskirts of the city, bordering the desolation of the surrounding desert. Above the clinic was a white sign that read DR. MIA SAHIB CLINIC, KANDA-HAR. We were in the shadow of a mountain, near the top of which was the historic site of Chihil Zina, or forty steps, which led to a carving in Persian by Babur, the founder of the Moghul Empire. The five-hundred-year-old carving proclaims the many conquests by Babur throughout Asia. It sits in a cave near the mountain's peak, the entrance of which is flanked by two stone lions.

It was a little past 7 AM, and the clinic still looked cool from night as the sun was beating its way into the rooms through a few of the scraggly wooden windows. I tugged the fabric of my *burqa* below my chin to adjust the screen covering my eyes. I squinted, trying to figure out whether the two men with Kalashnikovs walking in front of the clinic were Taliban or not. Grizzled men with guns were everywhere, and it was often impossible to tell whether they were religious police, former *mujahideen*, or just civilians. Ousi reassured me the men were not Taliban, so we entered the clinic.

Ousi walked me to the room where she administered vaccines to children, and we took off our *burqas*. We replaced them with large cotton scarves wrapped around the top halves of our bodies. In my family we called these larger scarves "prayer scarves," because we used them during prayer times to cover our hair and chest. I often thought that there was no point in wearing a scarf while speaking to God, because He is all-knowing and all-seeing, and it would make no difference to Him anyway how I looked. But somehow the scarf had become the symbol of being a Muslim woman. When I was younger, for example, people were always so surprised when they found out that I was Muslim but didn't wear a scarf. Now we were wearing these scarves simply to get out of our *burqas*, to be less modest, not more so.

The room in which Ousi gave out vaccines was small and sparse, with two old metal chairs, a rickety little desk, and a tall decaying wooden cabinet with broken glass doors for the medicine. I watched as she prepared her office for visitors, opening her black-and-white composition notebook, fixing syringes on the desk, and removing tubes of clear vaccine liquid from the cabinet. She brought in a chair for me from the maternity ward, as well as a glass of tea. I heard voices in the hallway, then her first patient, a young girl with blond hair and green eyes being held by her mother, wearing an olive *burqa*. The woman lifted her *burqa* to reveal her young yet very sun-beaten face, green eyes, and sandy brown hair. The *burqa* lay perched on her head, with her brown bangs scattered over her forehead. She had what we call "natural highlights" in America, something I and countless other women have tried to reproduce with chemical bleach.

This was the second time she brought her daughter in for her shots. Ousi encouraged her to tell the women in her family to bring their children too. "It's such a long journey to get here," she responded. "You know everyone doesn't think it will really help their children." She continued to explain the mind-set. "Besides, they say, if I survived and am doing well, so will they." There were people even less fortunate and less aware than this poor uneducated woman coming to a free clinic practically in the desert. She looked over at me as she thanked Ousi, and I realized that in the United States my role would have probably been explained to the patient, so as not to compromise her privacy.

The women and children flowed in, as Ousi left the room and came back with yet another set of patients. One woman waiting for her medicine turned to me and began to divulge her ailment: "I have a pain in my side that just won't go away. Sometimes I take herbs for it but it just aches and aches. The medicine they gave me doesn't even work so well. Since this pain has started I have so much trouble, when I try to go to the bathroom . . ." Before she could continue, I stopped her. "I'm sorry, Khala, but I'm not a doctor," I said, but she didn't believe me, even though I called her aunt out of endearment and respect. "You have to take care of me," she pleaded. Ousi jumped in. "She's not a doctor. Leave her alone." The woman left, upset and probably thinking we were lying to her because she didn't have any money to pay for medicine. Apparently she had been to the clinic before, but nobody could help her with the pain, except by prescribing painkillers.

A few other women mistook me for a doctor. Ousi thought that my glasses and fair skin made me appear that way. I apologized to all of them for not being a doctor, wishing now that I had gone to medical school so that I could be of use.

An older woman, appearing to be in her forties, walked into the room, looked around, and demanded that Ousi give her a shot.

"This is only for children," Ousi answered.

"But I am so sick, and so weak. I think it will help me."

"It's not serum, Khala," she said, raising her voice. "It's to protect children from diseases that they get, like when their legs die."

"But my legs are weak too. Who knows when they will die? Please just give me one shot," she pleaded, as she began to lift her sleeve. Ousi looked at me, as if to say "See what I have to deal with?"

"Khala, I can't give you this vaccine. Please go see the nurse."

The woman pleaded with Ousi some more, and finally turned to me, but by then I had learned my lesson. I pretended I couldn't speak Pashto, so she walked out.

Ousi suggested that I leave the room and look around the clinic. I had been nervous about causing a disruption at first, but now felt more comfortable with the patients. In the maternity room, there was a bare table, which looked like it was made of stainless steel, along with some gadgets laid out on a table on wheels, and a cabinet with a few trays of medicine. There were no doctors in the room, or in the clinic, as far as I could tell. There may have been a midwife, but there were no sheets, nor any medical equipment. If something went wrong with a birth, there would be little the clinic could do. I wondered why women would come to give birth here if they were so horribly equipped. I learned that even this was a luxury for the women that came. The privacy of a room rather than a tent, and the availability of Pakistani knockoffs of American painkillers, were good reasons to try to have a delivery at the clinic. At home the women might not even be able to cry out during childbirth, because it would be shameful for the men to hear what was happening.

I walked down the hallway to see the waiting area, near the entrance of the clinic. As I approached I heard the echoing voices of women gossiping, and children crying and playing.

When I drew nearer I saw that the hallway was overflowing with women, some breast-feeding their babies. There were also women outside the clinic, waiting in the morning sun. Some were squatting, others standing, and others sitting Indian style on the bare floor.

Women had traveled for many hours over dirt roads and alongside minefields to get here. Many, I was sure, had fought bitterly with their husbands and in-laws about whether it was immoral to leave the tents without their husbands, even for the clinic. Most had no doubt lost babies in past pregnancies, or seen their sisters or mothers die in pregnancy from lack of medical attention. Some had visible growths on their skin.

Most of the women were *burqa*-less, wearing only the brightly colored, ornate dresses of the Kuchi nomads and adorned in silver necklaces. Although women in Afghanistan were required to wear the *burqa*, Kuchi women were apparently exempt, especially because they rarely lived in the cities. Most Kuchi women never wore the *burqa*, because the Taliban's religious police rarely ventured out into the wild desert areas where the Kuchis lived, and because the Kuchi nomads were so rebellious and independent that even the Taliban didn't attempt to tame them.

This was the worst hospital I had ever seen. Looking back, I don't know why I had expected anything more, given what everything else was like in Afghanistan. In the United States, I thought hospitals were bare. I had grown up going to New York City public hospitals for care, where there were abundant medications, high-tech machinery, lasers, CAT scans, artificial organs, computers, endless files and paperwork, televisions in the rooms, clean sheets on the beds, and vending machines. But here there was nothing, just bare rooms, a dirty cement floor, no registration area, and no machines, linens, or paperwork. Just people. There must have been a hundred women waiting to be seen, yet there were only six women working in the clinic, judging from the van we had arrived in.

I walked back toward Ousi's office, distracted by an old woman who was crying out in anguish in another room. I slowed down to watch what the commotion was and found out why the woman was crying.

"Please give them to me. Please," she pleaded from the doorway to the medicine room.

"I can't give them to you. I gave you three for free last week and we're not allowed to do that, you know," answered the pharmacist coldly from the medicine room.

"In Allah's name," she sobbed, "what am I supposed to do? You are a Muslim, aren't you?" I stood in the doorway as the woman walked away, still weeping.

The pharmacist looked at me and shook her head, as if to say "Tsk, tsk, tsk."

"Poor woman cannot afford all the syringes she needs to take her medicine with," she explained.

"How much does it cost?" I asked.

The medicine was subsidized by the clinic, but it still cost patients something, and the amount she told me that it cost was equal to fifty-five cents.

"I'll pay it," I reassured her, and I ran the syringes after the old woman, who was already out of the clinic by now. I handed them to her and said I hoped she would get better. As I was running away, fearful of being caught without my *burqa* outdoors, I heard her praying for me, showering me with blessings of all sorts. "May Allah give you happiness and health! May Allah reserve for you a space in Heaven!" she shouted as she cried. I realized I was able to make a small difference in someone's life. Despite all the reasons I had to be sad at the clinic, I was filled with joy. At the end of the day, when all the money was counted up from the pharmacy, the grand total equaled fourteen dollars and fifty cents. The women who worked in the clinic said they knew it wasn't much money, which is why they felt even worse about patients who couldn't afford it. This was nothing in the

West. Indeed, I had bought simple lunches in midtown Manhattan that cost that much, if not more. I could easily finance at least the pharmacy section of this clinic. If I could do it, certainly there were so many other people who could do so with their resources. They could finance the whole clinic, and other clinics if they wanted to. They just needed to know about the opportunity, and the stark reality these women faced. There was only so much I could do, but if I got other people involved, we could really have an effect. I couldn't wait to start telling my friends about my experiences. In all my days in Kandahar, that was the day I changed the most.

Chapter 9

An American, My Own Way

They ever lie in wait, one to injure the other;
Hence they are, always, by calamity, remembered.

— Khushhal Khan Khattak, Afghan poet

The return to Quetta from Kandahar was numbing. July was turning into August and the six-year anniversary of my failed wedding was approaching as I returned to Pakistan, the place where I had been married. I had been away from America for less than a month, but my life was unsettled in a way that I could not remember. My divorce had been life changing, and after it was over I felt as if my body had been shaken forcefully. Now my world had been shaken as well. As if looking through a kaleidoscope, at one moment I saw a new world of opportunity and adventure as an American. By a simple turn of the magical cylinder, I saw another world altogether. I could not go back to America the same person I had been.

I always knew that a world like Afghanistan existed, but it was legend. It posed no real threat to me, and like a child touching an iron who knows it is hot, I had to go and see if Afghanistan was real. In doing so I had damaged my dreams of the land, of my own connection to it, and of my family's original home. I was left with a lingering feeling of guilt for having made it out of

Afghanistan, for having left my husband, for having lived my life. But I had also met a deep part of myself that I could not ignore. It was not the part of me I expected to find there. I had half expected to find out that I was really a Kandahari girl who made it to New York by accident, and that I should therefore go back and be the Kandahari girl. Instead, I found out that I had made it to the United States for a reason. I had made it so that I could have the power to do something, anything, about the people who didn't make it. I made it because I *would* do something.

Quetta felt like coming to America. We had survived, and we made it to the land of showers, music, and light. I instantly felt free, as much freer as I had felt restricted when I first arrived in Quetta from America.

Nothing had changed for Suraya, only the size of her belly. She fought with Aunt Lailuma and I about the shortness of our stay, accusing us of abandoning them, but the next day we were off to Karachi, retracing the way we had come. Karachi was as hot and sticky as ever, but even more liberating. I shopped for *shalwar kameez* outfits, gifts for Moor and my sisters at home. I left Karachi alone. Aunt Lailuma, Jan Agha, and the family would stay longer.

At the airport, a Pakistani guard stopped me to check my luggage. He found a clear plastic bag with white powder inside and looked up at me, shocked that I would be so stupid as to smuggle drugs in such an obvious manner. Afghanistan was producing a lot of opium, 70 percent of the world's supply in 2000.

The drug trade in Afghanistan was big, and Karachi airport was a major entry point to the world markets. The underground network of smugglers were mostly Afghan and Pakistani, and anyone who could smuggle a brick here, a couple of small bags there, would be elevated from poverty to riches in a matter of a few trips back and forth. I was stunned to discover that Muslims would engage in drug trafficking, especially since I had learned that Islam strictly forbade drug use. While Islam bans taking intoxicants of any kind, it technically doesn't ban growing or transporting them, although many authorities on Islam and mainstream Muslims agree that it is un-Islamic. Some Afghans told me the profit from the drug trade is "dirty," and that possessions bought with that money are unclean. The Qur'an calls intoxicants the tool of Satan and tells Muslims to shun them. But many Muslims feel entitled to more leeway when it comes to intoxicants other than alcohol, including anything from smoking cigarettes to growing opium. Even the word for intoxicants in the Qur'an is sometimes translated into English as "strong drink."

Whenever Afghans in America went back and forth too much to see relatives, we would suspect that they had been lured back by the "powder." When I was a young teenager, a man I knew growing up was suddenly arrested. My parents did not tell me why at first, but I later found out he was in prison on drug-smuggling charges. It was the first time I learned about the practice. Sometimes, I learned, the smuggler slipped the drugs into a family member's luggage, and even the person transporting them had no idea. Because there was no reliable mail system once the Soviet war began, Afghans in Pakistan and Afghanistan sent letters and gifts through friends and relatives traveling to America and Europe. An old Afghan woman in her late sixties, we'll call her the Afghan Grandma, was returning home from a visit to relatives in Pakistan when she was suddenly arrested at Newark Airport. The authorities found drugs hidden in her luggage. She pleaded her innocence, saying she had no idea anything was there. Her daughter, a respected woman in the community, took on the fight to save her mother and hired a lawyer to defend her. The Afghan Grandma spent almost a year in jail but was eventually released. The real criminal was the male relative who was coming back to the States with her. He had placed the package in the Afghan Grandma's bags without her knowing, thinking she could easily pass through the authorities because she was an old woman and therefore not suspicious. He also didn't think she would be arrested, but he soon learned that elders don't rule in America, the law does.

"What is this, young lady?" demanded the guard, as he shook the contents of the bag and began to open it. "It's powder for your face," I explained, "to make skin look white." I gestured as I spoke, as if rubbing the powder into my skin. The white powder was *safaida*, an ancient substance that brides use on their wedding day to make themselves appear fair-skinned. It was often overused, causing particularly ghostlike appearances in brides with red lipstick and rouged cheeks, the kind of getup that made my brother and I giggle when we saw pictures of weddings in Pakistan. When I had been in Pakistan for my own wedding, I vowed not to wear it on my big day, instead settling for leaving it on the night before. I recall going to the bathroom in the middle of the night and becoming afraid of myself after catching a glimpse in the mirror. *I* had become a ghost, in more ways than just my appearance.

The *safaida* had been requested by a cousin, who could not find it anywhere in America. Now my favor to her looked like it would land me in trouble. The guard was suspicious. He smelled the contents of the bag and gestured for another guard to come over. "It's just for skin," I said to the new guard, who was equally suspicious. I expected Pakistani men to know the substance, since their society was also obsessed with fair skin. They must have thought I was taking them for fools. They told me they didn't believe my story and began checking other people in while I waited. I was nervous. What if I had indeed been given the illicit powder, not *safaida*? What if *I* was being used as the transporter? Where was it better to be caught, in Pakistan where the rule of law is up to the individual policeman who captures you, or America, where I would be jailed for sure? They wouldn't speak to me, so I waited, wondering who else would arrive to question me.

I was going to be late for my plane, but I didn't want to upset him or give him any reason to hold me back. He was already ignoring me. I wondered if I should bribe him. Pakistani authorities were known for being corrupt. But that might get me into *more* trouble.

"What's happening?" I finally asked.

The guard waited until almost everyone had passed through the security checkpoint. Smiling mischievously, he turned to me and said, "But why do you need this? Your skin is already so white and beautiful. It is like milk."

I knew where this conversation was headed. "Look, it's not for me. I'm going to miss my plane." If I was thinking about bribing him before, now I was so angry with him that I wouldn't give him a penny.

"What are you doing here?" he asked.

"I'm getting on my plane to go home," I said, realizing I had become the entertainment of a crowd of airport guards. I took the clear plastic bag of *safaida* from the guard's hands, put it in my carry-on, and slung it over my shoulder, not looking at him. I walked away and continued to my gate, wondering if they would run after me. They didn't.

As we took off, I stared at a Pakistani newspaper. It was dated August 10, 2001. Exactly six years ago, on that very day, I had been preparing for my wedding in Karachi. Once again I looked down at the city of Karachi from the air. Based on what I had seen of Afghans' desperation, stubborn beauty, and unimaginable losses, I knew that my life was about to change again, in a big way.

On the plane, I opened up the newspaper to find a story about the Taliban raiding an aid agency that had been preaching Christianity. Two American women were being held on the charge of proselytizing to Muslims, a crime punishable by death. I thought about my own secret desire to work for an aid agency in Afghanistan. I had asked Ousi to take me to the headquarters of the Red Cross/Red Crescent, but she was afraid the Taliban would follow us home and punish us for speaking to foreigners. If I had been alone I could have taken the risk, but I would have been endangering our entire family, including the men, who might be punished for allowing their women to go out in the first place.

Reading about the Taliban's intolerance of charity workers, and knowing how difficult it was for Afghan women to be active in public, I knew that my hands would be tied if I tried to become an aid worker in Kandahar. I dreamed about building an organization in the States that could bridge the two societies, and combine the freedom to organize in the West with the ability of Afghan refugees to return to their homeland and direct charitable contributions where they are needed the most. Like many Afghans, my family believes deeply in charity and regularly sent money to Afghan relatives and educational charities working in Afghanistan and among the Afghan refugees in Pakistan. According to the Qur'an, God makes every act of charity grow from a mere morsel into a mountain, while those who hoard money and do not practice charity suffer on the Day of Judgment.

When I got home to the United States in August 2001, I began working in sports again, but I could not shake what I had just experienced. I wished I could be in Afghanistan. I wished I could do something. Nobody in the States seemed to be paying attention to Afghanistan. When I told my closest friends the stories of people I met, they too felt that something needed to be done. But what could be done with the Taliban? In my research I found RAWA, the Revolutionary Association of the Women of Afghanistan. I e-mailed and called them, asking how I could be involved in the cause from New York. When I read more about RAWA, however, I learned that they had Maoist roots, and was told that the Afghans in America, most of whom were refugees from the Soviet genocide of the Afghan people, would never forgive me for joining up with Communists.

Brainstorming on how best to help Afghan women, I called the Afghans I knew in New York, but they didn't have any leads. It was amazing that so many of our relatives, who have family in Afghanistan and travel back and forth, were still completely disconnected from the work of the international aid agencies and human rights organizations doing work on behalf of our people. I finally asked my father for help, and he suggested I call an educated elder in our community. The man seemed suspicious of me but gave me some names of politically active Afghans to contact.

One name the elder gave me was Laili Helms. He would give her my number but couldn't guarantee that she would call me. Later I read an article about a woman by this name in *The Village Voice*. She was a spokesperson for the Taliban! Not only did I find it ironic that the Afghan elder had, probably accidentally, recommended the Taliban's own spokesperson to a young Afghan woman interested in exploring human rights work, but I wondered how the Taliban would let an Afghan woman, head uncovered, act as their spokesperson. I was even more surprised that she would want to speak for them. Still, I hoped that she would call me. Maybe she understood something about the Taliban that I didn't. Maybe she had the key to knowing how to accomplish change within their framework. At one point I realized that I had seen Laili right before I left for Afghanistan, at a party in New Jersey, but I did not recognize her at the time and found out who she was only after she left. I was stunned at the time to hear that her husband was American, and the nephew of the former head of the CIA. When I investigated this woman later on, I discovered that before 9/11, she told CBS that the Taliban had to enforce strict laws to reestablish law and order in Afghanistan, because before they took power, Afghanistan was "like a Mad Max scenario" in which armed gangs kidnapped and raped

Afghan women at will. She claimed that most Afghan women were "happy" with the Taliban because they had suffered so much under the Soviets and the anarchy that followed their defeat.

When the Taliban first came to power in 1994, they were welcomed by some Afghans living in New York. Even Hamid Karzai, who became the transitional leader and eventually the president of Afghanistan with American backing after the fall of the Taliban, told an American reporter before 9/11 that the Taliban were "good, honest people," and his allies during the anti-Soviet jihad. He added that when the Taliban came to him asking for help in fixing the "unbearable" situation of anarchy, rape, and looting in Kandahar following the Soviet withdrawal, he initially provided them with money, weapons, and political legitimacy. But he broke with them after their policies became increasingly oppressive, and Pakistani intelligence began to take a more active role in the Taliban movement.[1] He then became an ally with America, one of the best-known anti-Taliban Pashtun fighters.

As the Taliban's policies toward women became harsher, and their edicts more backward, Afghan-Americans also began to question their newfound hope for a return of law and order to Afghanistan. Debates raged at Afghan dinners about the Taliban's intentions and the effect of their policies on Afghanistan. I witnessed one very heated argument between an Afghan man and a woman about whether the Taliban were good for Afghanistan. The man believed that the Taliban had restored some sort of security after the chaos of the early 1990s, and that they needed time to build society up again to allow girls to attend school. Like many Afghans, he believed that all the alternatives available at the time—communism, anarchy, and the Northern Alliance —were even more awful than the Taliban. The woman, on the other hand, argued that any regime that forbade girls to attend school was backward and would ultimately destroy the entire society. "What are they waiting for?" she asked, referring to the

Taliban's initial claim that they would allow girls to go to school when it was safe, but that they would begin with the boys first. At the time I believed that both of them were right, but after seeing for myself how harsh Taliban rule was, I realized how wise the woman had been to question their vague promises of future reform.

Unsatisfied with the lack of interest and action from the Afghans I spoke with, I decided to form my own organization with my sister and a few friends. We incubated the organization in my friend Vic Sarjoo's investment banking office. Vic had been supportive of my trip to Afghanistan, one of the few people who understood my desire to find my path. We considered each other siblings, and he had been instrumental in showing me there was excitement and opportunity in life when I was still depressed from my divorce. I felt especially lost at that time. There were so many options in the freedom of the West, but many of them felt empty. He helped to create a sense of community for me, one that I desperately needed to anchor me after my old sense of community was shaken and the rest of the world seemed like chaos. Vic didn't flinch when I told him I was going to Afghanistan, even though I know he must have been worried about me. He respected me, yet was the sort of friend who instinctively threw out his hand to protect me after suddenly braking when he was driving. When this happened I laughed because I knew that no arm could protect me from smashing into the front windshield during a collision, but it was an important sign of caring. It was something my father did, and in my gut I knew that Vic would remain a brother for life. I called on him for advice and comfort in my most desperate moments, like when a minivan hit my red Neon at an intersection one rainy night and sped off. Vic urged me to stay calm and be careful as I chased the car up and down the streets of Queens, furious over being taken advantage of. It was a reckless thing to do given the risk, but the van finally did stop, at which point I realized that the man might just kill me to avoid being caught for whatever crime he had committed. Fortunately, the man in a 1980s-style tracksuit jumped out and bolted into a side alley. I was never able to figure out who he was or get any compensation for the buckled hood of my car.

The organization was called YA-WA, for the Young Afghan World Alliance. *Yawa* is the feminine version of the Afghan word for "one," and was also chosen because it sounds like Yahweh, the Jewish word for God. I had thought of the name many months before I had even thought about going to Afghanistan, while fantasizing about starting an aid organization. YA-WA would be about young people who wanted to create change in Afghanistan. A majority of Afghans were under eighteen, and most of these were just children. Millions of Afghans my age or younger had never seen what peace looked or felt like. Most kids had barely attended school and had fought through their childhood for a country that now denied them the right to go to school or play games. Our parents' generation was getting older, and while we had to respect them, we also knew that they had little power in the face of armed men.

The purpose of YA-WA was to raise awareness about the plight of the Afghan people, foster understanding between Afghans and Americans, and ultimately to build a school in Kandahar, the stronghold of the Taliban. This school would offer a world-class education to a select few students who exhibited strong ability and dedication to learning. It would be an opportunity for children to learn about not just religion but also literature, science, and history. Inspired by the secret girls' schools run by RAWA, the school would teach these other subjects in secret, if necessary, and every few months we would bring in a *mullah* from the Gulf States or Saudi Arabia as a guest speaker to please the Taliban leadership. Unless a school included religion in its classes, the Taliban wouldn't let it operate. Because girls could not attend school after the age of eight under existing law, we would send tutors to their homes to continue their education, or so we dreamed. I was especially worried about these girls.

In Afghanistan I had witnessed the extreme dedication to learning of one of my cousins, Qais. The Turkish school he attended had finally refused to bow to the Taliban's control of its finances. Although the Turks were no longer operating the school, Qais continued to attend the school, now barely run by a group of Afghans. Most children in Kandahar, including Qais's brothers, were not as lucky as he was in earning a basic education. I saw so many smart, capable kids there whose energy and potential were going to complete waste. YA-WA was meant to invest in these children and groom the youth that would lead Afghanistan forward.

At first I desperately wanted to believe the toppling of the Twin Towers was an accident. As soon as I realized it was the result of a terrorist attack, I prayed it wasn't Muslims. From my car on the Long Island Expressway, I had just seen thick, black, filthy clouds rise from what would later be called Ground Zero. I was in shock. Even looking right at the havoc that had been wrought on *my* Twin Towers, I couldn't believe it was happening. I refused to believe it. Besides, America had been the place of safety to which my family had fled during the Soviet invasion of Afghanistan. Now the danger had followed us. I knew, however, that my immediate family was safe in Queens, and that my extended family had probably not been in the area.

Later that day I was standing on a street corner in Queens, waiting for a pay phone to call my friends in the city. All of the phones in my brother's office across the street, where I had come to first, were dead. The pay phone was in front of the deli I'd visit often to pick up breakfast or lunch. The place smelled of roasted chicken mixed with that old deli smell you could only know if you lived in New York. The office was located in Forest Hills, Queens, the most American part of Queens I had ever seen. Queens is the most diverse place in the world but unlike the very Asian parts that I was used to, many people in Forest Hills looked like they could have come from anywhere in Middle America. The people in line behind me looked at me with impatient eyes as I dialed number after number with no success. They were restless to try their own luck. I swung back to the end of the line and waited to try again. A heavyset limousine driver in elegant black slacks spoke into the receiver in a tongue I didn't recognize.

Sparked by the memory of the 1998 terror attacks on the U.S. embassies in Tanzania and Kenya, I had a gut feeling that the person behind this attack was probably Osama bin Laden. As I stared toward Manhattan, I thought, Oh my God. The United States is not going to let this go without punishment. This is probably worse than Pearl Harbor. I clenched my jaw. And Osama is in Afghanistan. What was America going to do? I had always wanted to be American, but during my recent trip to Afghanistan, just weeks before, I had begun to really accept and appreciate my Afghan roots. What would happen to the family and the people of Afghanistan whom I had just discovered, and whom I adored?

I started to imagine what the American government's reaction might be. If it certainly was Osama, how would we get him? A month earlier, when I was in Kandahar, it had become obvious that the Saudis were taking over the city. Occasionally, black SUVs with tinted windows, sometimes in a convoy of five or six, would tear through the streets and cause fear and curiosity among the local Afghans. Sometimes on a drive somewhere, in the dark, it would be difficult to make anything out, as the adobe houses were shrouded in darkness. But occasionally we'd drive past a compound and see light coming from the inside of the high gates. The walls looked like they were made out of strong metal, light blue in color, with a design engraved in metal on the outside, squiggly lines. The walls were probably ten or twelve feet high, like those surrounding many houses in Afghanistan, but these were unusually ornate. Yellow light. It's an unmistakable symbol of privilege. The type of symbol that gets people to wish they could know what life was like inside. The yellowish light shined from the inside of the fortress upward and illuminated the air around.

When I'd ask what lucky person's house or vehicle I had seen, the answer was always the same.

"It's the Saudis. Who else could afford to have these luxuries?"

To most locals in Kandahar, the Saudis were invading. They bought up the property; they lived reclusively, only venturing out to travel to some other reclusive location or purchase goods in the market. Women would sometimes remark that they had caught glimpses of the Saudi women—wearing all black, traditional Saudi *abayas*—perhaps as they were entering or exiting a vehicle in the market. Jewelers would remark that the Saudi men were frequent buyers of gold. To most people they were an annoying reminder of what wealth could do. Wealth they didn't have.

Initially I thought that perhaps some Saudis just liked Kandahar and decided to move there. Later I was told that this was all Osama's clan. These were his people.

Back from my first trip, I often discussed what I had found in Kandahar with the people around me. Over an AOL Instant Messenger conversation with my friend Nellie, I casually remarked that the Arabs seemed to dominate the city of Kandahar.

"They bought property there and lived reclusively."

"What?"

"I guess they were forming some community there."

"In Kandahar? Who the hell wants to live in Kandahar?"

"Well I mean, Osama's there, and he probably has a community surrounding him," I wrote back. "Money goes much further in Kandahar than it does in Saudi Arabia. It's probably a power trip."

"It's ludicrous to think that anybody would live there out of choice. Don't you get it? They were all probably criminals or exiles."

I stood on the edge of that street corner in Queens, thinking of Osama and all the Saudis who apparently lived in Kandahar. I began to wonder if that community was a network of Osamas, rather than some friendly neighborhood of Saudis who just decided to live in Kandahar City.

Still no luck on the pay phones. I walked across the street to my brother's office, where Agha would often be tying up the loose ends, the kind of help parents are good at giving. My brother, Babai, had been running an import business for years. I found Agha sitting behind a desk, as I often did, seeming not to be doing anything. He had the circulars from the supermarket with markings on them of the purchases to make. He also had unpaid bills, telephone and electric bills. His reading glasses were perched on his forehead. He was wearing a khaki plaid shirt that looked like it had been worn too much. He refused to buy new clothes for himself. Indeed this was probably a gift one of us had bought him for Father's Day, or something my mother had snuck into his closet.

The radio was playing in the background. I listened because there was nothing else to do. The announcer seemed to be giving a play-by-play of a horror story. He spoke in a concerned voice, but I could tell he was straining to have something to say. He was struggling to explain a crisis to his listeners that he could not even make sense of. It was all just unraveling. I could almost imagine this man sitting in a glass-walled studio, trying to sound calm as people were running around the studio screaming and crying.

The announcer made remarks about an incident in Pennsylvania. I was confused. The story was New York, wasn't it? Then I realized it was the Pentagon too. I felt for a moment the world was going to collapse. What next? This is definitely going to be answered with force. I spoke to my dad in Pashto, the language I grew up speaking at home, often being forced to speak it at the expense of English.

"Agha?"

"Ah?" This meant "What?"

"What do you think America is going to do about this?"

There was no response. I sensed he was processing.

"Are you worried about our family in Afghanistan?"

He frowned.

He looked up from the circular he was paging through. The perched glasses fell over his eyes. He lifted them again.

"America is powerful and does whatever it wants and what was done by these terrorists today was very wrong."

I never could get a clear answer from him. But then again, it wasn't a time of clear answers, just seemingly endless chaos and destruction. I went back out to the pay phones, this time dialing family in New York City I knew I could reach.

First I called Jan Agha, the uncle with whom I had just taken the trip to Kandahar a few weeks earlier.

Jan Agha seemed too calm on the other end. I couldn't tell whether he was in shock or simply reacting in his characteristically stoic manner to my obviously shaken-up voice. Speaking as fast as I could, I explained my revelation to him. "Tell your brother to get his family out of there *immediately*," I said as politely as possible, trying not to sound too commanding to my older, respected uncle. Indeed I was commanding. Jan Agha quickly dismissed my concerns, reminding me it was too early to tell what was going to happen, and besides, us Sultans were always too cautious. I was overreacting. I thought for a second he might be right, but got right back to the end of the pay phone line to call my other cousins in Queens and advise them to do the same for their families in Afghanistan. I called Basir, my father's stepbrother's son. His family was living in our old house in Kandahar City. They had cooked a feast the night that I visited and stayed over. That evening many of my female cousins around my age slept on the roof with me under the star-sprinkled sky.

When I told Basir to evacuate his family, he said he'd consider it and try calling home to see what their reaction was. Over the next few weeks, bits of information would trickle back to me by word of mouth about the family that had left Kandahar in anticipation of the day the United States started bombing. Amnesty International later reported that half of the entire population of Kandahar province had fled their homes in anticipation of the bombing.[2]

We all knew the bombing was imminent. But we didn't know what it would mean for our family.

I was to have lunch with my friend Nellie that day in downtown Manhattan. It was a lunch that I had been trying to schedule for months. Late that morning I was trying to figure out how I would get into the city for my lunch when everyone was fleeing. Deep down, even amid the chaos, I felt I could continue ordinary life. I was in denial. I got Nellie on the phone, and of course her answer was that lunch was off.

Two nights later, I got together with my friend Alice to have an early dinner—and to talk about what had happened to our city. We sat on stools in the window of the restaurant and watched people walking by on Twenty-third Street. Like many New Yorkers, I needed to interact with people that had shared the experience. After dinner I walked down Fifth Avenue with Alice, and kept walking south after I had dropped her off. I felt like I could not do anything else but walk down that avenue. I felt completely numb as I walked, as if I couldn't do anything but go straight. I didn't want to be stopped or talked to or see or feel anything besides what I was headed for: downtown Manhattan. Feeling only the intense pull of a magnetic force I could not explain, I had to see what had happened with my own eyes. The images on TV were all too Hollywood-like. Maybe it was just a stunt.

It was now nine o'clock in the evening on Thursday, and I was getting closer to the World Trade Center site. The acrid smell of burning electronics filled the air. I saw dust particles in the intense blinding yellow light of construction bulbs. They decorated the streets in misery. The flakes of dust were the first evidence to me of the destruction that had happened. They were witnesses—they had gone through it—I was walking *through* the dust particles that had witnessed what I was looking to get closer to. Were they parts of people? Were they pieces of the computers—the thousands of computers that must have been used daily by those people? Were they a part of the planes? Caught in the intense blinding light of the yellow construction bulbs, those specks of matter appeared to *exist*. It made everything seem more real.

All around me there were people, holding hands, chatting, hugging, and looking like stunned children. I got to a police barricade and, when no one was looking, ducked under it and walked on as if I belonged. I got to another barricade a few blocks later and walked through the little strip of sidewalk between the barricade and a building. This time an officer was checking someone else's ID. I reminded myself to walk like I belonged—but was so afraid someone would find out not only that I didn't live there but that I was a Muslim Afghan. If anyone found out who I was, I didn't know what might happen to me. Would I be labeled a conspirator? Someone looking to damage evidence? I wondered if I should announce myself voluntarily. That way if I was caught I couldn't be accused of hiding anything. It was times like these that I could most appreciate having more European features, and fairer skin, than the typical Afghan person.

. . .

Just a few weeks ago, in my hometown of Kandahar, I felt that I had to pretend I was a pure Kandahari girl. I had to behave like a local. If they realized I was coming from America, we might be harassed—expected to pay higher than ordinary bribes or not even allowed into the country.

That trip was also the first time I became acutely aware of the danger of being an American. I had left my American passport and any other papers identifying myself as such with family in Quetta. It was a very awkward moment, not because I felt like I was altering my identity but because of the value of an American passport in the Third World. All through my stay in Quetta, family and friends asked me whether I could somehow get them to America. Some even suggested, jokingly, that all I had to do was allow them to "borrow" my passport and claim that I'd lost mine. They then told me how they could try to alter the picture on the document. For them, a foreign passport was like a winning lottery ticket that someone had forfeited.

We were standing in front of a wooden cabinet. It was separated into three equal sections, each with its own door. The cabinet doors all opened with the same key—a key that Mohtarama, my eldest first cousin on my mother's side of the family, carried around with her at all times. The first section contained makeup, hair accessories, and jewelry that belonged to Mohtarama's married sister, Suraya. As I was handing my passport to Mohtarama, I felt like I was entrusting her with my entire future.

I pulled out that internationally recognized navy blue symbol of status and looked her in the eyes as I handed it to her. She laughed nervously as she opened the thick cover to reveal my picture. She passed her fingers over the plastic laminate and with her nail looked for the edge to see if it could be peeled off. Mohtarama said it might be difficult to alter the photo, but she could give it to a brother to take into the bazaar to see what could be done with it. Mohtarama and I had always made fun of people who were that pathetically desperate to get to America. But the thought of my claim to freedom floating around the bazaars of Quetta as I ventured into Taliban-controlled Afghanistan caused me to want to hold it close to my chest and never let it go.

. . .

I looked down at my sandaled feet, which were powdered by the dust that was raining down from Ground Zero. It was just like the dust that had powdered my feet in Afghanistan on dirt roads and desert paths, and amid the rubble of clay homes. Arguing with myself, and all the while afraid I'd get caught, I walked up to a corner where a row of tables had been set up, packed with protective masks, sandwiches, water bottles, and a few bright yellow emergency battery packs for cell phones. I asked a blond-haired woman with blue eyes and a baseball cap if I could help. She looked at me for a second and said, "Sure, I'm exhausted. You can take over if you like."

When I was much younger, I had once watched a bus fail to stop for my mother and me because she was wearing a *hijab*. Now there was tangible proof that people had good reason to fear Muslims. I feared misdirected anger toward my Muslim-American community.

But the woman just said, "You can take over if you like."

Now I was the person behind the volunteer stand—the last point to which any civilians could go. As I handed a peanut butter sandwich to a man in an orange hard hat whose face was powdered with white dust, he smiled, and it felt strange having him accept me. I fought the impulse to confess that I was an Afghan. Part of me felt that I could not say who I was and part of me wanted to say, "Here is a Muslim woman, an Afghan woman who feels this pain too." But I said nothing.

Even though it was difficult, I had always believed I could balance my sometimes competing Afghan and American selves and reconcile my two halves, my two worlds, and my two homes. Just as I had gone into Afghanistan knowing I must not be American, even if I wanted to, because it would endanger those traveling with me, I walked down the streets of Manhattan thinking, Today I must not be Afghan, or Muslim. Standing on the edge of that street corner, I knew in the deepest part of me that the white flakes of soot raining on Manhattan were asking me to choose. Would I be able to maintain the balance? And, I wondered, how and how soon could I return to Kandahar?

The next few days were spent in a haze, watching the news, thinking about our family back home. Muslim leaders, under pressure to show their respect for American lives, issued statements condemning the attacks, explaining that the hijackers had in fact hijacked Islam. Islam was a religion of peace. *Jihad* meant struggle within yourself, not killing innocent "people of the book," referring to the Islamic term that scholars argue means Muslims, Jews, and Christians—not just Muslims. Mostly the people that came forward were men from Arab countries.

But I did not hear of or know of many Afghans who were condemning the attacks. Instead, they appeared to go into hiding. I learned that parents were afraid to send their children to school, fearing the backlash. Many of my cousins remained at home for days after 9/11. An older cousin, who had recently come from Pakistan and always wore ethnic clothes at home and in public, was terrified. She feared being targeted for being Afghan, and because her father was conservative, she wouldn't dare wear American clothes. But she had a plan for distinguishing herself. She said, "You know, if I run into someone who thinks I'm Afghan, I'll tell them I'm Pakistani." I don't know that anyone would have bothered to ask, but she trusted that in America people would know the difference. A few other young Afghans I knew changed their names in school, asking their friends to call them by more inconspicuous names. Tahir became Tony, Yacoub became Jacob, and Mikhail became Michael.

Driving up 149th Street in Flushing after I'd dropped off a relative who my parents were afraid to let walk home in ethnic clothes, I passed the mosque. Something felt off. I made a -U-turn and as I drove back I realized the sign had been taken down—the one that read SYED JAMALLUDIN MOSQUE. Could it be that they too had caved in to the fear? First I felt sorry for them, and then I got angry. They were a symbol of our community, and while that made them a target, it also gave them an opportunity to send a message of tolerance, a place from which to proclaim our unity with the rest of America. Instead, like the Afghans that worshipped there, the mosque hoped to go unnoticed. A police car was parked on the corner. Were they investigating the mosque or protecting them from threat of backlash? The cops wouldn't speak.

Meanwhile, flags were unfurled across the city. Some were taken out of dusty attics; others were bought for the first time. Agha pasted a big flag on his SUV. "What are you doing?" I asked, somewhat condescendingly. The man who had told me growing up that I was not American, that I should not pretend to be American, suddenly had a big *American* flag on his SUV. What was more American than that? Sure, he read Qur'an out loud at the mosque, and most of his friends were Afghan, but Agha had a strong American side too. He spoke of the safety and opportunity America had provided us. "America has been good to us," he said, and it had a right to protect itself. We had cast our lot with America. Suddenly, *we* were America. But wasn't that what our family had been fighting this whole time, in a cultural sense? Being American? Assimilation? Losing our ethnic and religious identity? That day Agha admitted that America had let him be himself. Sure, there was pressure to assimilate, but who said anything to you if you surrounded yourself with people from your village in Afghanistan and made your children speak Pashto at home? Sara hardly spoke any English before she started school. My youngest sister, Aziza, spoke more because she had discovered *Sesame Street*, and by the time she was learning to talk it was harder to control the older siblings from speaking in English at home.

But I would not put a flag on my red Neon, a college graduation gift from my family. When I was a little girl, Agha would tell me that if I graduated college he would buy me a little red car. Red was my favorite color. When I got older, so did the story. It had been one of those things you hear as a child. I got married, got divorced, moved on. But a few days before graduation Agha handed me a key and told me to look out the window. There it was—a Dodge Neon in shiny, beautiful, fiery red, the color that I loved to paint my nails before going to a wedding. My car had a big red bow on top. I felt like a little girl again.

And here I was, refusing to put even a little American flag sticker on the windshield, as my father urged me to do. I felt very American, and that's exactly why I didn't want to stick a flag on my car. Instead, I would express my Americanness in other ways. I would buy tickets to fund-raisers for firefighters, speak out against terrorism, look out for suspicious packages, shop at the Gap, *and* speak up for ordinary Afghans. That was being American too. In America, we were allowed to do all of those things. That's what I loved about it.

But the community wasn't speaking up. I scoured the news for statements. YA-WA issued a statement condemning the attacks. There was nothing, however, from our leaders, our elders. I phoned one of the leaders in the Afghan community, Dr. Zikria, and he completely agreed that we needed to issue a statement. And would I draft one? *Me?* Draft a statement from the Afghan community?

I decided to take a stab, but in the meantime, shouldn't we have a meeting of the community? Yes, that was a good idea too, and he would arrange one, he said. A few days later his people phoned my father. "There will be a community meeting on Sunday," said the voice on the other line. "Bring your wife and your daughters."

The meeting was to be at an Afghan restaurant called the Mustang Cafe. The community, although fractured along ethnic and political lines, had met before under various banners, but as far as I knew, women were rarely present, if at all.

The day of the meeting, I was incredibly nervous. The first question was what to wear. Should I cover my hair? I wore the *hijab* to the mosque and when we expected to be around conservative men, but this was going to be a variety of community members, many of whom knew I don't wear the *hijab* at all. Would it be a sign of respect to wear it, or would it be hypocritical, a sign of bowing to pressure? I decided against the *hijab*, but made sure I wore a jacket long enough to cover my butt and wrapped an Afghan shawl around myself, a style I had acquired a few years ago. My sister Sara, sixteen years old at the time, accompanied me. We were both afraid the men would turn us away at the door. These men were my father's age, the guys we avoided while hanging out on Main Street, for fear they might realize our jeans were too tight, or something just as silly but embarrassing nonetheless.

When we got there, we were relieved to see a few older women in the audience, so we sat behind them. They were fashionable and spoke Farsi among themselves. Farsi is the language spoken by modern, educated Afghans. Pashto is the original language of the conservative tribal Pashtuns. I would conduct myself according to their norms. The entire meeting was in Farsi, so I barely understood a word. Sara tried to translate for me. Some people spoke in Pashto, which I understood better, except for when they tried to be poetic. I sat through hours and hours of the meeting, which began calmly but turned into an antiterrorism fest. One man after another condemned the Taliban and al Qaeda, and repeated the story of the Afghan wars. "Twenty-three years of war!" they all said, many of them with tears in their eyes. Ironically, in the section of the restaurant adjacent to us, the restaurateurs were watching CNN. The U.S. coalition had begun bombing Afghanistan that day, October 7. I watched with a friend, Haroon.

During a break in the meeting, the Afghans gathered around the television. Even though most of them supported the war because they wanted Afghanistan rid of al Qaeda and the Taliban, they were emotional. Little comfort can be gained from watching explosives fall on the land one calls home. War, a frequent visitor to these hospitable people, became once again their unwanted guest. With my newfound love for Afghanistan, I felt their pain. More important, I wondered how ordinary Afghans were handling the events. What were Khala Sherina, Nasria, Janaraa, Sulaiman, and little mousy Mamoon going to do? Would they stay in Afghanistan? Were they in danger?

In the weeks following 9/11, I became more active in my community, speaking about the plight of ordinary Afghans, particularly women, in Afghanistan. In November, I helped organize a fund-raiser for refugees pouring out of Afghanistan as a result of the U.S. bombing. When I visited the Pakistan-Afghan border in December to distribute the aid, I purchased thousands of dollars of oil, rice, and sugar for some of the thousands of refugees camped out there. I hoped to personally hand out the aid, but the refugees' desperation was such that I would have been trampled and crushed in the process, so I left the aid for the refugee camp workers to distribute. When I met refugees who needed operations or medicine, or limbless men pleading for food or money, I bought them what they needed, when I could. "May the doors of Heaven open for you," one man wished.

In late November, the Afghan community elected me as one of their representatives to the Electoral College of Afghanistan-USA, a group that would represent the Afghan-American community in Afghanistan's transition to democracy. Some of these delegates were later chosen to participate in Afghanistan's first Loya Jirga, or Grand Assembly, to select a transitional Afghan government in Kabul in June of 2002. The day the community voted, an elder came up to me, someone I didn't know by name but only by face, and said, "Son . . . what's your name?" When I told him, he nodded his head, walked back to his chair, and voted for me. That was the day I learned that the elders in my community were not only going to let me attend meetings, but they were also confident in my leadership. Men who might not let their wives work and arranged marriages for their daughters would let a *young* woman speak for their interests. That day, Sara and I drove on the expressway, radio blasting, laughing in disbelief. We never imagined we would witness a time when this would be allowed. Change was indeed possible.

I had already begun my new work. Two weeks after 9/11 and before the bombing of Afghanistan began, my organization, YA-WA, sent an open letter to President Bush. It read, "Mr. President, we implore that you consider the ramifications of military action on the people of Afghanistan. If it is determined that it is necessary to act, please keep in mind that this is a country that has been devastated by war for more than twenty years. We pray that military action by the United States does not add to the more than four million refugees and over one million deaths since the Soviet invasion." While I supported efforts by the United States to rid Afghanistan of its latest plague, I would soon find out how meaningful those words would be.

Chapter 10

Nasria's Story

No one has brought, by weeping, the dead to life again.

—Abdur Rahman, Afghan poet

My trip to Afghanistan to reunite with family paved the way for me to become a documentary film producer about the U.S. war in Afghanistan and its aftermath. I was a speaker at a film screening of *Kandahar*, a movie by an Iranian filmmaker about the life of an Afghan woman living in Canada who returns to Afghanistan after hearing her best friend planned to commit suicide before an upcoming solar eclipse, rather than live under the Taliban's oppression. It was a poetic and harrowing film, one in which the heroine, Nafas, is helped on her way from the Iranian border to Kandahar by a number of desperate people struggling to survive, but she never makes it to Kandahar, and the film ends with the feared eclipse.

At the screening, I spoke about my trip to Afghanistan just before September 11, 2001. I told the audience about the boredom and isolation of my aunt Khala Sherina and the six cousins I had never met before, living under laws that forbade them from going out. I explained how as a New Yorker, 9/11 had happened in my backyard too.

At the end of the event, a journalist came up to me and introduced himself as Jon Alpert. He asked about my family in Kandahar, whether or not I had contacts there, and if I would consider going back. I explained that I wished to see my newfound family again, especially to be close to them through all that was happening with the war. I wished I could be with them, as houses trembled under the thunderous bombing from the sky. Somehow I felt like I could protect them—because I am American—because American bombs couldn't kill Americans, could they? I wanted them to know that I had not turned soft in America. I wanted them to know that they were not alone.

Jon asked me if I would consider going to Afghanistan with him to film a documentary. A few days later he showed me the offices of his film company, where I saw several Emmy awards lined up in a display case. Every day since the bombing of Kandahar had begun, I had worried about Khala Sherina, Mamoon, Najib, Ousi, Janaraa, Sulaiman, and Nasria, wondering when I would be able to see them again. I could not get rid of the itch to go to them. In my mind I played out the moment when I would tell my parents that I am leaving to go to Kandahar, a city actively engaged in war. I wondered if it would bring back memories for them of the Soviet war. They would surely think that I am crazy for wanting to return to the place that they had fled, for the same reason I am now running to it. But I desperately wanted to be there. My father warned me that Jon would exploit my contacts and my naiveté, and get me to say and do dangerous things. He said I was young, reckless, and misguided, and I would regret my decision. But it was really up to me, he explained, reclining on the velvet-covered mattress at home, with his back to a pillow against the wall, one leg stretched over the other. It was the typical position he assumed after dinner, while sipping tea and eating *jalebi*, a spiral-shaped Indian sweet made of fried flour and covered in saffron-colored sugar. "May Allah guide you to the right path," he said.

Hearing this, I lowered my teacup, and the tea that was kissing my lips fell back into the cup. Agha's reaction was new. The choice was *really* mine? Truly? He had never been so resolved about my being an adult. He had always taken the position that I could or couldn't do something—rarely leaving me to my own decision, except the decision to defy him. This time it wasn't about disobeying. It was about his wisdom, his advice, and my judgment. It was also one of the first times in my life that I felt truly respected by my father. That alone made me want to refuse Jon's offer, but unable to resist. I accepted it the next day.

This journey would become the most adventurous and emotional of my life. The plan was for Jon and me to travel to Afghanistan with two associate producers, track down my aunts, uncles, and cousins, and find out what ordinary Afghans had lived through during the war and after the fall of the Taliban. We wanted to know if people were excited to be liberated, how their lives were changing, and whether women still had to wear *burqas* or stay inside the home almost all the time. Jon's daughter Tami, who was my age, would film the women in places men couldn't go. Brent Renaud would film everywhere else, along with Jon, and edit the documentary footage.

The night that we were to leave for Afghanistan, my family took me to the airport. There they met the film crew that I was joining. I quietly introduced our crew, as if their mere existence was a violation of my modesty. I was especially embarrassed when I introduced Brent, who was a young, tall, long-haired, good-looking man.

I could already feel my father's muscles tense as if they were my own. He must have felt that these people were going to take advantage of me. It made me want to be tough, to show that I wasn't going to fall for anyone's deception. He was wary of Jon and the crew, and believed that they would manipulate me and twist my words in order to paint their own political picture of the war in Afghanistan. Indeed, we had already met journalists whose line of questioning made clear that they wanted to get a sensationalistic quote.

I was still afraid of Jon too. I had learned to be wary of the media, a lesson learned from an ABC producer who had pursued me and then my father, tried to corner us in the interview and force us to make inflammatory statements, and later dropped us like a used henna rag when a better angle came along. Jon could crush me forever—my image, that is. If that happened, I might never be able to work on Afghan issues again. Then I would have to go into corporate work, or some other career far removed from Afghanistan.

Jon pointed his video camera toward my family as we walked through the automatic sliding doors to enter the airport terminal. Why did they have to call it a terminal? Such a bleak-sounding place from which to depart on such an important trip. As soon as my parents saw the camera, they scattered, finding their way to a corner of the waiting area, pretending to be talking about something important. I approached Jon, explaining that they didn't want to be taped. My parents had already refused to let the cameras into our home earlier, when Jon had asked to record our family life.

It was December 22, the same day that the new government headed by President Hamid Karzai took power in Afghanistan, when I boarded a flight with a man I barely knew, leading a crew of strange people to a war zone against the wishes of my family, with no idea of who we could speak to or how my Afghan family would react to us. I sat next to Tami. Together, we surveyed the Pakistani megacity of Karachi as we landed. We had to stay the night there before taking another flight to Quetta, the mountainous city from which we would drive to Kandahar.

. . .

By now I had taken the trip to Karachi twice before, once when I traveled there with my family to get married, and again with Aunt Lailuma.

Now I was on my way to Karachi again, leading a group of three Americans on a very different mission. I wondered how we would be treated. This time I looked much more like an American in my corduroy pants and a sweater, so that Jon almost seemed like a father to me. We arrived at 2 AM, and made our way into the hot, damp air of Karachi without incident.

I felt a rush as we drove through Karachi. I had entered the "other world" again, full of Bollywood music and new, mysterious people. I had to pay attention to everything. To play once again the game of who's your friend, who's your foe, and who just wants to sleep with you. This time the stakes were higher. Especially because we had entered a Muslim country, I felt that the crew members were my guests and I was responsible for them. It was only a few months later that Daniel Pearl, the *Wall Street Journal* reporter, would be killed in Karachi.

The airport hotel looked like a cheap Atlantic City motel but it would be fine for the night, that is, until Tami and I opened the door to our room and discovered an odd-looking insect crawling the walls. I reminded myself that we were going into a war zone—to face land mines, bombs, and Taliban—bugs should've been the least of my worries. We inspected our sheets and decided to take turns keeping watch over each other. I zipped up my sweater and covered my head in the sheets, pressing on the edges so nothing could crawl through.

An hour later I woke up and found that neither of us were keeping watch—but by then it didn't matter. The next day we would be farther from home, in Quetta, with a little more adventure and a lot more glamour. We were staying at the "posh" Hotel Serena, the best hotel in Quetta. I had heard my family speaking about this five-star hotel years ago. At the time, I never thought I would see it because I had family in Quetta, and anytime an Afghan has family anywhere, it is a crime to stay in a hotel.

It was Christmastime and a tree was decorated at Serena, complete with shiny metallic wrapped presents and bells. Reporters told us that the place was swarming with ISI, the Pakistani intelligence service that had supported the Taliban, and that our every move was probably being tracked. We quickly made friends with our CBS News hotel contact, who offered to help us get into Afghanistan, and even to hook us up with security. I had been calling Quetta for weeks looking for security, but hadn't found anyone I felt I could trust.

Quetta is located in Baluchistan, a province of Pakistan, but was overflowing in December 2001 with Afghan refugees and Pakistanis who spoke Pashto. In some ways I felt at home because I could speak the language, but never totally at ease. Quetta, derived from *kwatta* in Pashto, means "fort," although one BBC journalist called it the "wild border town." This was the city that the Taliban had been fleeing to through the porous border as the war on terror had begun. Part of the traditional Pashtun homeland, or "Pashtunistan," it was handed over to Pakistan after the country won its independence from Britain.

In the 1980s, the CIA and Pakistani ISI made Quetta a base for anti-Soviet Afghan guerrilla fighters, and it remained a haven for conservatives and fundamentalists, although in recent years it had been considered a party town, compared to Taliban-controlled Kandahar. The Taliban got their start in *madrassas* in Quetta and received their first financing from the Quetta transport mafia, which was tired of being shaken down by warlords on its route to Kandahar. My cousins spoke about lines of traffic developing on the road to Quetta before the Muslim holiday of Eid, as young men tried to leave Kandahar to celebrate over the border, where they could play music, play cards, and just escape. The Taliban caught on to their plans, though, and blocked their access to Pakistan when Eid came around again. When Afghanistan's current president Hamid Karzai began to organize an anti-Taliban opposition, the Taliban murdered his father in Quetta in 1999.

My mission on this trip to Quetta was to find my family, so I called my cousin Suraya. I told Suraya I had brought American people with cameras this time. Her family invited me over, but said the Americans should tour the city while I was out. I understood, and the thought of failing to persuade any of my Afghan relatives to cooperate with cameras was the fear I had woken up to every night since I had agreed to come. My biggest fear wasn't being killed, but returning to America without footage that revealed the charm and sorrow of Afghan life. I needed Afghans to open up to me on camera the way they had in private, or their stories would remain hidden from the world forever.

Suraya's uncle arrived at the hotel to lead us back to their house. We drove behind him through the humid evening air, down several unpaved alleys with no street signs, to a series of squat one-story walled compounds that housed many Afghan refugees. I imagined long-bearded Taliban taking shelter in the compounds, indistinguishable from the other Afghan refugees who had fled across the porous Afghan-Pakistan border.

Reuniting with Suraya and her family was different this time. There was a palpable distance in the air as we spoke about family. They were suspicious of me. I was now the American coming to expose them and to put their daughters on TV. I wanted them to speak with me on camera, but the eldest man in the family, Gul Agha, said "it wasn't for them." He explained that they were uneducated, refugees, just trying to get by. I felt cheap, as if I were acting the sweet producer to get them to say yes.

But their views were so important. They had lived under harsh conditions in Afghanistan, and now in Pakistan, where they could be hauled off to jail for any reason if the corrupt authorities suspected they could benefit from a ransom. They were denied health care unless they could pay up front, and they couldn't find work. Homes and apartments in Quetta were packed to the doors with Afghan extended families. This was the reality for the Afghan refugees, and it had only gotten more crowded as thousands fled the U.S. bombing. The whole city was flowing over from the flood of refugees.

Gul Agha told me to visit my other cousin, Nasria. Like Mamoon, Najib, and Suraya, Nasria was on my mother's side of the family. At first I thought Gul Agha wanted me to visit Nasria's family so that I would leave his family alone. But I realized he wanted me to hear their story when he shook his head and made a *tsk, tsk, tsk* sound, which Afghans use to indicate pity. "Something awful has happened to them. You should go and see for yourself." My mother had told me in New York that some of Nasria's family had been injured or possibly even killed while fleeing Afghanistan during the war. I didn't know who had inflicted the harm, or any other details. Gul Agha gave a phone number of an Afghan that lived close to the home she was staying in, who would fetch her when I called.

After we had dinner, Gul Agha and Suraya expected me to stay with them through the rest of my visit to Quetta, but I explained that I was working. "Then come back here at night," they argued. "Why stay in a hotel when we are here? Don't you want to stay with us?" they asked, almost in chorus. I could tell they were uncomfortable with the idea that I was staying with Americans. The idea of a good Muslim girl staying overnight in a strange place with "infidels" was something unconscionable to the men, who naturally wanted to protect me. To them, no Americans could come close to family. Beyond that, Muslim tradition had trained them that a woman shouldn't travel unless accompanied by a male relative.

Back in my hotel room, I dialed Nasria's neighbor. I hung up and waited for her sister Rabia to be summoned. When I called back, Rabia told me that I should come right over to see the family. I told them I was with a camera crew and that I wanted to interview them about their escape from Afghanistan. She said the men would have to answer about that, but that I should come anyway. I was nervous, but I darted out of my room and knocked on Jon's door, across the hallway. He was excited that we would finally speak to someone. We were to travel to a gas station twenty minutes away, and would be met there by Nasria's male relatives.

We drove for what felt like an hour to the outskirts of the city. There were no streetlights and the darkness made me feel trapped, as if we were in a cave. I wished someone could have told me what happened. I didn't want to have to guess. I worried that Nasria herself may have been injured or killed. After all, I had not spoken to her since I had arrived in Quetta. Perhaps they wanted to tell me in person. I wanted to question her sister on the phone, but was afraid of being rude, and it was better to see them anyway.

We pulled up to the gas station, where a small van was waiting. Nasria's husband, Mohammed Rasul, came out and greeted us. We followed the taillights of his van through narrow dark streets until we came upon a large rusted green gate. I kept my eyes on his rear lights, forcing my eyes to squint, so that the red turned into a blur in the darkness, and then opening my eyes to regain focus. I did this over and over. I couldn't bear to think about where we were going. Mostly, I was worried about what Nasria would think about my coming to them with American men in their moment of tragedy. How could I face them? What could I say? What would the men of the house think of me? I realized I had come with no gifts. Not even chewing gum for the young girls. I clenched my fists in regret.

As the car slowed I reminded Tami that the rules for filming were different now. This time we were to ask for permission first, not to be forgiven later. I also warned her against shooting secretly, even if she was sure they wouldn't notice. The last thing I wanted was to offend them. Although I had met the women before when I was in Afghanistan during Taliban times, on a day trip from Khala Sherina's house, I had never seen most of the men of Nasria's family. I assumed they were conservative, like most of the Pashtun men in the area. The women stayed home and wore *burqas* outside, and the men of this family worked as mechanics during the daytime.

Mohammed Rasul stepped out of the driver's side and welcomed us into what looked like a crumbling house. He led us to a room where the women were waiting. I took my shoes off, fixed my scarf, and lifted the fabric draped over the opening to the doorway. I let out a loud and reassuring *Salaamwalaikum*, as if to affirm my Islamic identity. More girls and women than I can remember existing in their family filled up the room. The women stood up with their backs to the uneven walls and the girls were in the middle of the small rectangular room. They ranged in age from one and a half to sixteen. There were probably fifteen people in the room. I suddenly felt shy, not knowing if I should kiss each one separately, wishing my mother were here so that I could follow her actions and otherwise be passive. This time I had to lead.

All eyes were on me and I was worried I might say or do something wrong. The worst thing would be if I insulted them or unknowingly made a mistake in Pashto. Tami said hello to all and they smiled at her. As soon as we sat down Rabia asked me how my family was, a required formality among Muslims, and then launched into their story.

"Look, Masuda . . . look what they have done to us. Can you believe we are the same people you saw so few months ago?" Rabia went on. "What kind of a war is this? Who do they think we are? Are they really trying to get Taliban or are they kidding us?"

Tami pointed at her camera and asked in English if she could film them. I asked them in Pashto, saying I would understand if they didn't want to.

"No, no, it's fine. We have never spoken to journalists. But we will tell you what happened, Masuda. For you, we will speak," said Rabia. She explained that she had not been at the scene of the bombing in Kandahar, but went on to describe it as if she had seen it with her own eyes. She had pieced the story together, having heard it many times from her sister, Nasria, and her ten nieces, scared little girls who needed to describe to someone what had happened to them. She had been their therapist. Rabia was the only one who could listen and really comfort them. She relayed the family's story to me. Nasria and the little girls were all sitting in the room listening intently, nodding their heads in agreement and watching as my mouth opened and I gasped.

Rabia explained that the family had been attacked, at night, in their farming village. They had left Kandahar City, where I had met them, because when the U.S. bombing started on October 7, 2001, they were afraid for their lives. The Taliban were said to be hiding in buildings next to where they lived, compounds they had inhabited openly before. At night the ground would shake and one night the sound of a forceful bomb nearly deafened them. After that sound many of them heard silence, then ringing in their ears. They ran out of their home for fear that it would be bombed, but the target had been a house a few doors away. That was the night the eldest man, Nasria's father-in-law, said they should leave. They packed up whatever they could into a few station wagons, one of their own and two others borrowed from the mechanic's shop in which they worked. Some of the men rode on their motorcycles.

In the middle of the night, no earlier than 2 AM, all forty of them jammed into the white vehicles, children crying, and headed in a caravan to the village where they would be safe. It was two and a half hours away, a tiny place called Chowkar-Karez dozens of miles north of Kandahar, which was a good hour off the main road into the desert. The village had no lights, and because nothing grew on the farm during that time of year, the men would go to the city during the day to work and come back at night with bread, cooking oil, and vegetables. Rabia turned to Nasria, who nodded her head at me as if to reassure me that the story was correct. Rabia went on.

About two and a half weeks later, when the children were put to bed, before midnight, they heard a loud boom, similar to what they had heard when they were in Kandahar City. The sound of bombs is a pretty familiar one to the Afghan ear.

Nasria's daughter-in-law Almasa ran to the doorway to see what had happened, Rabia recounted. A young girl, about eight or ten, suddenly interrupted Rabia. "Then a rocket hit Almasa and she fell into two pieces." I held back my tears, as a little girl crawled over to me. I picked her up and sat her on my lap. "I saw it . . . then there was blood everywhere," the young girl continued. Nasria chimed in, beginning to sob: "She was pregnant."

"How many months?" I asked, trying to imagine what Almasa might have looked like in the doorway—hoping the answer would be that her fetus hadn't yet developed very far, but wondering why I had even bothered to ask the question.

"Almost six months," Rabia lamented, and started to sob again. She gestured with her head to the little girl on my lap. "That's her daughter—and that one." She pointed to another girl who was pulling the scarf off Rabia's head to cover her own. "She's almost three years old." Tami focused the camera on the girl in my lap.

Nasria took over to explain what happened. "We immediately picked up the little children and began to run out of the house."

Outside, they first saw a motorcycle on fire. Huge balls of fire were hurling into the air, and then falling to the earth. The trees of the village were ablaze. They ran to avoid the fireballs, in every which direction they could go, not knowing which way to run.

At the same time, shots were being fired at them. Some kids were holding hands, others lost track of each other. "I thought it was the end of the earth, the day of *kaymat*," whispered Nasria. She went on. "We were running, and they were shooting from above. Right on our heads! There was a plane above us, shooting."

"Who was shooting?" I asked, still trying to get the story straight.

"The Americans," she said in a deadpan tone. That was what I suspected, but I needed to ask because I didn't quite believe what I'd heard, and I needed to make it clear to the cameras. But still, somehow I didn't get it.

"The Americans?" I asked again, still refusing to believe what I'd heard.

"Yes, the Americans," replied Nasria, thinking I was repeating it for the cameras, but I was in shock.

It took me a few seconds, but then I was struck by a moment of understanding. I knew what had happened. The Americans meant to target Taliban or al Qaeda but the bombs missed their target. This had happened before. Even Americans had been killed by bombs going astray. After air strikes were called in by anti-Taliban fighters in Kandahar, a "precision bomb" killed at least two Americans and injured twenty.

"All these girls were there that night. They all ran."

I looked around the room. All eyes were on me, except for the oldest girl, who was looking at the floor. My eyes fixated on the two girls sitting in the middle of the room. "Were you there?" I asked. They nodded their heads.

"Talk to her, don't be shy," ordered Nasria.

The young girl picked up the edge of her scarf and put it in between her lips while the older one fixed hers, adjusted her legs, and began to speak. "We ran out of the house. They were shooting at us," she said in a hushed tone.

"You were running?" I prodded her. She nodded her head.

"Talk to her. Don't nod your head." Nasria repeated her orders.

"I was running with Alia. I was holding her hand and then she told me she was tired and she needed to stop and sit, so we did."

"Alia is her cousin," Nasria explained. The camera and my eyes went to Nasria and then back to the little girl.

"When we sat down, she asked to put her head on my lap. And then I saw blood running from her head, down my knee and on the ground." I felt like a big rock had sprouted in my throat. This girl was telling me this story with the coldness of a New York City police officer at the scene of a crime.

"Then I asked her to get up, but she did not say anything." My eyes bulged and I stuck my neck out. I was hoping she would be able to continue and not make me ask for more details. I didn't want to force her to talk. "I picked her head up and put it on the floor, and then I got up and started to run again." She gestured picking up the head from her knee, while sitting Indian style, with her legs crossed. I couldn't imagine what it must have been like for her, a ten-year-old, to find someone dead on her lap and have the instinct to leave the body and continue running. I hated that I had to lead this discussion. I didn't feel like speaking to her. I only wanted to hear what she had to say.

"Where did you go?" I asked.

"I ran and I ran and then I found a ditch and I jumped into it. Then I stayed very quiet until the morning."

Nasria, clearly directing this conversation, joined in again. "Show her where the bullet hit you." The little girl was clearly embarrassed. "Show her, it's okay. We're all girls here." She lifted up the leg of her pants and turned to show me the back of her thigh and smiled nervously. Tami asked her to hold it. Then Nasria asked the other girls to show me theirs, and one after another they lifted a sleeve to show a wound on the arm, a long chemise to show one on the back, and another pulled on the neck of her chemise to show me her shoulder. All of them had been hit. A firestorm of bullets, cutting through the night, had pierced almost every single one of them.

Nasria pointed to her upper lip. "They got me here." I had noticed something strange about her lip, but I couldn't remember if that had been there before. Many of the wounds looked like they had healed, though some of the indents in the skin were craterlike impressions. Nasria's wound on the lip was the most exposed of all.

"What I don't understand," continued Rabia, "is why they had to do this to us. What did we ever do to them?" At this point it had become clear that the attack had been carried out by American or coalition forces, because the Taliban did not have air power. "We weren't at war with them. We were just trying to live our lives. We're not Taliban." I nodded; she barely noticed and continued.

"Ask this girl with you." She extended her chin out in Tami's direction. "Ask her why we would have been targeted. Did they think my sister and her family were Taliban? What made them think that? Then when they were running out of their homes at night, didn't they see that there were women and children? Why did they continue to shoot? Who would do such a thing? Now some of them are lying in hospitals in Pakistan . . . some are there and some are here." Rabia was very angry, and boy did she have a mouth on her. Nasria, by contrast, was incredibly soft-spoken, and perhaps still in shock.

It had been two months since the attack, in which nineteen members of the family had died. In one night, Nasria had lost her sixteen-year-old daughter, her pregnant daughter-in-law, two brothers-in-law, and fourteen nieces and nephews. I felt like I was being gently interrogated and asked to account for what had happened. Tami and I were the only thing close enough to Americans Nasria's family had met, and Tami did not understand a word they were saying. I had a hard time believing them, even though I had just heard their story and seen their wounds with my own eyes. I felt responsible, as an American.

"It must have been a big mistake. It had to have been. Did they come to apologize?" Rabia asked rhetorically, letting out a sarcastic laugh, while Nasria made a *tsk* sound to indicate a negative. I was surprised. Then I realized that the U.S. forces that night may not have realized it was a mistake, or were too afraid to come to them afterward, thinking there were Taliban about. It seemed odd to me that no one had come to check on the success of the attack. I needed to contact someone when I got back home to find out what had happened. These people definitely deserved an apology at least, as well as help with treating the injured in Pakistan and rebuilding their village.

I asked Rabia what could be done now. "Well, we have incurred so many expenses from this tragedy. We need the hospital bills of the injured to be paid, and our village must be rebuilt." I was impressed by her straightforward answer, and she carried herself with the perfection of a longtime activist in front of the camera. "We also want to know what happened. We want an explanation and an apology." With that, I thanked them for speaking to me and promised to carry their message to the United States.

Before I left, Nasria pulled out a few pictures she had hidden under her knee. She asked the camera to be turned off and showed me pictures of her sixteen-year-old daughter posing in front of a television next to a bouquet of flowers, and another of her with her arm around her adolescent sister. In all the pictures Nasria's daughter had her long hair pulled back, with a twist of hair hanging over her forehead. She was very skinny, and clearly loved to pose for the camera. Finally, Nasria showed me pictures of her daughter-in-law as a bride, and of a row of nine of her nieces and nephews. Three of the children had lost a parent, three had fled Afghanistan after the war, and three had died that night in Chowkar-Karez. They were all younger than seven years old.

In some ways Nasria's daughter reminded me of my own sixteen-year-old sister, Sara. I wished I could show the pictures to reporters and television cameras, to prove how absolutely innocent and human this girl was—but the prohibition of conservative Pashtun culture and Islam would not allow it, and I wasn't about to argue with Nasria.

As I left I kissed every single woman and girl good-bye, three kisses, alternating between cheeks in the traditional Afghan style. I'm not usually an affectionate person, but at the moment all I had to offer them was a pat on the shoulder and a tight hug. I felt completely powerless, but so disturbed that I knew I would never be the same. I was losing my innocence fast. I had come on this trip partly because it was an adventure to uncover the truth, but what I had found meant that people were treating me as an adult and asking me to help them as if I were actually capable of doing it.

I entered the men's room and braced myself for another round. This room was full of men and boys, though not nearly as many people as in the women's room. Jon had been sitting with them, waiting patiently while we spoke to the women, and was now eager to hear the family's story.

I told the men that I couldn't believe what the women had told me. The men's story began the same, but the hurt seemed to run even deeper. This time I had Jon to guide the questions. He waited for me to catch my breath, and then directed me to ask who the eldest man, Nasria's older brother-in-law, had lost.

He replied, "My daughter, my daughter-in-law, my brother, my nephew, one of my cousins, another cousin. Three grandchildren and a nephew." I repeated after each one mentioned. I did not know how to respond to this list. It was said so coldly, without any emotion, almost as if we should have known already. He continued, "In the morning, my young son told me there were sheep slaughtered on the ground. Afghans were familiar with the sight of freshly slaughtered animals. When I walked over I found that it was all *our family,* body parts scattered all over the bloody ground."

I couldn't hold back another second. I translated for the camera, barely able to speak. I burst into tears. I was so embarrassed to be seen in such a weak state. They, who had been there, spoke so matter-of-factly, while I cried.

Nasria's husband was eager to tell his side of the story. "My daughter died," he declared. He was a handsome man, with glasses, which were a rare sight in Afghanistan these days. Few people wore glasses, because few ever saw an eye doctor. He was quite young. Nasria had certainly aged faster than him.

"I ran out with her, we were together . . . but she was shot. So I carried her on my back as far as I could. But when I stopped running and put her down I realized she was dead." He looked down, almost frozen. I imagined what it would have been like to carry my sister Sara on my back and then look at her lifeless face. I could not bear it anymore. I could not hear another awful story. I could not take one more nauseating detail.

"What can we do now?" I asked the eldest man. He paused, looked me straight in the eyes, and said, "We want to know how this happened. Why were we chosen? What was the logic for choosing us? We're not Taliban, we never supported the Taliban."

"I have no idea, but your questions are important," I said.

"Ask him." He pointed his chin toward Jon.

"He doesn't know. He's a journalist," I explained.

"Well, ask him to find out. All of you can help us find out what happened. We heard the Americans were paying Afghans to find the Taliban targets for them. We don't know why anyone would pick us. We have no quarrels, no problems with anyone. But if this is how we were chosen we want to know who it was. We just want to know his name."

The old Afghan way of revenge was in their hearts. Yet they were incredibly calm—almost chillingly so.

"Just his name."

The women had asked for aid. They somehow had moved on, but the men wanted revenge, a concept of Pashtunwali. The clear difference between the strategy of the men and women was typical, but still noteworthy. Jon nodded his head, indicating his understanding, while I explained their wishes. He had a way of sympathizing and showing emotion that defied any language. The compassion on his face made me want to hug him right there. He told me to reassure them that we would look for answers.

On the way home Jon and Tami expressed their sorrow. This had not been the first time this sort of "accident" had happened. Jon explained how he dodged bombs in Vietnam when he was reporting from there. He was incredibly understanding and it was at that point that I really began to trust him. "We need to get to the village and see it for ourselves. Then we need to get to the base and try to get some answers."

"The base?!?!" I said, aghast. "How are we going to get on the base?" The American base was located in Kandahar airport, just outside the city. It was in the middle of an active war, and it was where the U.S. Marines were stationed in the south of Afghanistan.

"We'll find a way. We're press, remember? I just hope they don't look up who I am. They might kick us off if they find out." This was not the first time Jon had gone fishing for information where he wasn't welcome. I thought he was exaggerating for effect, but I soon realized he was serious when he asked Tami to prepare the replacement tapes in case anybody tried to confiscate them. Before we left, he had labeled blank tapes with titles so that they would appear to be our footage. They would be presented instead of the originals in case we were caught taking footage we weren't supposed to have.

The next day we set out for Kandahar, from our cozy hotel in Quetta. We were told we required Pakistani escorts to take us to the border, and because we hadn't arranged for security, we were happy to oblige. The senior police official in Quetta pulled up to our hotel as we were packing the cars and waved to Jon.

Jon summoned me and I began to translate, saying that we were journalists.

I could tell the official was checking me out from the window of the car, but this was par for the course in Quetta. The only thing that bothered me was how obvious this man was about it. Clearly an official of some power, he was perched high on the passenger side, his round belly and thin, well-groomed mustache signs of status among skinny policemen. In Pashto, he asked me what room I was staying in. My first thought was that he wanted to send protection for me, and that he didn't realize I was with Jon and we were all going to Kandahar. He repeated, "I'm asking *you*. What room are you staying in tonight?"

"Umm, I'm leaving the hotel. I won't be here." I felt like saying he would never have a shot with me and who did he think he was that I would just give him my room number. But I knew better than to insult a man of power in Quetta. The police in Pakistan were notoriously corrupt, and I recall reading that Pakistan was routinely ranked as one of the most corrupt countries in the world. The police chief then wrote his number on a piece of paper and handed it to me.

"Call me if you need anything, and definitely call me when you come back."

The man had no sense of shame, and I was sure that at his age he must have had a wife, or two. After a "good-bye" to Jon he sped away. Jon smiled at me.

"He was nice."

"He gave me his number and said to call him."

"Oh good, we should." Did Jon not understand what had just happened to me? That a gross Pakistani police official tried to pick me up? Could he be that naive? "He asked me what room I was staying in. He tried to pick me up." It was then that Jon agreed the man was a scumbag. It was then that *I* realized that I must trust my communication skills and instincts in the journey forward.

We headed to the border, with four Pakistani guards in the van close behind us. I felt both instantly safer and yet in more danger watching these men in the side mirror as we drove. We were supposed to have left at the break of dawn, but now it was 8 AM and we had a six-hour trip ahead of us. Moving from the Afghan border to Kandahar, three hours' driving distance, would be the most dangerous part, and we needed to hire security at some point, after we got over the border. There were reports of bandits along this road, some allegedly affiliated with the Taliban. It was like gangs of New York, only it was gangs of Kandahar, and American journalists would be a prime target. In fact, hundreds of Afghan refugees, many from Kandahar, had badly beaten British journalist Robert Fisk on the road from Quetta to Kandahar, just a few weeks before we traveled the same road.

As we drove, the roads got narrower and dustier, and the shops got sparser. The trip always made me feel like we were going back in time. With each mile traveled, conditions got worse, but it felt good to be going "home."

Our driver, Mowin, was a Pakistani from Baluchistan province who spoke English, Urdu, and Pashto. He blasted Bollywood music as we drove, even though Jon repeatedly asked him to turn it down. Mowin told me stories of driving journalists along the road. "Westerners are so naive," he admitted. "And the women don't understand our culture at all," he explained. He described how one jolly woman he drove around would always make faces and laugh at people in other cars. On this same road, she had made faces at a man sitting in the back of a pickup truck driving just in front of them. Mowin pleaded with her to stop. Nothing good could come out of this, he warned. But she kept laughing and making faces, and the man in the truck became very excited as a result of all the attention. He made faces back, and soon enough pulled his bottoms down, which as you can imagine freaked her out! Mowin remarked that he had been embarrassed for her, and that she still didn't understand why making faces at men was not a good idea in Afghanistan. Mowin later told me this same woman had rubbed her breasts up against his arm while he was driving. He clearly had enjoyed her indiscretions, even if they were annoying when directed at other men.

Mowin's stories faded in and out, as I thought about what it would be like to visit the U.S. base. The most important thing was to keep going, and to drive while it was still light out. At least this time we had air-conditioning and only had to deal with the dust that infiltrated our AC system. When we arrived at the last Pakistani checkpoint to get our exit visas stamped, Brent, our young editor and cameraman, realized he didn't have his passport. He had forgotten it at the hotel desk, not realizing that they were holding it, as they do in some foreign countries. Inside the checkpoint office, the Pakistani police checking passports pointed to the cell that Brent could be held in if he didn't have a passport. It was a small square room, with high ceilings, large enough to hold two or three prisoners standing. It had once been painted lime green, but the dirt, the dust, and probably the criminals had worn it out.

We were in a real bind. Everyone except Brent now had their passport stamped and that meant that we could only enter Pakistan one more time, on the way back from Afghanistan—so we could not accompany Brent to the hotel in Pakistan to pick up his passport. We really did not want to send Brent alone, especially now that the guards were gone, but neither could we wait, because the area we were in was incredibly hostile to foreigners, and except for the immigration station there was nowhere else to go. No hotels, no restaurants, and, worst of all, no places to pee.

Our only options were to either leave Brent behind to travel to the hotel and wait until he returned, or all turn back. Neither option was good. In the meantime, we tried to call the hotel in

Quetta using our satellite phone, but even that couldn't catch a signal. We walked over to a pay phone outside to try our luck, but the phone was dead.

As we gathered around our car trying to get our satellite phone to work, frustrated, Afghans waited in line trying to get into the Pakistani station to get into the country. They carried their lives wrapped up in colorful sheets, hurled over their shoulders. Their feet were dry and cracked, their turbans frayed at the edges and dusty. They were so tanned compared to my alabaster skin. They stared at us resentfully as they walked, but all I wanted to do was run up to them and say that I was really one of them. They looked like they wouldn't have approved of me, an American "collaborator," anyway.

We stood there for half an hour, trying to get the phone to work, but we were to have no luck and no better plan of action. It was going to get dark soon, and then we would really be playing with fire. Then, just as we were dialing the hotel yet again, the dust flew into the air and a speeding black four-by-four stopped short of us. It was our Pakistani fixer triumphantly waving an American passport out of the passenger side window. We were saved, but the long delay meant that the road to Kandahar would be traveled in the dark.

Chapter 11

From Ground Zero to Ground Zero

With the strong one, either keep your distance or your peace.

—Pashto proverb

As we crossed into Afghanistan the metal bar was lifted by an armed man in Afghan clothes, but with no discernible difference from the average citizen. Mowin instructed us to stay seated in the car while he took care of our entry visas. It was December 27, 2001, and Afghanistan was still at war. In fact, it had only been a few days since Hamid Karzai had been inaugurated as interim leader, so he would have to deal with whatever authorities now had control of the border. "Roll up your windows and don't open the doors for anyone," Mowin ordered. As we watched armed men surround our vehicle and emerge out of mud huts, our goal was to remain calm. I pulled out my peanut M&M's and turned to our crew, who were sitting in the backseat.

"These guys don't look happy. Think they like the new government?" Jon joked even under the most intense pressure. That's how he had dealt with fear in the other countries he had visited. I dealt by eating chocolate.

There was a tap at the window and I jumped. When I turned

around, it was Mowin. "They want one hundred dollars per person for the visa."

"What?!" Jon had the same reaction when I translated, but we had no choice but to pay. It was the most expensive country Jon had visited yet, and that included prior visits to Afghanistan as well as Iraq. I wondered if Mowin had secretly taken his cut. Even though he was our driver, there was no way of knowing where his loyalties would lie. It would have cost another hundred dollars per person per day if we took the security forces offered to us at this checkpoint, but not knowing these men and having just been charged an exorbitant fee by them, we decided we would probably need additional security to protect us from these guys even if we did hire them. Needing security from your security was a novel concept, only to be discovered in a place like Afghanistan.

We could hire guards at the first Afghan village on the road, suggested one of the journalists we met on our drive to the border. As we left the border area, we realized we were being followed by a white station wagon. At first we thought it just happened to be behind us. Besides, there were so many white station wagons that it took a while for us to realize it was the same one behind us the whole time. We began to get nervous. Could it be the same men that surrounded our car while we were waiting for Mowin to get us our visas? We sped through the streets to try to lose our followers.

We saw the village approaching in the distance, and just as we pulled in through the large metal gate the white station wagon turned into another street. We had lost them for now, but there was no telling what would happen when we came back out. We needed security—fast. We drove to the center of the courtyard, where a couple dozen young and middle-aged men were milling around; many were armed, and all eyes turned to us as we stopped. This time I got out of the car and asked for their commander, whom I presumed to be a local warlord and former anti-Soviet guerrilla fighter. "He's out for prayers. What do you need?" said the eldest man seated under the tree, cleaning a Kalashnikov.

"We need security. We're journalists and we're going to Kandahar."

He immediately ordered a young boy to get the commander. They invited us into the compound for tea. As I walked I tried to act tough, as if I weren't at all affected by the loads of men armed with Kalashnikovs near the entrance or the hallways. The rooms of the building were full of even more men. We were seated in a room with two single beds, their frames comprised of rusted metal, and cups of fresh green tea were poured into small clear glasses. The glasses were the same kind we had when we lived in Kandahar, only smaller. I remembered when we used them in America, I could read the MADE IN FRANCE imprint on the bottom. I pretended to drink the tea, taking small sips, thinking only of how dirty the cups might be in a compound full of guerrilla fighters.

A group of five men walking past in the hallway stopped in the doorway and tried to start a conversation with me. One of the guards got up to close the door, but by then the men were already filing into the room. "So where are you from? Who are these Americans? How is it that you speak such perfect Pashto?" It was clear that it had probably been a very long time since a woman had entered the compound, and one that spoke English and Pashto was even more of a sight. More and more men wanted to enter our room, but by now it was full and the guards inside were pushing against the door to stop others from coming in.

After some commotion, there was a knock at the door and a whisper, "*Commanderr di.*" A large, very tanned bearded man entered. The commander appeared to be in his mid-forties, and had surprisingly round, soft eyes. A few men leapt up to offer him their seats, and he was instantly poured a cup of tea. The men around him became suddenly quiet and reserved, and the

Masuda Sultan

commander asked us about our mission. He told us the road to Kandahar was very dangerous. Only a few days ago some French journalists had been attacked and beaten black and blue, their cameras smashed. "The people on this road are like animals. There's no predicting what they'll do. And you're a young woman. They may let you go because you're Afghan, but these people will be in trouble." He went on to explain that the last two journalists had taken ten men with them.

He then suggested we take twenty guards, since there were four of us. Twenty men at forty dollars a day would have been way too expensive, however. After some haggling, we decided to take six. They packed into a land cruiser with a sticker on the back that read SUICIDAL TENDENCIES in red with a black background. My main concern was that these same men would plan an attack on us on the road, or that they wouldn't be able to protect us in our time of need.

I thought of a few plots they could come up with. One: They could just stop us on the road, take our money, and leave. It would be more than enough for each of them and might even make them rich by their standards. Two: Another car of men from the same compound could stop us and take our money, pretending to be unassociated bandits, and our men could pretend that they couldn't do anything about it. Three: Bandits could really attack us, and our guards could refuse to defend us, or just leave. There were probably many other plans they could have thought up, sitting in that dusty compound, but I chose not to dwell on them all.

The sky was rust orange, with deep red streaks like the blood of martyrs, and we were headed to Kandahar with a group of strange armed men with suicidal tendencies. Their vehicle led us, kicking up dust, especially when swerving to avoid big rocks on the unpaved road. I never figured out how to drive on this road. Sometimes the driver would drive up on the edge of it, riding the wave of rocks like a skilled surfer, and the car would tilt; other times he would swerve from side to side, making S shapes as he went. When we rode too close to the guards, the dust clouds from their car would rush up, swirling around so thick that we couldn't see anything ahead of us. But the driver never even slowed down. It was during those moments that I most feared another car would be on the other side of the clouds of dust, about to collide with us head-on. I wondered how many accidents must have happened in such a manner. Somehow this didn't seem at all risky to Mowin. The only thing he was worried about was losing our guards. They kept speeding off into the distance, almost as if they didn't want us to follow them. If something happened, they would have no clue that they had lost us.

Chasing a group of armed Afghan fighters on the dark road to Kandahar was beautifully ironic. Mowin hit the pedal after a cloud of dust cleared and they were nowhere in sight. When we saw the red taillights, he hit the gas even harder and started honking his horn. The guards' car stopped and they rolled down their window. Mowin rolled down his and asked them to slow down. They told him to speed up; *this was Afghanistan*. Mowin shouted at them that they wouldn't get one Afghani (local currency) if they didn't do their jobs. The bearded driver nodded and rolled his window back up. Money was one thing they were serious about, especially because they had to answer to their commander.

The drive lasted three hours, and by the time we got to Kandahar we had been on the road for over twelve. The smell of flatbread in the air, so aromatic that you could taste it on your tongue if you closed your eyes, reminded me I was home again.

We headed straight for the CBS compound, parts of which had been hastily constructed with wooden planks. Many journalists had set up shop in Kandahar, but NBC had been driven out after their compound was shot at in the middle of the night. Inside the brightly lit rooms were laptops, other electronic equipment, satellite phones, and mostly blond-haired women and men playing cards and drinking beer at a white plastic picnic table.

Through the crack of a door near the entrance I caught a glimpse of several rough-looking Afghan characters crowded into a small room, seated on the floor, being served Afghan food. Those must be the guards, I thought.

We were served a much-needed meal of Afghan rice and lamb and then introduced to the Afghan man who made the CBS operation run. His name was Jamil, and he was a nephew of the new chairman of the Afghan Transitional Administration, Hamid Karzai. Jamil was a soft-spoken young man with a scar on his wide face. He wore elegantly embroidered light jade–colored Afghan clothes and had an elegant demeanor, almost presidential himself. Incredibly confident and respectful, he immediately focused on me, called me sister, and asked if I had eaten. He said he would make sure I would be well taken care of, and that I should have no worries. I was to call him day or night, like I would call on my own brother.

Jamil made me feel instantly at ease and reminded me of what I absolutely loved about Afghan men, when they rise to the best of Afghan tradition. Really, it was the way proper Muslim men were to treat women, he was charming and full of respect. I thought that he would be our fixer too, but he summoned his younger brother, with less English experience and less of a presence, to accompany us. Jamil explained that he was being paid three hundred dollars a day by CBS, but we decided to pay his brother Fazl half that because he had far fewer contacts and experience. Fazl was shyer, but he had the same indentation on his face as his brother, the kind that was obviously caused by sand fly bites, which carried the Leishmania virus.

Fazl led us to a compound nearby that had "Oxfam" written on the gate. A handsome bearded man opened the gate and blurted out, "Welcome to America!" followed by a boisterous hearty laugh. His name was Haroon. He showed us around the house, which was easily big enough for us, our guards, as well as him and his guards.

When Haroon leaned over to ask me whose daughter I was, I got a whiff of the vodka on his breath. Some people had gotten right to drinking at the first sign the Taliban were on their way out. Haroon recognized my father's name immediately, and he proudly informed me that he had lived in Washington, D.C., for many years, which explained why his English was so good. I felt better knowing that we had landed in good hands.

Two nights later, I was excited about calling my father on the satellite phone to report that we had arrived in Kandahar and were in good hands. "We're with your good old friend, Haroon."

"What?! Why did you go there?!"

"What do you mean, it was where the Karzais took us. It's fine."

"You shouldn't stay there. . . . He . . ." There were crackling sounds on the phone.

"I can't understand you, Agha, speak more clearly." The phone went dead. I dialed frantically to find out what he had to say, but I couldn't get through. I felt like Abdul Haq, the Afghan military commander who entered Afghanistan after 9/11 to fight the Taliban but was surrounded by Taliban forces while he was desperately trying to call in an American air strike. He kept dialing until he was killed.

It didn't work, so I walked downstairs to find Jon laughing and drinking tea with Haroon. I asked to speak with Jon upstairs and explained my conversation with my father. Jon didn't think we should worry. "What are we going to do? Leave? It will be fine." The next day, Jon asked Haroon about his story in private, and Haroon admitted that he had been arrested for punching his wife in a drunken stupor. Months later in New York, I found out from the Afghan community in Virginia that Haroon had actually been jailed and deported for raping a Vietnamese cleaning lady. I also learned that he was not really connected to Hamid Karzai, probably more of an embarrassment to the Karzai family than their representative. In Afghanistan, the truth could often be only somebody's version of a rumor. I should have known to be suspicious.

The second day that we were in Kandahar, a man walked out of our house and approached us as we were waiting by the cars to begin our day, asking if he could use our satellite phone. Before I could question him, Jon held it out to him and he was dialing. After he was done with his call, he walked over to me and said the building we were staying in didn't even belong to Haroon, and he had just made a call to find a way to get Haroon, and us, out of the place. He then had the nerve to hand me passport-sized photos of his entire family and asked me to get them to America. The photos would be ready in case I was able to get them passports. I told him I couldn't get him there, but he insisted that I hold on to them. I later learned that Oxfam was a European aid agency doing health work in Afghanistan, and that this was indeed their former headquarters. He was a doctor with the agency, attempting to reclaim the building so that they could begin operations again. I carried his family's photos in my bag for a long time, not wanting to give up on the Afghan spirit of taking a chance, and believing in luck, even when it seems that God has turned His back.

The next few days were spent exploring, trying to find my family and setting ourselves up in Kandahar. Everything needed to be arranged from scratch. We needed to hire a cook, buy or rent dishes, purchase groceries, and figure out how to get our laundry done. Haroon hired us two cooks, who turned the backyard into a kitchen, and soon all the elder men in the neighborhood were being "wined and dined" on our dime. The day that Haroon took us out to buy fruits and vegetables, he rode in his forest-green old convertible, with the top down, playing a Pashto song about *watan*, or the homeland. An Afghan flag hung from each side of the vehicle, and Haroon drove around like the king of the land. As he drove down a one-way street, cursing in Pashto, telling the children and cart pushers to get out of his way, he explained to Jon that he had been a cabdriver in Washington. He drove up to an electronics store and priced a $150 washing machine, urging us to buy it because soon we would be out of clean clothes. We declined and decided instead to hire someone to wash by hand.

Word had gotten out that there were foreigners staying in Haroon's house, so Afghan men who wanted work began to visit us. One Afghan man offered to do our laundry, and Haroon approved of him, so we loaded up a bag to be brought back the next day. The man came back two days later with a shopping bag full of neatly folded clothes and asked for twenty dollars. "Twenty dollars?!" asked Tami, making a face. "I don't pay that much in the U.S. for *dry cleaning*." I felt sorry for the guy, because he looked almost embarrassed as we inspected the clothes. The socks were drenched, and the T-shirts were still wet. He explained that his pregnant wife had tried to wash them as soon as they received the bag, but that there were too many and by the time she was finished it was past prime noon drying time, so they decided to get the clothes to us before letting another day pass. I was impressed with his sensitivity to timeliness, despite the fact that he was a day late.

"I'm sorry, sister. We don't do laundry. Fate has brought us to a state where we must do what we can to earn some money. Forgive me. They will be better dried next time." Somehow I believed him. He seemed to be so ashamed as he spoke. I wished we could give him more than twenty dollars, but we weren't here for charity and Tami was already irked because it seemed like yet another money grubber on our journey. I couldn't blame her. He was hoping I'd understand his predicament, and out of kinship agree to pay him the total sum. After some negotiation with him, and then some with Tami, I convinced both of them that fifteen dollars would be a fair compromise.

Masuda Sultan

• • •

Once we were set up, we made several excursions into Kandahar City to explore ordinary Afghans' experiences during and after the war. The biggest initial shock was the ruins of almost all of the roads and buildings in the city. Homes and government buildings lack doors, roofs, and even walls, while many solitary walls rise from the dust where buildings once stood. The people of Kandahar bitterly expressed to me how ashamed they were at the condition of their city, declaring that it had once been a beautiful city, before the wars. Many old women, grown men, and small children begged us for a little money, food, or medicine everywhere we went. A man in the bazaar told us it took him three months to earn thirty dollars, and showed us his blistered and cut hands as evidence of his hardship.

Our first destination was the stadium, where the Taliban had carried out monthly executions of murderers and other criminals for about four years. Our fixer claimed to have seen thirty to thirty-five public executions there over the years, as well as ten to fifteen amputations. The groundskeeper told us the Taliban judges would sit in the dignitaries' platform, and the accused would wait near where a soccer goal should be to be shot or have their hands chopped off. "It's the worry that's caused my beard to turn gray," he told me. He didn't agree with what the Taliban had done, he said, but he had to feed his family somehow.

Next stop was the bazaar, where a shopkeeper proudly announced to us that he was selling just as many *burqas* as in Taliban times. I picked out a pink *burqa*, which cost me twelve dollars. When I wore it out into the street, I felt protected from being ogled by the crowds of men and young boys unused to seeing women out without their *burqas*. All of the Afghan women in Kandahar (except for me and a few Western women) still wore their *burqas* outside their houses. Even though there were no more Taliban religious police to beat them for going uncovered, they had to cover up to placate their husbands and fathers, and to avoid being kidnapped or assaulted in the street by criminals.

We visited shops selling televisions, music CDs, and DVD movies for the first time in years. *Titanic* and *Rambo* had always been favorites, as were many Bollywood classics, and now *Invasion U.S.A.* with Chuck Norris was selling well. The Taliban had outlawed all of these technologies of entertainment, not to mention kite flying, playing cards, and dancing. The city had no hope when I visited in August 2001, but was now experiencing a real rebirth. Money changers, butchers, and bakers were all doing a brisk business. The people in the city were very optimistic about the future because the Taliban were gone and a new government was being built.

As we approached the Ministry of Education building, where I hoped to obtain permission to visit the girls' high school where my father had taught chemistry for years, we saw piles of books being stacked outside by several large men in olive-green turbans. The men had retrieved hundreds of books for Kandahar's schools that had been stolen by the Taliban for use in fundamentalist *madrassas*. They promised that in the new Afghanistan the religious books they had reclaimed would be an important part of, but no longer the whole content of, the education of Afghan children in the city. Inside the ministry, officials reported that the schools had been reopened about ten or fifteen days before our arrival in the city. Large sums of money that should have gone into the schools had been looted and converted to the Taliban's own use, they maintained.

Inside the Zarghoona Ana lycée for girls, opened before 1950 but shuttered entirely during Taliban times, I found young girls struggling to make sense of why the Taliban made them stay home for the past eight years, rather than go to school. "We begged our parents to let us go to school, but they told us the schools were closed," one girl related. "They wanted us to stay home because it was dangerous," another remembered. "They didn't like it," was all one could say. Some teachers recounted to me that they hadn't held classes in twelve years, since the Soviet withdrawal and the start of the civil wars of the 1990s. Teaching is considered a noble profession in Afghanistan, so the reopening of the schools represented an exciting revival of public life in general, especially for women.

It was only the third day since the start of school in Kandahar, after years of no school. Although it was a lycée, or secondary school, the Zarghoona Ana school was welcoming girls of all ages, from four or five to eighteen. Some girls had trudged several miles through rubble and war wreckage to get to class. Back in school, the girls proudly told me they dreamed of becoming doctors, teachers, and journalists. In the hallways during recess, throngs of little girls giggled, playfully jostled each other, and screamed in happiness to be together again in school. They had worn their best clothes, brightly colored scarves and flowing tunics in pink, neon green, scarlet red, and turquoise.

At Mir Wais Hospital, a squat tan-colored structure with glass windows, we learned about the price paid by some Afghans for the joyful sounds of children laughing in school, and of the music blaring from the CD kiosks in the bazaar. In the intensive care unit, the head nurse at the hospital informed us that many people with injuries from land mines, cluster bombs, and unexploded ordnance were filling the beds. A child complained of being sprayed with shrapnel during the war. Another lost his hand and much of his feet after picking up a bomb that failed to go off on impact. A girl named Maimona and her little brother had suffered through the deaths of five family members, and the amputation of the brother's penis in the hospital. He looked under five. "I had to pick the body parts of my family up off of the ground after our home was bombed," their mother mournfully declared, biting her lip.

. . .

After visiting the bazaar, girls' school, and hospital, we began the search to find my family. I found out that Khala Sherina and her children had fled Kandahar for Quetta, so I decided to start with my parents' old home. I hoped to see my aunts, uncles, and cousins on my father's side, most of my mother's family having left for Pakistan.

I told Fazl, our fixer, the name of the street where I thought our house was. When I visited the house with my aunt Lailuma during Taliban times, my cousins were living there and had prepared an enormous feast for us. Afterward, we slept on the roof and admired the sky for hours while they enthralled me with stories of what our family life was like when I was a child.

We stopped at the first shop on the edge of the street, a small, decrepit indentation in the clay wall with long green raisins and other dried fruits in sacks out front. The shopkeeper pointed in the direction of the house when I said I was the daughter of Sultan Mohammed, teacher and Qari. We asked again at another shop, where a man sitting in front who recognized my father's name greeted me warmly and left his shop to walk me to the house. "Of course I know your father. I'm his cousin. I remember you well." He had a dark tan on his face, and his eyes looked almost like they had been lined with kohl. His turban was loosely wrapped on his head, making it look like a woman's head scarf, and he wore a warm, familiar smile with perfectly clean white teeth. I later learned a grain of truth about him too. When I returned home and showed the tape to Agha, he said the man was the village thief!

We passed little girls playing in the street. They watched us lumber by, their mouths gaping open with curiosity or even awe, stopping in their tracks or leaning their backs to the walls on the edges of the narrow, crooked, khaki-colored street, almost as if some aliens had come down to earth to visit them. Only twenty years ago I was one of those girls, and if I had stayed one of those girls would probably have been my daughter, coming home to tell me they had seen Americans with cameras walking into their play area. That it could easily have been me on that street was a feeling I could rarely escape, whether walking down Shikapur Bazaar or sitting in a Starbucks in midtown Manhattan sipping on a caramel Frappuccino. In those girls' eyes I could see myself, but to them I was an intruder on *their* street, a strange woman sans *burqa*, but surrounded by a sort of *burqa* of Americans.

My father's "cousin" led me to the doorway, and I got so caught up in the excitement I didn't realize he had left before even saying good-bye, or its Pashto equivalent, "May you encounter good things on your path." I swept in, looking forward to surprising my family. Surely they would never have expected a visit from me only a few months after my last, especially since it had taken me twenty years. "God knows when we'll see you again," they quipped after my last stay. "It has taken you twenty years to come to us once, when you leave will it take you twenty more years to come again?"

Jon and the crew were waiting outside until they received clearance from me that there weren't any women around. I entered the large central courtyard and regarded, from across the square empty garden, a tall man wearing a very long pale gray shirt with his belly bulging from underneath, looking almost pregnant, with his hands clamped on his waist, waiting right by the doorway to one of the rooms. He did not look familiar, but I greeted him warmly anyway and approached him as closely as decorum would allow to get a closer look, thinking that maybe I didn't remember him from my August trip. He did not budge, only stood taller, as the towering elder male of the house. He was clearly uncomfortable, however, and was probably guarding the room where the women were hidden. I wondered what must have been going through his mind as a strange uncovered woman with a camera strode up to him.

An expression of consternation and doubt crept over the

man's face as he explained that the family that had rented the house to him had left town, and he didn't know where they were. I looked around again at the courtyard. Suddenly the house was less recognizable, the layout of the yard a little less familiar. It felt like a deserted town from a Western movie, with balls of tumbleweed rolling in the wind. How could my family have left this house to strangers? Under what conditions must they have fled? What must it have been like for a house full of elders, women, and children to suddenly have to vanish? I wondered if my father's relatives had fled in the night, just like Nasria's family.

After I asked permission to film the bedroom where I was born, Jon and Tami joined me inside. I pointed to the corner where I had been told in August that my mother gave birth to me. When my mother saw the documentary she called me "shameless" for being so explicit, she was embarrassed so much. I wasn't sure if it was that I spoke about her giving birth at all, or the fact that it happened in the corner of a fairly empty room in a private home, that made it seem so primitive and therefore shameful. What was there to be ashamed of? I thought. We didn't go to a hospital. For whatever reason, that's who we were. It didn't mean we were primitive or somehow undeserving of hospital treatment in a more modern city like New York.

I never understood why people, especially Muslims from Third World countries, were embarrassed by the state of their lives back home. Somehow people always found something "civilized" to hang on to when they described their past. They would boast that their mother wore a short skirt in conservative times, or their father was a government official, or that they were born into some recognized tribe or family, even if nobody else recognized that tribe or family. Coming from Kandahar, I didn't have quite as much to brag about, and I didn't care to make up fabulous stories. One time, when I was growing up in Brooklyn, my friends in junior high school were comparing the names of the hospitals they were born in, and when all eyes turned to me I proudly said that I was born in a house. They looked at me as if we must have been the basest of humans to give birth in our own living rooms, but that's just the way it was in Afghanistan, and in many other places. A hospital existed in town, and although we could probably afford it, there wasn't a compelling reason to go. You only went to the hospital if you had complications that thousands of years of experience from the midwives and elders couldn't fix.

As we left the bedroom, a tiny, frail old woman with a red scarf and a peasant dress came to the door with a broom. I smiled at her and she was eager to speak. When she found out who I was, she threw her arms around me and explained she helped take care of me when I was young. I shot footage of her, but she would only let me get her sweeping the floor. She seemed ancient to me. The fact that she was still living and still working in our old house through all that had happened in the country was incredible but, sadly, a predictable result of her extreme poverty. I gave her fifty dollars, but I wish now that I had taken care of her better, as she had cared for my brother and me when we were infants. I recall that her family was extremely poor, and that my father gave them the land across the way and built them a small house. They kept a large dog tied near the door, which in my memory was the size of a bear, its growls frightening me to my core in nightmares, even after I became a teenager.

By the time we were outside the house, there was a small group of people gathered outside, probably made curious by the security guards waiting there for us. An elder man on a bike waited with some children. "You're Qari Sultan's daughter?"

"Yes, I am. *Salaamwalaikum*," I said, walking toward him to kiss his hand. "Do you remember us?"

"Of course, Qari Sultan went to America. How is he doing over there?"

I would hear over and over again that we were the ones that left the neighborhood, making me wonder if there was lingering resentment about that. "Uh, he's well. He sends his *'salaams'* to everyone," I replied, and moved on.

As soon as I turned around, an elderly couple standing in another doorway were signaling for me to come over. Their broad smiles and gestures were so welcoming that I found them hard to resist. The woman waved the edge of her scarf at me. "Come in and have tea with us. Come in. Come in." We walked in and sat on the elevated platform outside the main room, in the courtyard. "Of course I remember you," she happily announced. "You were a little girl when you left. You would play on this street, and call out for your brother to come home for lunch all the time. You were so precocious. Do you remember me?" she asked, her voice rising to an almost childish tone. But I could not remember her, and I admitted I didn't. I wish I had said yes, to lift her spirits, but I could not lie. She came to my rescue, saying, "Of course you don't, you were such a young girl when you left." The love emanating from this woman was overwhelming. I wished I could stay overnight and get to know her. I had come home. Home was where your neighbors remembered you twenty years after you had gone, never really expecting you to return again. In my family there was always a hope, or at least a dream, no matter how unlikely, that we would return to our home in Kandahar someday. Our neighbors on the street knew better than that. Somehow they knew that once we were gone, it was almost impossible that we would return again. I always wondered how that affected their feeling of self-worth, their feelings about their surroundings and the value of the lives they led. Surely it must have been sorely depressing to know that anyone who left your town, and usually it was the more wealthy and more educated that did, almost never came back.

Another woman in a *burqa* squatting on the floor with her back to the wall asked me to come over to her. She lifted the edge of her *burqa*, revealing a somewhat low-cut dress despite the presence of Jon. The way she lowered her *burqa* for Jon and me, but kept it raised in the direction of everybody else, was like she wanted to be seen but wanted to show the rest of her family that she was covered. She recalled inviting me over to her house when she saw me playing on the street because I was the fairest girl around, and giving me gum and warning me not to tell the other girls where I got it. With the cameras rolling, she joked about not wanting to wear the *burqa*, but rather wishing she could walk around the streets like the American women do. "We want to be like you. We wear this because we have to, because it's the tradition of our fathers and grandfathers." It struck me that she portrayed the tradition as belonging to the men, not to her mothers and grandmothers.

I had begun the day feeling like a foreigner in a deserted town, but within an hour I had been welcomed with love by the village that had raised me. I only wished that I could tell these people that I remembered them and their generosity, just as they remembered me.

Chapter 12

Ask DOD

Blood cannot be washed out with blood.

—Afghan proverb

I wanted with all my heart to avoid the village where Nasria's family was bombed—but Jon would not let it be. "Let's visit the bazaar one more time," I pleaded, hoping it would be impossible to go to the village. Anything but the village. But, alas, it could not be avoided. Jon wanted to see it, to film it, to show the world the village where my family had perished. I thought it was somewhat sick that we were doing this. What did people need to see? Did people really need to see ruins in order to believe? Wasn't the word of my family enough? There was something quite gross about journalism in that respect. I knew that showing was different from telling, but I didn't know if I could stomach it.

We rode first thing in the morning to the home of my cousin Janaraa, who was also related to Nasria, so we could pick up a few men from the family who knew how to get to the village. Tami and I walked in to see the women quickly, and they were full of joy, just as I had remembered them.

Janaraa pulled the scarf off of Tami's head, somewhat aggressively, reminding her that the Taliban were gone. Tami smiled nervously, aware that going around without a scarf would not be a smart move, Taliban or not. It would not be the first time local women encouraged foreigners to go out without a scarf, hoping that by doing so they could clear the path for other women. It was one issue I had been wrong on before. This was tricky territory. On the one hand, foreign women were expected to respect the local culture by dressing modestly—wearing loose clothes, with long sleeves that reached up to their wrists, dresses that hung down to their ankles, and a scarf wrapped around their heads, covering most of their hair. Sometimes, when Western women would wear something inappropriate by those standards, locals made sure to point out their disapproval to one another on the street, or to whichever Afghans might be accompanying them. One time, two Asian women were walking down the street in a busy bazaar in Kabul, wearing tight blue jeans that highlighted their behinds. I watched as older men gave disapproving glares, and caught glimpses of men and boys pointing, laughing at the foreign women on the street. Even Afghan women, such as those working in government ministries, would point out to me that if foreign women wanted to work in Afghanistan, they should dress in such a way that didn't call attention to themselves. These professional Afghan women argued that the wrong kind of attention sets back the cause of women's rights because Afghan men will criticize them for wanting to associate with such loose foreign women—or, worse, wanting to be like them. The dirty little secret is that many Afghan women, especially young women, did indeed want to dress like American women, short sleeves and all. But first they wanted education, financial independence, and health.

I introduced myself to a group of men from Janaraa's family that came out to greet us. We only needed one person to guide us to Chowkar-Karez, but instead, a group of men packed into a station wagon and we headed out as a caravan. One of the elders rode with us and explained that his son worked in a fried chicken store in Albany. We laughed about Afghan men and the fried chicken business.

As we drove along the road toward the airport my stomach began to knot up. The trip itself was dangerous, as we were driving through an active war zone, and a caravan could be a prime target. But my stomach pains were about the fear that I had about visiting Chowkar-Karez. I had some desire to see it, I realized, just as I had felt the desire to walk down as close as I could get to the site of the World Trade Center disaster, despite the fact that I knew what had happened. I just didn't like that I was sort of ordered to go and that my first sight of the village would be on camera.

The station wagon ahead of us slowed down, and headed off-road, right into the desert. How they knew when to turn was beyond me, as there was no sign or obvious marker. We all stopped after turning and were told to put Afghan flags on the antennae of our cars so that we could be recognized from above by the American air force. How Afghan flags distinguished us from the Taliban, who could easily plant flags on their vehicles, I didn't know, but any precaution we could take was worth it. We rode up and down the desert pathways, sometimes going straight, other times turning a few degrees, then following straight ahead. Aside from two rocky khaki-colored mountains in the distance ahead, there was the same desert all around us. I lost my sense of direction, not knowing which way we had come from or where we were going.

What a cursed land, I thought, gazing out on the cracked earth and craggy rock formations. So desperate, so desolate, yet so contested. Looking at it, I could not understand why anyone would fight and give up his life for this land. Not even a cactus could grow in this desert. Occasionally we would see a circle of mud houses, or a young boy on a donkey riding by. With no visible drinking water or vegetation, it was a wonder how these people lived at all. Without a car, it was impossible to get to a village for groceries or meat. What could you survive on in a barren desert like this?

That people could live in the middle of nowhere, with just about nothing, meant that most of my possessions were probably unnecessary. What a simple life it would be to live on a herd of goats. No trends to worry about, no neighbors to keep up with, no constant shopping. It struck me that the average Westerner is constantly buying one thing or another. Even I, not a big shopper, seemed to be routinely carting home bag after bag of food, clothing, books, dishes, you name it, all the time. Like little ants, day after day, we work so that we can carry more and more loads of goodies home. We all have that hoarding mentality, even though we live in a land of plenty. And the older we get, the more we accumulate, until one day we die and all of it has to be gotten rid of one way or another. Then all that stuff is someone else's burden. I always wondered what would happen with all the "things" that would be left over after people die, especially as the population in Western countries increases, and each of us acquires mountains of possessions. Wouldn't it be amazing to leave nothing behind? To have given away or consumed all you have, except for your thoughts, writings, and pictures? That's how I wished to go—with just about nothing, just as I came.

"This is it! This is it. This is it." We had driven an hour into the desert to find the rubble we were looking for. The village was larger than I expected, and some parts of the circular outer wall were still standing. The houses were reduced to piles of flattened clay, or even to mere dirt. Broken and burned-out branches could be seen dotting the perimeter of the village, and the most striking thing of all were huge cone-shaped craters in the earth, large pits big enough to devour whole vehicles. Later I learned that two-thousand-pound bombs had hewed the craters, plowing into the earth with incredible force.

I expected this place to be devoid of life, but a man in ragged clothes was rifling through the remains of the village when we arrived. I was disgusted to see that someone would steal from what was left of this bombed-out village, but my relatives recognized the man. He was a farmer that lived in the village, still rummaging through the rubble to pick up mementos from the flattened rooms of his home. The desperation was overwhelming. He too was surprised to see anyone coming back to visit, but was eager to speak with us. Once I made it clear that I was interested in his story, he lit up like a flame. He wanted to speak with us, so we immediately rolled the cameras.

"Do you see that tree?" He jabbed a finger toward a tall branch protruding from the earth in the distance, hardly an intact tree. "That's how high they were. It's ten meters. Ten meters! They were shooting at women and children from an airplane at ten meters!" He got louder and louder as he spoke, directing his anger at me. "Why did they do this to us?! Why?!" I had nothing to say to him. "Why would they shoot at women and children?! They obviously could see them!" He dropped to the ground, pointed a finger to his head like a gun, and pretended to shoot himself. "Like this." Then he rolled over in the rubble, as his turban unfurled, to demonstrate his rolling away from the bullets. "They kept shooting!!" His cries sprayed us like bullets.

He got up, and I was so ashamed to have seen a grown Afghan man have his pride reduced to this extent, rolling in rubble in front of strangers. He screamed, "I have no wife anymore, no more children except this one," pointing to a young boy about six or seven next to him squatting on the highest point of the rubble. The man walked over to him, picked him up from under the arms, and threw him down to the mound of rubble on which he stood. "What am I supposed to do with him?!"

I felt like crying for the boy. He said nothing, only slowly got up, embarrassed. I wondered what must have been going through the boy's head. Truly it must be the worst feeling in the world for a child to know that his mother is dead and gone and he is a burden on his father. Worse yet, what would he be thinking years into the future, knowing that his childhood had been stolen, along with his mother and siblings, by Americans in big planes in the night? Would this boy grow up to be America's enemy? I hoped not, but all indications were that he would, from his perspective, have good reason to be a young reckless fighter, out for revenge. Besides, it's the Afghan way. The old man offered to walk us over to where other women had perished, nomadic Kuchi women, who happened to be passing through on a different occasion. The farmer said their bloodstains were still spattered about. We declined his offer.

We plodded through the rubble, as our guides showed me where the rooms of each of our relatives once stood. In the rubble my eyes caught a single pair of slippers, a piece of a head scarf, and the remnants of broken baby bottles. I noticed a bit of green sparkle in the rubble. I walked closer and as I tugged on the tiny pink pom-pom attached to it I realized it was a miniature handkerchief, the type that is used to symbolize the commitment of a girl's family to the family of her future husband. It was the centerpiece of a wedding game young girls played in preparation for the second most important day of their lives. One of my cousins picked up the nipple from the bottle. "There were a few young children killed that night. Imagine what it must have been like. They're running, being shot at in the head from above." Although I had heard the story many times by now, I knew it was therapeutic for my relatives to retell it, looking for a new perspective on what had happened.

My cousin turned to the sun, squinting, and held up two fingers, his pointer and middle finger in the air to block out the bright white ball of fire. "You can't hide the sun with two fingers. You can't hide the truth. You can try, but you can't." He continued, in a slow voice. "What do the Americans call terrorism? What is it? Is what you have seen here and heard for yourself not terrorism?"

I stood frozen, not sure if I should even try to say anything. The man had a point. "How is it that shooting innocent men, women, and children in the dark of the night while they are running for their lives is not terrorism? Right in the head," he said, curling his index finger back at his head as if it were a trigger aiming down on him from above. "It's very simple. It's terrorism when the United States calls it so, but not when it perpetrates it." I could have argued with him, contrasting intentional attacks on civilians and horrible mistakes, but I just listened. This was probably what most of the Muslim world thought. It was certainly what al Jazeera would play on their airwaves, but it would have been called propaganda in the United States. Up until that point I was very sensitive to the propaganda of others, watching mostly mainstream U.S. news and filtering out the "other." But it was then that I realized that this truth—their truth—would have been considered propaganda in the United States. If I wanted others to believe in my story, my truth, I would have to begin believing in theirs. There really was no avoiding *this* truth.

After surveying the whole area, the guards and the rest of the men unrolled their turbans on the floor and sat on them, peeling cucumbers and oranges. "Sit down and speak with us. Tell the Americans to sit," said Janaraa's husband, Sulaiman, waving at Jon. I was bothered by the fact that they thought it was appropriate to have a meal next to the site of so much grief. Besides, how could you have an appetite after walking in the corpse of a village? It was like eating after death. But Afghans had grown so accustomed to death and destruction that to grieve one moment and laugh the next wasn't considered disrespectful. The fact was that no matter how awful the tragedy, it was beyond their power and they had to keep going.

The conversation turned to humor as Sulaiman said he heard I had visited Paris. "But why didn't you go visit your uncle in London?" he queried. How did he know I went to Paris? I had traveled to Paris with some friends to have fun and take in the sights, the type of trip that my parents usually hid from our relatives. Now a relative I barely knew was asking me about my European excursion in the middle of the desert in Afghanistan. For a group of people so disconnected from the rest of the world, their gossip propagated at lightning speed. Note to self: They will know about your life choices before you even make them. I explained that I didn't really have time to visit my uncle, not wanting to disclose the truth, which was that my uncle's wife had not wanted me to visit, as she was in one of her bouts of mental illness. She had become the consummate germophobe, and my presence would have driven her to even more madness.

Sulaiman started laughing. "Yeah, we heard the crazy didn't want you to come. We need to find your uncle a new wife." I laughed nervously. Not only was he on top of all the latest gossip, including my secret vacations, but he had a sense of humor about it all. Many of my relatives would joke about finding a new wife for my uncle, saying he should only come back to visit Afghanistan, and they would take care of finding him a bride. This was my family, one moment walking among the remains of a village, the next speculating on a second marriage. Life, marriage, and death. These were the dates that mattered, just as my mother's grandmother Koko had told me.

The next day, we headed out to the airport base in Kandahar. As journalists, we intended to find out how so many civilians could have been cut down at such close range in Chowkar-Karez. I had spent this whole time being afraid of the Taliban and al Qaeda, but now my fear turned to the American military. Kandahar airport, which was located just outside the city, had been converted to a U.S. Marine base. Equipped with our CBS IDs, the plan was to arrive for the daily press conference, then spring some tough questions on the unsuspecting marines that handled press relations.

As we sped along the main road to the airport, we saw the carcasses of burned-out petroleum trucks, turned over off the side of the road. Our driver pointed and said, "American war." A few hundred feet ahead, there were large chunks of what used to be an airplane, and an overturned tank. He pointed again and said, "Soviet war." It was as if time had stood still, and many awful moments had collapsed into one another. In the miserable south of Afghanistan, destruction had been wrought by both major superpowers of our time. In one war they had been practically fighting each other, while in the other war, the United States fought those who had once been on its side. Why did the superpowers feel so drawn to Afghanistan, and would this ever end?

As we pulled up to the elegant white archway that was the airport gate, complete with bullet marks, the first thing that struck me was the group of Afghans, extremely rough and local-looking, bearded and armed, sitting with Kalashnikovs at the only entrance to the airport. Had we chanced upon some secret attack? Where were the Americans, anyway?

But wouldn't you know it, the Afghans were guarding the American base. I wondered what sort of due diligence had been carried out to find out the history of these men. You couldn't exactly do a background search in a country where most government buildings were burned-out husks. Waiting for what felt like hours at the gate, I struck up a conversation with the ragtag band. "How do you feel having Americans in Afghanistan? Do you like it?" I asked, in Pashto. My manner of speaking made it obvious that I too was from Kandahar.

"Do *you* like that they're here?" the chief guard shot back.

"I live in America, and I asked *you*."

"Whether we like it or not they're here," said another.

"But tell me how you feel about it. I mean you're guarding them, so you must approve." I hoped that by putting it this way I would get a clearer answer.

"What do you want us to say?" said the chief, annoyed that I was talking him into a corner. The gate then opened slightly. A marine peered through and asked everyone to submit his or her passport. Jon was sure that once they knew he was a producer of gory battlefield footage from Vietnam to Central America to Iraq, we would not be allowed in. If this happened, I was to go in and ask my questions, camera or not. This trip was part documentary, part truth gathering.

A few minutes later, the marine came back, opened the gate, and called each one of us by name, including some of the other journalists that had gathered around the gate. We were all let through. Our cars were to wait outside, as we piled into two camouflaged army vehicles. We were driven to a checkpoint, where we went through a metal detector and were thoroughly searched. Then they led us to the main airport hall.

I had heard so much about Kandahar airport, from my father who had flown through it a few times, and in the news, especially during the war, when the United States captured it from the Taliban. A lieutenant walked us over to a corner, and we gathered around him. He pulled out a piece of paper, read a statement indicating how many Taliban had been captured, describing how the major offensives had gone down, and praising the cooperation of the new Afghan government, which was well protected in Kabul.

I felt the top of my head getting warmer and warmer under the light blue *hijab* as the seconds went by. Was I even allowed to ask about my family's village? How would I phrase my question? Would they kick me out? I hadn't even practiced what I would say, but after a few questions from the male journalists, such as "What's the mood amongst the troops?" or "What about the artillery cache you found up in Zabul province?" there was a silence, and I took a deep breath and started. "Um. I have a question," I said as I gingerly raised my pen. "Firstly, I want to say I appreciate the efforts of yourself and everyone here in ousting the Taliban. I'd like to know what happened in that village in

Chowkar in the middle of the night. Apparently there was some kind of an attack by the U.S. Nineteen members of my family were killed. They were offered no explanation. It's been about two months, and I'm wondering if you'd had any time to investigate that."

The lieutenant, a handsome young man who incidentally looked almost like a young George W. Bush, fell silent for a second but barely flinched. "Ma'am, we weren't even here at that juncture so I couldn't tell you. A question of that nature should be directed at DOD [the Department of Defense in Washington]."

What he meant was that the base had not been set up, and his particular division had not been in the Kandahar area when the attack happened on October 22, 2001. What I have since learned of these operations is that information is scanty and is rarely shared, even among the troops. Everything is on a need-to-know basis, and you don't need to know much if you're being told to aim at the strange-looking man in the turban and shoot to save your life before he takes yours.

Question time was at an end, as the lieutenant turned to the rest of the group and asked if we wanted a tour of the base.

We weren't kicked out, but we weren't given any answers either.

The young Bush look-alike showed us around the base, showing us some samples of packaged meals they sometimes ate when on the road, and taking us outside to where the marines sat in tents in the heat, some at work digging trenches. We were not to veer off the main path and placed our footsteps carefully for fear of the land mines. All the tents were khaki-colored, and they were lined up all the way to an invisible line in the sand, far beyond which stood a barbed-wire fence.

As I watched the marines sitting outside their tents, eating and playing cards, I couldn't help but think of the Afghan tents I had seen on my way into the country. When we were driving I had noticed a solid line of white in the distance, and watched it thicken and grow more detailed as we descended the mountain-side near the Afghan border. We could see endless dots of tents in the plains of the desert, as far as the eye could see—these were refugees fleeing the bombing. Some of them had been lucky enough to cross over the border, on the other side of which the United Nations agency for refugees was handing out tents and supplies. On the Afghan side of the border, however, the tents were made of wooden sticks planted into the earth and covered with various tattered rags. These were the most fragile type of homes you could imagine—often, the old clothes and other bits of fabric stretched between the sticks provided little cover. It was the newest, barest definition of home I had seen yet.

This war had relegated both the Afghans and the Americans to living in tents, each afraid of the other, but claiming they weren't each other's enemies. None of the marines I talked to had been off the base since they had arrived, and they knew nothing of Afghan culture or life. They were told to shoot at any-one coming anywhere close to the fence, which loomed in the distance. When I asked how they would distinguish an ordinary Afghan from a Taliban or al Qaeda, I was told they would look at the facial features to determine friend or foe. Look at the facial features! You couldn't even see anything close to facial features at the distance of those fences. I didn't know who to feel more sorry for. The Afghans were dealing with a fearful bunch, who didn't know who or what to shoot at, while the marines were so ill prepared for war that they didn't even seem to know who the enemy was.

In front of another tent, there were a few marines smashing their axes into the earth, apparently digging a trench. One of them looked friendly, and we began to chat. I asked him why he was here, in the middle of the desert. He said that every time he lost sight of his purpose, he would remember the World Trade Center. Being from New Jersey, he had visited it hundreds of times. I mentioned that I was a New Yorker, and that I had lost family here in Afghanistan as a result of a U.S. attack on their village. He stood silent, lowered his gaze, and said that he lost friends at the World Trade Center and that was why he was here, in Afghanistan.

Another army official came over and said he would guide the tour henceforth. He walked me over to where the helicopters and gunships were stationed, nodded his head toward them, and said these were probably the types of aircraft that "killed your family."

As the guide walked me over to the planes to give me a closer look, I felt it hard to be silent. "I want to say thank you for getting rid of the Taliban, but my family was killed in this." He answered, knowing where I was headed, "I suppose it would be hard to put it in perspective." I should have stopped there, but I continued. "Do you have any idea what the methodology for picking this target was? I mean, why?" But the words back seemed almost scripted. "Couldn't tell you, don't know. Don't have any information."

Chapter 13

Changing the Rules

There is a path to the top of even the highest mountain.

—Pashto proverb

When I returned to the United States, I found out that the attack in Chowkar-Karez had been explored in the press and that the Pentagon had even issued statements defending its actions. Reporters who visited the village quoted a man named Mehmood saying: "I brought my family here for safety, and now there are nineteen dead, including my wife, my two children, my brother, sister, sister-in-law, nieces, nephews, my uncle."[1] Villagers described being bombed for an hour around midnight and told journalists that they were fired on while trying to flee their houses. Anywhere from twenty-five to a hundred people died in the attack. Secretary of Defense Donald Rumsfeld, asked to explain what happened to these people, responded: "I cannot deal with that particular village." Later on, however, Pentagon officials said that village "was 'a fully legitimate target' because it was a nest of Taliban and al Qaeda sympathizers. 'The people there are dead because we wanted them dead,' an official said." Those words would ring in my ears nearly every time I thought or spoke publicly about what happened that night.

Soon after the Pentagon issued its statements, Human Rights

Watch issued a report discounting its claims, based on interviews on the scene with the survivors of the attack.[2] The *Washington Post* later reported that a "dozen witnesses" confirmed that
the village suffered "a mistaken attack on civilian refugees."[3]

Jon and I knew we had powerful footage of my family telling
their story, and of the devastation of the village. Eventually we
edited the footage into the scenes of Nasria's story; bombed-out
homes; and visits to Kandahar's bazaar, girls' school, and hospital into a documentary we called *From Ground Zero to Ground
Zero*. We entered into negotiations with CNN and FOX News,
but couldn't find anyone that would air it. A FOX News producer who viewed the footage even laughed at us for thinking
we could get the civilian casualties issue aired on television during a war in which "American boys were fighting thousands of
miles away."

But we finally got our break. Bill Moyers, who had just started
producing his own show on PBS, agreed to feature our documentary on his program, including the most controversial material—
the stories of the deaths and injuries in Nasria's family, and the
interviews we had done amid the rubble in Chowkar-Karez. The
day that PBS aired our footage, the *Washington Post* published a
feature story entitled "NY Afghan Navigates 2 Shattered Worlds,"
which explained my difficult position on the war. I told the
reporter, "I'm not a pacifist. I think there are times when war is
necessary. And this was such a time." The fall of the Taliban had
certainly been a triumph for the women in Afghanistan, no
longer denied an education or the right to work as a matter of
law. But I was under no illusions that the liberation of Afghan
women, seven years after the Taliban occupied Kandahar, had
been anyone's priority. And I knew that outside of a small elite in
Kabul, most Afghan women still had to wear *burqas*, could not
freely choose whom to marry, and remained as poor and illiterate as ever.

After the *Washington Post* profile, more and more television networks aired our documentary. CBS's *The Early Show* only agreed to put it on after its executive producer personally met with me. Jon thought that I would make a good impression as a native New Yorker with reasonable views on the war and its aftermath. I talked about baseball with the executive producer, sounding as mainstream and nonthreatening as I possibly could.

Soon, the offers flowed in. Our documentary was aired around the world, including in Japan, Italy, and Canada. Even Oprah featured it on her show about Afghan women after the Taliban. My little sister Aziza, who appeared early in the documentary seeing me off at the airport, still loves to brag about how she made it on the *Oprah* show. Later that year Phil Donahue interviewed me live on his show. He was fascinated to find out that even though I was a committed activist for Afghan civilian victims, I had voted for George Bush and supported the U.S. efforts to rid Afghanistan of the Taliban. I emphasized that I did not want our government to turn its back on our Afghan allies by failing to recognize the plight of civilians who suffered during the war.

I hoped that with all the attention the documentary was receiving, the U.S. government would agree to investigate the incident in Chowkar-Karez. But I did not feel that the administration really addressed the issue until the families of the World Trade Center victims joined the movement for recognition and aid to Afghan civilians. A few days after I arrived in New York from taping the documentary in Afghanistan, I appeared on a radio show called *Democracy NOW!* with Amy Goodman. Her staff told me that a woman named Rita Lasar, who had lost her brother at the World Trade Center, would be on with me. The night before the show, I worried whether she would be angry with me, or feel that I was justifying what happened to her brother and others like him by speaking of the deaths in Chowkar-Karez. As soon as I sat across from her, I realized how wrong my assumptions had been.

When I had arrived at the *Democracy NOW!* studios in the attic of Jon Alpert's firehouse studio just a few blocks from Ground Zero, there were camera crews from NBC, CBS, FOX, and the Associated Press. A reporter literally cornered me, asking whether I would be happier if the Taliban were still in power, and did I not think that America should defend itself? I knew I could handle an obnoxious reporter, but I wasn't sure how I could deal with a bereaved family member of an actual victim.

But on the show, Rita and I cried together and embraced, consoling each other for the losses in each of our families. Rita said, "Masuda and I are the same. There's no difference between us." Her brother, Abe Zelmanowitz, was on the twenty-seventh floor of the north tower of the World Trade Center. He stayed until the very end with his friend and colleague Ed Beyea, a quadriplegic who could not go down the stairs in his wheelchair. Abe refused to leave even after Rita's other brother called him and pleaded with him to get out. At the national memorial service for the victims of 9/11, President Bush eulogized Rita's brother Abe, calling him a hero who sacrificed his own life to save the life of another victim. The next day Rita wrote a letter to the *New York Times* objecting to the president's invocation of her brother's name as a cause for war. Rita later went to Afghanistan along with other family members of 9/11 victims who advocated a peaceful, law-enforcement solution to terrorism. There she met civilian victims of the war in Afghanistan and saw what she called the "devastation and horror of what happens to innocent people when bombs fall—anyone's bombs, anywhere in the world."

Instead of exchanging accusations, Rita and I became like family. She visited my home for dinner and made friends with my sisters and Moor and Agha. Rita became the grandma I never had, always full of love, wisdom, and encouragement. I never imagined a grandma like Rita existed, but then I could never have imagined the circumstances that brought us together.

I was especially touched by Rita and the other family members of 9/11 victims who decided to turn their efforts to helping the people of Afghanistan. These families and I both lost innocent loved ones in senseless violence. This, along with our shared desire for peace, became part of our common bond. I joined with the organization they founded, September Eleventh Families for Peaceful Tomorrows, and Global Exchange, a human rights organization based in California, to lobby Congress for aid to the civilian victims, what we called an Afghan Victims Fund. Based on discussions with Afghan human rights organizations and Marla Ruzicka, a friend on the ground in Afghanistan, we advocated that each victim's family receive $10,000 in aid to obtain medical attention, rebuild their home, and provide for their children. We estimated that this would cost the United States only about $20 million if two thousand families applied for assistance, a modest amount compared to the $30 million spent every day on the war.

Working with Rita's organization, I learned of the unique status people associated with 9/11 now had in our country. We instantly got appointments, and people listened to what we had to say. I was amazed to see congressional staffers crying with us, or putting their hands on Rita's shoulder and offering to help. I learned that even high-level people in the State Department felt sorry for the innocent Afghans who had suffered so much, because most of them supported the United States and wanted the Taliban gone. This was the human face of the American government.

Only a few people were hard on us, such as the legislative assistant who told me Muslims didn't appreciate what Americans had done for them in Somalia, Bosnia, and Kosovo. Another high-level government official pointed out that al Qaeda and the Taliban weren't helping 9/11 victims. "But we're not Taliban," I shot back. America was better than that, and that's what we had to show the world. At the State Department, the most senior official at the meeting burst out laughing and, mocking our plea for aid to America's Afghan friends and allies, said, "I didn't know there were any friendly Afghans!" A stillness fell over the room. He did not know there was an Afghan sitting across from him among the concerned faces. I knew the 9/11 family members expected me to speak up for my people, but I was afraid to embarrass him and ruin a shot at gaining a supporter of aid to Afghan civilians. They waited. I fought myself for a second, then raised my hand a little and said, "Um . . . I'm a friendly Afghan." He seemed shocked and quickly turned to how much the United States was doing for the Afghan people already.

While most government officials I met with expressed sorrow over the deaths of innocent Afghans, they believed that direct assistance to survivors would be unlikely, due to the Pentagon's refusal to admit mistakes in a way that might provide a basis for legal action. Nevertheless, Bianca Jagger, a human rights advocate who traveled to Afghanistan and who happens to be the former wife of Mick Jagger, encouraged me to use the word "compensation." I truly respected her insistence on boldly standing up for what's right, but we were told over and over again by government officials that this language would lead us only to closed doors. To overcome this resistance, we emphasized in our lobbying and during press appearances that neutral terms such as "assistance" or "aid," rather than "reparations" or "compensation," could be used. I met with Zalmay Khalilzad, an Afghan-American who later became President Bush's ambassador to Afghanistan, and he suggested we use the term "targeted assistance."

I believe our press campaign for an Afghan Victims Fund really helped change U.S. government policy. In January 2002, when four families of 9/11 victims returned from a trip to Afghanistan, we held a joint press conference on Capitol Hill in which we presented the proposal for a $20 million fund for Afghan civilian victims of the coalition bombing. The families had met with Afghan president Hamid Karzai, who told them: "People have suffered, let us help them out of compassion." President Karzai expressed his support for the fund again when we met him on Capitol Hill while we were lobbying for congressional aid. Subsequent editorials in the *New York Times*, the *Washington Post*, and the *Boston Globe* supported the creation of an Afghan Victims Fund. By June 2002, an opinion poll by Zogby International found that 69 percent of Americans endorsed the idea of providing targeted aid to Afghan war victims.

As a result of our efforts, we learned, the Afghan Victims Fund became a major issue in the Bush administration. A State Department official called it a public relations nightmare that had been elevated to the level of Dick Cheney's staff and the National Security Council. A Defense Department spokesman acknowledged that aid to civilians was being reviewed, but maintained that international law provides "that nations are not liable to compensate civilians killed in the normal conduct of war."

We continued to push, and when a wedding party in Uruzgan was bombed in July 2002, I organized a protest in front of the White House. A few hours later, the Associated Press reported on the protest, in a newswire entitled "Bush calls Afghan president after U.S. bombing of civilians." The article described me as "[s]houting 'No more innocent victims' over a bullhorn," and said that President Bush called President Karzai to express condolences about the deaths of forty-four civilians in the incident.

Our campaign for an Afghan Victims Fund eventually succeeded. We persuaded members of Congress, led by Senator Patrick Leahy, to earmark $134 million in a 2002 spending bill for International Disaster Assistance, including "repairing homes of Afghan citizens that were damaged as a result of military operations." Language in a 2003 spending bill also directed that additional funds, possibly millions, be provided to Afghan "communities and families . . . that were adversely affected by the military operations." Officials in the Pentagon, State Department, and U.S. Agency for International Development (USAID) have worked with Senator Leahy's office to identify communities in which Afghan civilians lost family members or their homes. About $2.5 million in such aid had been provided by May 2003, Senator Leahy's office reported.

Helping civilian victims of war, which we were initially told nobody would support, had apparently become U.S. policy. During the more recent war with Iraq, Congress earmarked millions in aid for Iraqi civilians who were killed or injured, or whose homes were damaged. The military has reportedly distributed $2.2 million to resolve thousands of claims for compensation in Iraq. U.S. commanders have authorized payments of up to $2,500 to families of dead civilians, up to $1,500 to injured civilians, and up to $500 to owners of damaged property.[4]

Our advocacy may have affected policy in other ways, some that we may never know about. Kenneth Bacon, a former Pentagon spokesman from the Clinton administration, told me that the rules of engagement, or the methods by which a target is selected and attacked, might have changed within the military in response to our work but that these are changes we may never know about because it's secret military information. For example, the military might be less likely to attack a village based solely on information provided by local tipsters who may hold a grudge against a family or tribe that lives there. I may never know how Chowkar-Karez was selected as a target, but it is possible, even likely, I'm told, that the selection of new targets will be carried out differently in the future.

The existence and mishandling of civilian casualties has been a target for criticism of U.S. policy, and has fueled hatred for America, ultimately making us less secure. Along with other human rights activists, I have argued that Americans should show the world that it values the lives of innocent civilians, and that it is prepared to help those unfortunately caught in the crossfire. The success of the campaign for an Afghan Victims Fund in coming together and persuading Congress to act is hopefully making this country a little bit safer.

I also feel very lucky to have found more family and love in the face of so much tragedy. I found the grandmother I was looking for when I met Rita Lasar. She has revealed herself to my sisters and me as a wise, feisty woman in her seventies who is hip enough to live in the East Village, and who has also adopted Afghanistan as her cause for life. Although no money has reached my own family members yet, I hope that other families of innocent victims will benefit from the kindness of Americans who cared.

Chapter 14

An Afghan Women's Bill of Rights

I will be a servant of God, rather than of man.

—Afghan woman at V-Day leadership conference

Perhaps some of my most cherished moments of working with Afghan women came when I became program director of Women for Afghan Women (WAW), and I took the lead in organizing a conference on women and the Afghan constitution that was held in Kandahar, Afghanistan, in September of 2003. This was the most challenging and fulfilling project that I had ever worked on. Although as an organization we knew that we wanted to hold an event that would enrich the lives of Afghan women, this left us with many options in terms of location, participants, subject, format, and funding. By the end, we had experienced almost every problem Afghanistan was facing as a nation, but we had also learned how to begin to solve some of them, and how to cope with the rest.

I had always dreamed of going back to Kandahar and doing a women's project there. Sometimes I would imagine arriving with truckloads of food, as far as the eye could see, other times I'd fly overhead and drop condoms and birth control pills to the earth, or bring in a band of professional masseurs to massage every pain out of every aching, torn muscle of these women's bodies. Then I wanted to go to the mountains in the north, to travel the landscape of such deep lush green that if you cut into it with a knife, thick green blood would seep out, where women walked up mountains so steep that I thought they would fall off. I wanted to go to the east, to Jalalabad, where people with accented Pashto called children "animals," and west to Herat, where my grandfather once lived in an eleven-bedroom house with his fashionable Herati first wife.

During WAW's second annual conference, held in New York City in November 2002, I realized just how much our help might be needed there. The conference brought together women from Afghanistan and the Afghan diaspora to discuss the achievements and challenges of the year since the Taliban had fallen. Several women leaders from Afghanistan told the conference that the situation of women remained desperate outside of Kabul, where the warlords held power and were gaining strength each day through massive funding from abroad and the lucrative proceeds of arms and drug trafficking. Hangama Anwari of the Afghan Women Lawyers and Professionals Association described how many innocent women in the provinces had been jailed for years and undergone rape and abuse without being able to answer the charges against them. While the Taliban were no longer around to forbid women from getting an education or seeing male doctors, teachers went unpaid for months, classes were held outside in the hot sun and chilling cold of winter, and hospitals functioned without adequate medicine and equipment, so surgery had to be conducted without sterilization or anesthesia. Fatima Gailani, a women's rights activist and spokesperson for the Afghan resistance to the Soviet invasion, even told us that religious conservatives were campaigning to revive some Taliban-style laws in the new Afghan constitution, such as demanding mandatory dress codes for women.

Sima Samar, the minister for women's affairs in President Karzai's government, also expressed her concern that women needed to play a more active role in drafting the new Afghan constitution and building a new democracy. She talked about upcoming elections and wondered if women would feel safe to come out to vote. But first, how would they register to vote if they didn't even have identification cards? A generation had grown up without any documentation. Indeed, even I didn't have a birth certificate. I was often asked for this document in New York, and whenever I told an authority figure that I didn't have a birth certificate, they scrunched their eyebrows, muscling their face into disbelief. "How can you not have a birth certificate?" a woman once inquired suspiciously, as if no one could possibly travel out of their mother's birth canal without that piece of paper handed to them on the way out. This was a common question. "If I don't have a birth certificate," I asked the woman, "how can you tell that I was really born?" This would usually get me out of the bind. Then I would explain that I was born in a place and a time when witnessing an event was enough to prove it had happened. Records were secondary.

In America we took these systems society had created to structure and understand itself for granted. We forget that it took thousands of years of slow, methodical state building. Identification, licensing, the census: all of these procedures for regulating the interaction of society were virtually nonexistent in Afghanistan.

I not only did not have a birth certificate, I also never knew the exact date of my birth. I grew up thinking I was born on January 6, but when I was thirteen my father told me he believed he miscalculated my birth date when translating it from the Islamic lunar calendar to the Western solar one. He had estimated the date under the intense pressure of the war, standing in an unfamiliar office in Pakistan where he had desperately tried to get us visas. When we redid the calculations from the lunar calendar, we got April 6. For that whole time I had been celebrating my birthday on the wrong day, thinking I was a

Capricorn. I now celebrate it on the correct date, but for a while I had two birthdays a year—my real one and my fake one.

Now the quirky detail that I had grown up with was coming back to haunt Afghan women's ability to participate in a budding democracy. All Afghans eligible to vote had to be registered one by one, whether they had any papers or not. Some women at the conference suggested identity cards. But in a country where women's faces must be hidden, pictures on ID cards were hardly the answer. Besides, what were the Taliban, who were lurking in villages and cities in the south, going to do to women on whom they found ID cards, proving they had "cooperated" with the Americans? Would raising their voices for the first time make some women forever voiceless?

Afghan women needed to quickly come together to form a plan to deal with their political future, a topic being decided, it seemed, mainly by foreigners involved in the reconstruction process. What if we could propose a conference like the one in New York to be held in Afghanistan, I wondered, outside the protected bubble of Kabul where internationals drank wine and beer at Thai restaurants that were patrolled by cute European men called peacekeepers? I began to believe that it just might be possible to hold an event in the Taliban's crib. What better place to start than Kandahar?

To explore the possibility of holding a women's conference in conservative Kandahar, I traveled to Kabul in March of 2003 to attend a conference organized by Eve Ensler's organization V-Day, which brought together Afghan women leaders. At first I was skeptical of American women like Eve Ensler, who I could just imagine telling Afghan women she was there to "liberate" them. I imagined her in a pink cape as she flew down to these women, who would be gathered in a crowd on the rooftop of a building, awaiting her arrival. What would Afghans think of a woman whose name will forever be associated with "vagina"? I could barely imagine explaining to any Afghan why I was there with the "liberators," let alone what the word "vagina" meant in English. I didn't even know the proper word for vagina in Pashto, or even the word for sex for that matter. Whether it was my curiosity that took me, or the part of me that feels God will one day bless any act taken to advance the cause of women, I went. In that moment I imagined God as a New York Jew, shoulders shrugging, unimpressed as I explained that I thought it would help me advance our cause—but tolerant.

I went to the event, sponsored by V-Day, and learned that all of my assumptions had been wrong. An Afghan woman working with an American woman, who played second fiddle, as it was called, conducted the leadership conference. There I met a woman I fell in love with. That was the first thought that occurred to me when I saw her speak, so that's how I tell it, even though it was not romantic love. Her name was Afifa Azim, and she led a network of organizations called the Afghan Women's Network. She is a wife, a mother to six children, a human rights leader, extremely feminist, and very Muslim. Beyond that, she possesses a love and understanding that I have seen in few people in her position. Most people I know in women's rights work have become cynical, frustrated, and apathetic. Afifa remains optimistic and has the wisdom of a whole village rolled up into one petite and humble woman. At the event there was no talk about vaginas or women leaving their husbands, but rather about ending violence with strength, beauty, and even Islam. I spoke to every woman I could, stealing moments while sitting in the room waiting for the day to begin, during lunch, and even outside on the streets.

Swelled with inspiration, I traveled to Kandahar, where I stopped a woman walking down the street with loaves of bread bundled on top of her head, wrapped in cloth that matched her *burqa*, and asked her what she thought about law, voting, and women's participation. First she told me the men could speak for her in such complicated matters as the law, but as we spoke I learned she was a servant in a local minister's mansion, and she confessed that if she could rule Kandahar average people would be better off. She saw my camera and asked for me to take a picture, even though no part of her body was showing except for her hands. She said that at least there would be a picture of her remaining after she had sunk into the earth and joined it. I got her address, which was a complex series of turns from a main intersection to her home, and told her we were organizing an event for women like her. We wanted average women, illiterate women, as well as women who had already made their mark in the field of human rights.

Kandahar was beginning to see spring, and the garden behind the house where I stayed was producing fresh lettuce and refreshing cucumbers. The purple carrots added to our salads from the garden made me wonder if there was blood in the soil. I was staying with Afghans for Civil Society, and the bravest women I had ever met, next to local Afghan women. Sarah Chayes, an American who used to report for NPR before she decided to stay in Kandahar, led the organization, and Rangina Hamidi, an Afghan-American woman, led its women's projects. Rangina was the woman I would be if I could bear living in Kandahar. But the place felt suffocating, long days of devastating stories and no entertainment. Still, I was looking forward to shaking up the local scene.

At the time I didn't know how difficult that would be. The first step was the departure for Kabul of an advance team, which I led. My colleagues Manizha Naderi and Fahima Vorgetts joined me on the team. Manizha is another Afghan-American who fled Afghanistan when she was very young. She barely has any memories of the country of her birth, but her identity is strongly tied up with it anyway. Fahima is a lifelong women's rights activist who sells Afghan arts and crafts in the Washington, D.C., area and uses the profits to finance girls' schools and agricultural and vocational projects for women's economic independence. For Manizha and I the irony was that our own relatives had never been politically active women. But perhaps this is what inspired us with even more passion. The three of us set out to organize our Afghan sisters, aunts, and mothers. We were to meet up in Kabul in two weeks with a Hindu Indian woman named Sunita Mehta who had cofounded WAW, an American Jewish woman named Esther Hyneman who had lived through the women's rights movement in the United States, and several volunteers from New York, mostly Christian American women.

Convincing the financial backers of the conference that holding a women's conference in Kandahar wasn't a suicide mission had been a challenge. Afghanistan was experiencing the most violence in the south since the war had begun. Taliban attacks on international aid workers had risen from one per month to one every couple of days. In July, the State Department warned Americans that travel in "all areas of Afghanistan, including the capital, Kabul, is unsafe due to military operations, land mines, banditry, armed rivalry among political and tribal groups, and the possibility of terrorist attacks, including attacks using vehicular or other bombs." Since that warning, more than four hundred Afghans have died at the hands of the Taliban or other factional fighters.[1]

We clearly needed to hire security guards. But our advisors argued over which warlord's men were actually safe to be around, or whether we should even let the local government in Kandahar know we were coming at all. President Karzai had just fired the previous governor of Kandahar, notorious warlord and fight-dog trainer Gul Agha Sherzai.

We found Gul Agha in Kabul, where we were given an appointment to meet him at a compound in Wazir Akbar Khan, a wealthy neighborhood. Behind the walls rose a building with a facade of large flat rocks of various brown colors like one would find in the suburbs in America. Inside the house were rooms full of men in Afghan clothes seated on cushions arranged around the perimeter of the rooms, drinking tea. They were all gathered to see Gul Agha, some of them to show support, others to discuss business proposals, still others to be part of his posse.

Gul Agha was a hulking bear of a man but warmed up to our delegation. As we explained our plan to gather women in Kandahar, he expressed his support, nodding vigorously, saying it was a good thing we were planning. While he listened he unwrapped one candy after another, popping them in his mouth and sipping tea. In those moments he hardly seemed like the warlord the media made him out to be. Indeed, he promised to help us in any way we needed. An older distinguished man dressed in a suit took my information, as he told me he knew my father from the old days in Kandahar. We were escorted out by a younger man, also well dressed, who told me he too was a Popalzai, and that we were therefore related. He called me his sister and offered me an apartment to put up our guests in.

Eventually we reached out to one of President Karzai's brothers in Kandahar, who provided us with a handful of heavily armed and rather shaggy-looking militiamen. They would camp outside the Afghans for Civil Society compound for the entire week of the conference. At first I passed by them warily, until they asked me to take their pictures one day, but they revealed themselves as big-time softies, posing near the brightest pink flowers they could find.

The day before the conference was to start, about thirty Afghan women from the north and east of Afghanistan gathered in Kabul to fly to Kandahar together, where the women from Herat planned to join us. I was surprised to see that the nicely dressed Popalzai man from Gul Agha's compound was dressed even more impeccably at the airport. He looked like he had stepped out of a European fashion magazine, with a navy blue suit and silver French cuffs. Before he left us at the airport, he declared, "Whatever you need, sister, money, vehicles, places for these guests. Just let me know." He offered to escort us to Kandahar, or send a caravan, but I politely declined. His kindness was overwhelming and reminded me why I loved my people so much. While tribal relations and conflicts had created so much hostility and pain for Afghans, it also created a kinship so powerful that I was overcome with it. I felt a bit guilty for being so thrilled to be part of this club. As a modern woman and feminist I should have shunned tribalism completely, but the beauty of that connection was part of what attracted me so deeply to Afghanistan. Here it didn't matter what books I had read, what my salary was, or even how pretty I was. I longed for that team dynamic in America.

Shortly before we were about to leave, the United Nations travel personnel in Kabul told us that the plane we had planned to take had lost an engine and couldn't take us. The road to Kandahar was considered very unsafe at the time, even though it was the number one reconstruction project in Afghanistan. The new highway was even closed down for most of its official opening day in December, after the United States had mobilized fighter jets, attack helicopters, and snipers to guard the U.S. ambassador and President Karzai during the opening ceremony.

The women insisted on going to Kandahar, however, so we persuaded the United Nations to allow us on one of its regular flights to Kandahar the next day. As we descended toward Kandahar airport, I thought of a story my uncle Jan Agha told me about traveling within Afghanistan during the Soviet occupation. At that time the road from Kabul to Kandahar was so dangerous and suffered so many battles that often the only way to visit family in Kabul was to fly on the Soviet-supplied military helicopters of the Communist government. When Jan Agha heard that his mother in Kabul was deathly ill, he boarded one of these helicopters to visit her. But it was struck down by *mujahideen* fire over a snowcapped mountain. Jan Agha was the only survivor, jumping out just before the crash and breaking his arm. He managed to walk to the nearest village, where he worried that whoever had downed the helicopter would suspect him of being a Communist and kidnap him, or worse. Once he explained himself, however, the *mujahideen* helped him recover enough of his strength to return home.

On the drive from the airport to Kandahar City, a familiar-looking man sat next to me, asking me if I remembered him. I didn't, although his face looked hauntingly familiar. I was embarrassed for not remembering. He wouldn't tell me who he was, however. He only spoke of how hurt he was that I couldn't recall his name. When it was time to part, he told me that he was the doctor we encountered at Oxfam when we went to film the documentary. He had given me passport photos of his family in the hope that I might be able to help them come to America. I was crushed. I hated letting people down, even though I told him when he gave me the pictures that there is no way to obtain a passport for an Afghan family using their photographs alone. He was bitterly disappointed, and for a second I wondered if he might try to hurt me. I didn't tell him that I still carried around his pictures, and that they were in the JanSport backpack sitting in my lap as we spoke.

When we arrived in Kandahar, more than thirty women were filling up the empty halls of a large compound we would call home, with even more women joining us later. At the conference, we conducted a series of workshops in which the women shared their stories of the brutality and crimes they had suffered during all the years of war, condemned the propaganda and culture of violence that prevented women from enjoying their rights, and expressed hope that disarmament and education would put an end to the violations against women.

One of our speakers was Tajwar Kakar, the deputy minister of women's affairs in the Karzai government. She traveled from Australia, where she was living as a refugee, to Afghanistan during Taliban times to meet Mullah Omar himself. She came as an elder to their foreign ministry in Kandahar. They were amazed that a woman like her would even have the courage to stand up to them, let alone unleash her fierce tongue on them. She told us the Taliban seemed like tough guys at first, but to her they were just young wimps. She said she took off her *burqa* in front of them and held it out to them. "Give this to Mullah Omar and tell him it's a gift from me," she said.

Many of the other women's stories were just as unbelievable. A pregnant human rights activist who had come from Mazar-i-Sharif had been pregnant twenty other times in her life, but only a third of her babies had survived. Another, a gynecologist, told us how many women in her city are forbidden to see a doctor at all. Others had seen their children be kidnapped by the Taliban. Sometimes the women's ignorance of the world was shocking. One of the women from Kandahar hired as a cook asked me whether it was true that women in America lived to be two hundred years old.

After debating the role of Islam and women's rights for four days, the women unanimously agreed on their vision for the Afghan constitution, called the Afghan Women's Bill of Rights. Their first demand was mandatory education for girls and women. They also demanded equal pay for equal work, freedom of speech, the right to divorce according to Islam, and bans on giving away young girls in marriage, domestic violence, sexual abuse, and exchanging women as compensation for crimes between families (which Pashtuns call *bad*, or "blood price"). A reporter who covered the conference for a leading newspaper in Britain summarized the women's vision more forcefully: "They ask that they should not be sold into slavery, that they should choose who to marry and that they should be offered an education."[2]

The women were literate and illiterate, urban and rural, Sunni and Shi'a, Tajik, Uzbek, Pashtun, and Hazara. As an editorial in the *New York Times* later put it, they had come together from "some of the most desperate corners of Afghanistan" to produce an "extraordinary document" in the Bill of Rights. Other conferences had been held on women's rights in Afghanistan before, and other lists of rights had been adopted by Afghan women before, but none of them so directly addressed the most difficult issues in Afghan life, let alone in Kandahar.

Chapter 15

The Prisoner and the President

The possession and control of desirable commodities,
especially zan, zar, zamin (woman, gold, and land)
is closely linked to the perception of a man's honour.

—Amnesty International

In Kabul, we arranged for a press conference, which was attended by leading Afghan women, such as Fatima Gailani, daughter of the spiritual Sufi leader Pir Gailani. Ms. Gailani was one of two members attending on behalf of the Constitutional Drafting Commission, the thirty-five-member body, seven of whom were women, that drew up the new Afghan constitution. She endorsed the Bill of Rights and proclaimed that the draft constitution would include them: "I am proud to say that what the women in Kandahar and other women have asked for, they are all in the constitution of Afghanistan. We were not alone in the commission, there were not just seven of us, we had you all there."

Later the conference participants presented the Bill of Rights to the minister for women's affairs, and to the full Constitutional Drafting Commission. We arranged for it to be distributed to each of the thirty-four provinces in the country—over six thousand copies by one human rights organization alone.

One lasting legacy of the conference, I hope, will be that Afghan women even in remote parts of the country will use the Bill of Rights to provoke debate and organize for local action to protect women's rights.

After the press conference, I arranged a meeting of some of our conference participants with President Hamid Karzai, which ironically was scheduled for September 11, two years after the catastrophe in America. Americans, foreigners, and UN workers were warned not to go out in Kabul, because of the symbolic significance of the day. We took along our new friend Mushtaba, a young child in dirty clothes who sold books about Kabul to foreigners passing by on the street. The guards of the presidential palace stopped him from entering with us. He had been our guide throughout our stay in Kabul. We had to argue with the people at the Chinese restaurant to let him in, because they thought he was a pesky street child who had followed us. Now, at each checkpoint on the way to see President Karzai, a large hand grasped his little body to stop him from going forward, but each time we pleaded that he should be allowed in. Security was tight: when we arrived at the rectangular table at which we would share tea with the president, I noticed that a number of American soldiers were pointing automatic rifles at us from behind a glassless window frame at the top of a nearby building.

When President Karzai arrived with his entourage, he walked directly over to Mushtaba, shook his hand, and greeted him warmly. The women presented the Afghan Women's Bill of Rights that they had drafted together, which Sunita and I had rushed to have framed in time for the meeting. We were surprised to learn that he had already read the document, after members of his security group, who had also been sent to provide security for our Kabul press conference, presented it to him. To me, this signified that not only were his men alert and independently helpful in getting the important message to him, but that he himself had been interested enough in the issue to have read it. President Karzai proclaimed his support for the principles the Bill of Rights had set forth and announced that half of his appointees to the Constitutional Loya Jirga would be women. Over tea, cake, and cookies, he was cheerful and light-hearted, remarking that the disempowerment of warlords was something he himself would like to see too. He even teared up speaking about how Afghan women had suffered for decades, first under the Russians, then during the chaos that followed, and finally under the Taliban.

That night, I heard screams coming from the living room in our Kabul guest house. I walked over to the women who were pointing at the television, where our meeting with the president was being replayed on Kabul television first in Farsi, then in Pashto. Mushtaba told us the next day that the people in his village had seen him with the president, his face beaming with pride.

The conference received favorable coverage in the international press, even making it to the State Department's Web site. More important, the Afghan press eagerly covered the event, while a Kabul newspaper asked our permission to reprint the Afghan Women's Bill of Rights, rather than us pleading or paying for coverage. After returning to the United States, we lobbied Congress to support a bill dedicating $60 million to programs promoting the rights demanded by the women in Kandahar, especially health care and education. Although the funding passed, we and other groups knew that the money would not go very far unless it went to Afghan women on the ground, rather than to expensive international consultants' salaries, travel, and security. If asked, many women in Afghanistan would tell you that $60 million would be enough to pay for education and health care for all, in a country where teachers and doctors make only about $500 to $1,000 per year. But they wonder whether they will see any benefit.

• • •

During the conference in Kandahar, the task of managing forty-five women's living, eating, and interaction had fallen to us. Some women fell ill due to the intense September heat, while others wanted to take more time to tour the city. As the days passed, the women began to bond and to trust me.

At night we danced, first to women's hands beaten on the bottoms of the buckets taken from the bathrooms. These are the hands, I thought, that had wiped tears when mothers learned that their babies must return to the earth. Even the sick, moaning in bed from heat exhaustion or because it was the first time they were away from their families and could reflect on their lives, rose like the dead to join us in the dancing. By the end of our stay we were both laughing and crying together, as the electricity came and went.

When the new governor of Kandahar found out we were in town, he was insulted that we hadn't alerted him to such an ambitious event. Even though we had visited him and informed him of our efforts, he hadn't realized what a big event it was until a few days had passed and news spread. He invited us over for a feast and told both of his own wives to visit from Pakistan to greet the large delegation. He sat at the head of a table as long as those in the Harry Potter movies, and spoke about how respect for women was central to Pashtunwali and Afghan culture. I sat with his daughter on the floor and heard her complain about having to wear the "shuttlecock," as she called the *burqa*.

Afghanistan had welcomed us. Still, we had to be careful. Some local Kandaharis believed that we were prostitutes or on some other evil mission for the "infidels." The thought occurred to me frequently that anybody passing on the street could toss a grenade over the walls, or drive a car through the gates. But we were here.

Rangina and I read the Afghan Women's Bill of Rights aloud to the governor as many of the women looked on proudly.

When we got to the fourth item on the list, however, there was an immediate uproar from the group. It looked as if everything we had worked for would fall apart. The fourth on the list was the right to remarry no sooner than two years after a woman's husband has disappeared, an all too common event in a society scarred by war and fractured into a thousand refugee communities. The women erupted into a firestorm of debate, some shouting, "Seventy years!" "Three years!" "What about Islam?" or "We have suffered enough!"

Meanwhile, Malalai, the sole female cop in Kandahar, who carried not only a pistol but sometimes a Kalashnikov, looked at us, winked, and said, "Two seconds." Besides being a wife and a mother of six, Malalai had been a cop from the age of fifteen, when her father suggested that his daughters follow in the family tradition. Her career was interrupted during the Taliban's seven-year rule over Kandahar. She had fled to Pakistan after hearing the Taliban were on their way to arrest perhaps the only armed woman in Kandahar. Malalai calls herself "one of the guys" and sometimes walked around without a *burqa*. She was often the first officer sent into the home of criminal suspects, because in Pashtun tradition the policemen cannot see the women. She warned the women that men were at the door, and in cases involving women, she questioned them and acted as their advocate. She was afraid of no one.

Malalai recruited me to work with her on pressuring another very powerful military commander Zabit Akram to invite his wife to the dinner he was hosting in honor of our group. The commander was one of Gul Agha's men, a shy and very kind man despite his gruff, brutish appearance. We began to ask him about his wife's absence as soon as we arrived at the dinner. In typical Afghan fashion, he talked about how she refused to come, even after his repeated requests. Malalai suggested we try to convince her ourselves, which made him a bit nervous. But he couldn't refuse our desire to see her, because that would be like admitting *he* had forbidden her to come. So as Malalai hopped into his soldiers' SUV to retrieve her, I followed.

When we arrived at the commander's modest home, very much like any other home in Kandahar, with a large courtyard and decaying adobe rooms, I wondered if his nervousness sprang more from the embarrassing state of his home than fear about our meeting his wife. His wife was just as surprised to see us. She was also a large woman, with short curly black hair and dressed in a pink nightgown like American grandmothers wear around the house. She seemed to be astounded that her husband was aware of our mission to bring her to the dinner, and that he had even agreed to it. Her face lit up in disbelief as we told her, and she giggled with her hand cupped over her mouth. She wanted to speak with him on Malalai's mobile phone to ask his explicit permission. "Do you really think it's okay?" she asked, sitting cross-legged, Indian style, facing us. "Really?" She must have been reassured by the voice on the other end, because as soon as she got off the phone she stood up to get ready.

Malalai laughed, telling the woman her husband said she didn't want to go. The woman looked at me and said, "*He* was the one that didn't want me to go," as if to clarify any misunderstanding. Then she scuttled away, lifting a drape over a doorway.

This was an extremely common tactic among Afghan men. Whenever a woman wasn't allowed to go somewhere, she would lie and blame herself when questioned, saying she didn't want to go or was too busy with the chores.

As the drape fell behind the commander's wife, a petite woman entered the room and greeted me politely, looking down at the floor as we spoke. By now Malalai had left the room and I was left wondering who this petite woman was. As we made small talk, she told me she was the commander's second wife and had married our host after his first wife could no longer produce children for him. She was young, with bushy raven bangs, and seemed very sweet and soft-spoken. She already had four children, however, and her gaze remained demurely lowered in my presence. As we spoke, I noticed that one of her eyeballs was a little off center, and I wondered how much emotional pain that must have caused her.

The first wife walked back out into the room, in a black glittery dress. "What do you think of this?" she asked me as she lifted the sides of her skirt to show me. "It's beautiful," I said, wondering why she was dressing as if she were attending a gala event. She was taking this invitation a little too seriously. She handed me a gray hand-embroidered scarf wrapped in a clear plastic bag. It was customary to give gifts to new acquaintances, although not quite necessary.

Malalai rejoined us, prodding us to finish up and return to our host. "Come on, we have to go. Where's your makeup? Your jewelry?" As the woman applied her eye shadow in the circular living room mirror, she asked my beauty advice: "What about this color? And is this too much?" she asked. In America my sister laughed at me for my fashion crimes, especially for applying crooked liner to my lips, creating a four-inch-square patch of blond hair on the top of my head instead of the highlights I was going for, and misapplying my self-tanner, which resulted in long zebralike streaks. But to this Afghan woman, my life in America made me more of an authority in the room than Malalai, whose makeup was applied impeccably.

"It's my turn tonight," the first wife added, which made dressing up and going out all the more exciting for her. Although she wanted to wear only a few bracelets, Malalai encouraged her to wear all of them. By the time we left, our large woman in the pink sleeping gown had turned into a princess in a glittery dress, bright red lipstick, and enough jewelry for a small village. As we walked out toward the car, two of the petite woman's children pleaded to go with us. Their mother refused to give them permission, but they insisted they were going anyway. She argued with them, objecting that it was a dinner for adults, not a place suitable for children, but as they jumped in the car with us, their mother's appeals sounded more like a test of loyalty than an expression of concern for the adults' event. "Don't you love me? Are you going to leave me here alone?" she asked. To her son she pleaded, "What if someone comes to the door? What will I do?" Afghan women from conservative families did not answer the door. A man in the house or the children would answer it, in case there were unrelated men visiting. The boy wasn't moved, replying simply that his uncle was already home.

As we rode to the mansion, I sat in the back with our new friend, and she gripped my hand tightly. Earlier, she mentioned that none of the female aid workers that were her husbands' friends ever came to visit. "I'm going to tell Sarah to come and visit me next time she comes to see my husband," she said, refer- ring to one of the women she knew about. She had heard that while I was there the other day, American aid workers visiting the mansion had dived into the pool. They kept all their clothes on, respecting the culture, but dove in anyway to show that life was to be lived. The stunned Afghan women quickly huddled around the American women as they emerged from the pool with their clothes sticking to them, and wrapped their scarves around and around their shivering wet bodies.

"Have you ever seen this mansion?" I asked.

"Oh no, never."

"Well, there are a lot of women there that are going to be happy to see you," I said. She let go of my hand, fixing her large scarf, which was wrapped over her body and framed her face. As she adjusted the edge of the scarf over her face so she could peek through a small opening, she told me that this was the first time in twenty years she was going out to see anyone outside of her family. She gripped my hand again, this time holding on even more tightly. "What about the workers in the mansion? How will I get past without them seeing me?" Like most Pashtun women, she had been raised under *purdah*, which in Pashto literally means "curtain," as in the curtain used to divide the men in the house from the women. It is a concept in Pashtunwali in which men and women are segregated, and women banned from showing themselves to men.

Malalai assured her that we would park the car very close to the entrance of the house, then surround her and walk quickly inside. "What will people say if they hear that the commander's wife was at the mansion?" Malalai, in her defiant style, pushed the back of her hand through the air in a dismissive gesture and said, "Dzzza!" which means "Get out of here!" When we arrived, we rushed our new friend into the house, and I held her hand as we walked, with one hand under her elbow, because she could not see the path in front of her with a large black scarf covering her face. I struggled to sustain my balance under the pressure of her heavy weight against me. I found it funny that two young, attractive women whose faces were showing were hiding this older, larger woman whose delights must remain hidden at all costs. I'm sure the workers in the garden must have wondered what fine specimen of woman remained covered, judging from the two women around her.

When we arrived at the large room filled with cushions laid about on a marble floor, our friend went directly to the corner of the room, away from the doorway, sat among the other women, and turned her face to the corner. As the women around her greeted her, she lifted the edge of her scarf to speak to them, and lowered it again when finished. Sarah later told me she hoped the woman's husband did not beat her when they got home. Even though he had agreed to her attendance and he seemed to be the nicest man we met in Afghanistan, she could be beaten for acting on his permission. She should know his rules. He controlled her access to the world.

When we heard about another place that controls women's access to the world, the prison in Kandahar, we decided we had to pay a visit. We went to the new chief of police with Malalai and introduced ourselves to him and his minions as we waited for the prisoners to be escorted in. As we waited, a delegation of men were brought into his office and began to speak to him without any recognition of our ongoing meeting. The chief ignored us, until Fahima spoke up. "You know, we had an appointment with you and you should really finish with us before you take other people." I braced myself for his reaction. Judging from the men around him, this was probably the first time anyone had spoken to him this way. He thought for a second. "You are correct," he responded, and adjusted himself on the velvet couch, turning back to us. Had I just witnessed a graying man who probably spent his whole life without being spoken to in such a way by a woman suddenly accept her complaint? Whether it was an act for the "foreigners" who accompanied us, or a true recognition of his mistake, his acknowledgment that Fahima was right made me realize that even these conservative men would sometimes listen when their errors were pointed out.

Three of the women prisoners were escorted into the chief's office to meet our delegation. Each was more of a victim than a criminal, although they had been accused of a variety of serious charges. The chief told me that one was accused of murder, another of leaving her husband and children to run away with an unrelated man, and the third of traveling alone and doing sexual favors for men.

After the officers left the room, the women began to tell their own stories. Initially very cold and impassive, they quickly became very emotional, weeping and nervously picking at their *burqas*. We asked if we could take the prisoners back to our compound so that they could visit with the other women just for a few hours and, as the Pashto saying goes, "have their minds on something else." Two of the women looked younger than twenty, and one wore a *burqa* that was torn and tattered beyond repair.

When we got back to the compound, the terrible truth of what happened to these women came out. The runaway, Lena, was rail thin, with soft, flowing brown hair and light freckles sprinkled across her nose and cheeks, and she repeatedly bit her lip in fear or frustration. She was an orphan who had left an abusive uncle to pursue her dream of an education and the ability to find work in Iran. She had been detained for traveling without a *mahram*, or male guardian, and had ended up in this prison in Kandahar. She grew angry as she related the details of how she ended up in prison, wrinkling her forehead, throwing up her hands, and shaking her head vigorously.

The pregnant woman, in prison with her seven-year-old son, tearfully recounted being sold to an abusive man with no arms. Her high-pitched voice crackled with despair, her words interspersed with sobs and sighing. She begged us to find her a proper home to give birth in and care for her older son, perhaps one of our homes. The prison lacked facilities for any kind of medical care, let alone childbirth. If there was any electricity in the building, I didn't see it being used.

The last prisoner was named Rosia. She was a tough girl with a quiet exterior. Utterly without passion or even interest as she spoke, her parched lips curled in suspicion of our group's intentions. She had been widowed but then remarried against her will to her husband's brother, raped repeatedly by her live-in father-in-law, chained and only allowed out to do chores, and finally falsely accused of killing a toddler nephew that had fallen down a well.

None of the three prisoners had ever been to school, and all were illiterate. Lena stared deeply into her visitors' eyes and declared that she just wanted to be released and attend school, like she would have done in Iran. As Carlotta Gall from the *New York Times* feverishly took notes, Rosia erupted into tears and asked me to be the sister she never had. Like from a cracked eggshell, the emotion, tears, and dirt all flowed from this previously stony-faced girl who had seen so much. Prison, she said, was the only place where she felt safe from her in-laws.

We resolved to do something for these women, but there were no lawyers and no trials in this place, simply the pointing of a man's finger toward a gate, which remained locked until the man decided to open it again. Even worse, we were to leave for Kabul the next day. We resolved to take Lena with us if we could. It would be impossible to take the other prisoners with us. Lena had family in Kabul, which made her case much simpler than theirs. I was worried about taking on the project, because anything that involves women that are considered "bad" by Afghan society carries great risk. But the thought of not doing anything seemed even worse.

We made a 7 AM appointment with the lead prosecutor in Kandahar. We pleaded with him to let Lena return to Kabul with us, but he refused to release her.

We were interrupted by a visit from an Iranian prisoner who had run off with an Afghan man. The prosecutor seemed to take pleasure in watching her tears flow and refused to release her until she had cried like she would never have a chance at being free.

After he released the Iranian woman, the prosecutor turned his attention back to us.

"Why should I trust you with my prisoner?" he asked.

"We are an international women's rights organization," I responded.

"How do I know you are who you say you are?" he threw back.

"We have business cards and identification," I said.

"How do I know what you will do with the prisoner, how could I entrust her to you?" This was his way of asking what evidence there was that we wouldn't traffic her to another country or place her in a brothel.

Then a man sitting next to the prosecutor asked me where I was from.

"Kandahar," I responded. But that was obvious from my Pashto.

"What street are you from?" he asked.

This was a question I wanted to avoid, but at least he had not asked me my father's name.

"Qazi Ghulam Street," I said.

I shouldn't have told him. "You're Qari Sultan's daughter!" he exclaimed. I was in too much awe to deny it. He could tell he was right from the look on my face. Recognizing that I couldn't do anything but admit it, I asked him how he knew. "Qari Sultan was one of the first to leave from our neighborhood. We lived near that street. Of course I know."

The tension in the room seemed to settle into my stomach. Now they knew who my father was. This was serious. There was no such thing as anonymity in Kandahar. What would happen to Agha when he came back to Kandahar to visit after twenty years? What would he be told by the people in the place where he was still a legend? I was worried about trampling carelessly through the place where he was the last of many generations building up a name. It was the one part of Agha's life that I tried to stay away from. It was sacred. Now I would destroy it in one fell swoop. I hoped that Agha would understand someday.

The prosecutor summoned me to his desk. "Read this," he instructed. It was a letter from the Pakistani consulate in reference to doctored prescription drugs made with counterfeit labels, in which the consulate agreed to conduct an investigation, along with the Kandahar attorney general's office. I read the letter to him, once again feeling like a child in Brooklyn, ordered by my parents to translate an official letter from Immigration that I felt out of place reading at all. The words were always difficult, and official letters had a complicated way of saying simple things. Now too the letter was hard to translate at first. It was written in Pakistani English, the outdated British kind that used extraneous words like "hereto" and "wherefore."

We began to get desperate. We were going to be late for our flight, and we had promised the commander who hosted the dinner that we would meet him and allow him to take an extra seat we had under the name Marcelo Gonzalez, an assistant film-maker who could not stomach more than a few days of heat, danger, and drama in Kandahar and departed. So we began to cry. Sobbing, we asked for his mercy. Perhaps the prosecutor needed to feel like he had broken women down. Whatever did it, he drew up a letter that we all signed stating we would take Lena and bring her back to her family. But her family was abusive, and she refused to take us to them when we arrived in Kabul, and there was no shelter to take her to. When we took Lena's case directly to President Karzai and asked him what should be done about women like her, he said that he would endorse an effort to build shelters to house them. We eventually found Lena such a shelter in Kabul, with a new family led by a loving Afghan woman who had adopted other children too.

We flew down the road to the airport at the U.S. base, Lena in tow, and the plane that was about to take off with us turned back around to pick us up as we waited on the tarmac. The pilot, annoyed that we were late, became almost enraged when he saw that our large suitcases could hardly fit in the back of the seven-passenger plane.

As we flew into the air, the backs of our heads pressed firmly against our seats, the plane refusing to level up because of the weight of our luggage in the back, the pilot told us we may not make it to Kabul. It was 1:16 PM, and the Kabul airport was due to close at 2 PM for reconstruction, leaving us less than the hour we needed to get there. If that happened, we would have to land somewhere else and wait for the airport to reopen, hoping to have enough fuel to last us. Zabit Akram, or the man posing as "Marcelo", looked scared. He was on his way to Kabul to meet with President Karzai and ask for a bigger job. The plane felt like it was struggling. Lena's face was yellow with fear. She gripped the seat in front of her and pressed her head against it. It was the first time she had ever flown on an airplane. The sound of the engine sputtered like a heavy man panting up a flight of stairs. I looked down at Kandahar from the air, admiring its warren of mud walls, like a cross between a maze built for rats as a scientific experiment, and rows upon rows of sand castles whose spires have been eroded by the crashing waves of the ocean.

Lena lifted her head, staring at Commander Zabit Akram sitting across from her, and began to speak with him in Farsi. They began to argue. The commander turned to me and said, "She's a loose woman. She came to Kandahar to be with a boy. Her parents are in Kabul."

Lena looked at me and told me *he* was the man that had put her in prison. "When I was brought into his office," she said, "he ordered them to throw me in prison until my family came for me." She was angry, and her voice trembled as she spoke to him, surprisingly defiant. I suppose she felt confident that we would protect her.

"She's lying," the commander said to me, as if I were now the judge. We were in much too small a plane to begin fighting, but I enjoyed Lena's audacity.

"He's lying," she said.

"No, she's lying."

I turned to Lena, put my hand on her shoulder, and said that I believed no one but her, and that life would begin anew when she got to Kabul and began her studies. She shot him a look of satisfaction, and we resumed our concern for the plane's angle. The adrenaline rush in the prosecutor's office that began the day felt like it was pumping through my system again. Moments like these made me believe that change is indeed possible. Even so, they were very rare.

I looked out the window at the thick fluffy clouds that surrounded us and thought about Rosia, whom we had to leave behind. Like Rosia, the prisoner of Kandahar, I can't leave

Afghanistan behind. She was, and may still be, a prisoner in the physical sense, caged within dusty walls and iron gates. The key to her freedom was with a guard who had left his prison duties and disappeared. I left Afghanistan in a physical sense long ago, but I can't seem to escape it emotionally. Afghan culture has shaped my parents' morality and ideals, and therefore my own. I am enamored with the city because neither I nor my parents should ever have left it alive. At the very least, we have a duty to return. My aunts and cousins call Kandahar home, and need not only our help but our love and presence in their lives. They want us to save them, to take them away from the rubble and their thirst. In that way, they too are prisoners of Kandahar.

Afterword

In many ways, little has changed for the average Afghan woman. She still wears a *burqa* and, more important, is still poor and has little access to health care, education, or even clean drinking water. In a city like Kandahar, she has less than a 10 percent chance of going to school or learning to read. She is more likely than women from any other nation in the world to die while giving birth, and her children have a one in four chance of dying in their infancy.

I am optimistic, however, that things can change as long as the United States truly honors its commitments to Afghanistan. This remains an open question, as international attention to Afghanistan has dwindled since the war.

I continue to work with Afghan women, knowing that by combining my university education and ability to communicate with people in the West with an understanding of Islamic attitudes and Afghan culture, I can do much from America. In New York and Washington, I have been able to rub elbows with heiresses, celebrities, Harvard professors, members of Congress, and even the former president of Ireland, Mary Robinson. This has never been an empty exercise for me because I have always approached these interactions with the same purpose: Persuade people to devote their precious time and energy to helping Afghan people improve their lot. I treat face time with anyone that can make a difference the way a struggling actor treats an audition. At the very least, those I contact in my work will have learned about Afghan women and may tell others about what is happening, others that may actually *do* something. I sometimes imagine myself as an irrigation canal, bringing water from where there is plenty to where there is none. The better the places that I go, the more that will reach the other end.

Immersed in all the excitement of the conference in that compound in Kandahar, despite all the dreaming and wishing and hoping that filled our magical days there, the fact that my own aunt Khala Sherina was not even allowed to attend gnawed at me like a nasty insect in a beautiful forest. I expected that she might not be allowed to participate in the conference, but I had hoped she would at least be allowed to visit. I had gone to her house one morning to pick her up, even if just to have tea with the women, but her husband would not allow her to travel with me to the conference site. When he told me that she was too busy with the laundry to join us, she agreed, but later whispered that she had really wanted to visit the conference with me. I left swallowing quickly to avoid tears, but I knew that even if I insisted on taking Khala Sherina with me that day, she would have to deal with the repercussions on her own long after I was gone.

Most women's rights work happens in the public arena, addressing the law, opportunities for education and work, and the ability to travel and receive health care. But how do you change women's most intimate space, and the power exercised over them by their own families? What do you do when the law changes but a husband refuses to let his own wife take part in a "liberation," or a father his daughter? Worse, what do you do when they don't want you to see or speak with "their" women? People like me enter women's rights work hoping to make big changes in many people's lives. But I have learned that change will come person by person and not all in one earthquake.

While watching a BBC program about Nelson Mandela, I learned that although he initially took a nonviolent approach to fighting oppression, he later got military training and, leading the African National Congress, began attacking the (mostly unoccupied) government buildings that kept his people down. I often relate, in my mind, the racial apartheid of South Africa to the sexual apartheid that takes place in Muslim countries, where the systematic denial of basic freedoms to women is common practice.

Change is certainly possible and in some ways inevitable, but change is slow for women. They do not resist fiercely enough, it seems. But they also fight from a more difficult position. In the quest for black rights in South Africa, the leaders at least had their families to support them. They acted as one unit against another, hostile unit. They ate, slept, and lived with companions who believed in the same struggle. In other words, they had family support. Women, by contrast, often feel alone in their time of greatest need. I think this has to do with the fact that historically, sons have married wives that enter and live with the husband's family. The result is that a man usually enjoys a family that shares his interests, whereas women, having been married into other families, are sometimes disunited. They were moved to a different team, so to speak. In this new team, there are many new players, the in-laws, who are not as likely to protect the woman's interests. The fact that women's unity has been broken up in this way has, I believe, contributed to their weak position in the affairs of the world. Despite this, women have a strong sense of family and community, and can relate to each other based on these bonds.

Women have resisted their subordination, nonviolently, and mostly when wealthy or highly educated. (Even though poor, uneducated women have resisted oppression and fought injustice in countless ways, women's liberation movements are most often led by women who have some education, and some resources to invest.) But what if women resisted the way that men have done? I have sometimes imagined a secret force of women who threaten to destroy government buildings unless their claims are heard. Or to destroy the property of male leaders who stand in the way of their freedom. It worked for the blacks in South Africa, why wouldn't it work for women?

I know it is not popular or proper to say these things. I am reminded of the feminist militants good girls like me are so mindful not to be like. We pride ourselves on being different from "those brutal men." And we have made much progress in recent years, nonviolently. But there are so many places where change for women is barely happening, or where the situation is getting even worse. How long do women have to wait to be freed from enslavement? Cooking, cleaning, serving, marrying, giving birth, all without any choice in the matter. The consequences of a choice made in the context of freedom are easier to bear than those forced upon us.

Freedom for Afghan and Muslim women has to happen as much in the law, where the multitude of restrictions imposed on them must be addressed, as in the deepest, darkest places in women's minds. Afghan women must believe, truly believe, that real freedom is possible. The kind of freedom you have when you believe you have a choice. This is something many have yet to understand. My friend Rangina Hamidi, an Afghan-American working with the most desperate women in Kandahar, and bringing fresh hope to them, says that predestination is the overarching theme in the women's lives. She says: "Many women believe that God willed them to be secondary beings and that God wants them to be the 'slaves' to their 'masters' (men), so when a woman ends up in an abusive relationship with a man, the response of the community is *'wai da dera bad-qismata da'* (she has a bad destiny)." She laments that this attitude, particularly in the rural areas, has twisted "the minds of the people here into thinking of themselves as just dolls being acted on—rather than active participants in life and society."

This is the mind-set that needs to be challenged, at a core level, in Afghanistan and all over the world. I believe that even those Afghan women who are exercising their new freedoms by removing their *burqas* and going to school aren't quite convinced that true freedom will happen. They are going through the motions, but they live in fear. Their fear is not misplaced. They have seen the horrors faced by those resisting—acid thrown in their faces, lashings and beatings, and even murder. These are the consequences women face in the quest for even minor freedoms.

One way things will change is if women learn that God has not meant them to suffer, and that their safest sanctuary, Islam, indeed wants them to have the freedoms and life that they dream about. They should be educated, work, and be free to marry whom they wish. They should not have to endure repeated abuse and pray to God that one day it will end, the day that life itself does. Rangina echoes the feelings of Kandahari women, the same feeling that I grew up with—that you must fear God to the utmost. He is an angry God, not a loving and understanding God.

While writing this book, I was accepted to a master's program in government at Harvard, and as I complete it I am nearing the end of my studies. Since then, I have become just a little more careful while driving, or walking alone at night. My life is finally wonderful and I don't want to mess it up. I once secretly thought that I might even get accepted to Harvard if only I weren't being held back in my marriage, and now that dream too has come true.

It is because so many Afghan women have so little hope that they can truly be free and accomplish anything that they are careless with their lives, their health, and their well-being. Many of them try to change their lives, sneaking off to visit relatives they've been banned from seeing for one reason or another, or wearing a dress with a slightly shorter hemline than allowed (in the presence of women only, of course). But they are deathly afraid of doing anything that will be seen as disruptive. My friend Vic says people behave much differently if they believe they are carrying a winning lottery ticket. If people think that they will accomplish great things in life, they will take more care over their choices, and their destiny.

During my marriage, I contemplated suicide to end the feeling of having no options. Although I always had many options, the "worst" of which was to run away and begin working to support myself, I still had this tight grip over my mind that I couldn't do that. Somehow, I believed that I wasn't "allowed" to be free because of the hold some power had over me. That power was simply myself, I realize now—my fear of failing, my desire to be a "good girl" and the most unselfish person, my determination never to be accused of acting shamefully. I would never have attempted suicide if I really felt I could one day meet the man of my dreams, travel the world, and go to Harvard. As one wise Afghan woman told me, "Hope is what keeps us going. Hope keeps us alive."

I believe that the same phenomenon is happening today in Herat, where girls routinely set themselves on fire in order to escape their forced marriages or difficult lives. Some may hope, like I did, that after death everyone will realize how awful things were and finally feel bad about what they had done. For these women, sometimes surviving can be a fate worse than dying, because it means having to heal from severe burns all over their bodies in a place that has no way of caring for the scorched. I am under no illusions about the vast difference in opportunity between myself and my sisters in Afghanistan and other predominantly Muslim countries. It is because I believe in their strength that I choose to partner with them. I truly believe that a collective earthquake will occur when their dignity and power is realized. It will be with this earthquake that we will uncover a great threat to the type of terrorism the world has seen since 9/11.

I am frequently asked my position on the U.S. war in Afghanistan. "Do you feel it was justified because it did, after all, liberate women?" I am asked. I know that the war was not worth it to Nasria and the rest of my family that suffered. Their lives have hardly changed since the end of the Taliban, and they must continue on without their dearest ones. I find their courage and hopeful attitude a sign of great strength. Having seen the extremely negative consequences of the war on them, but also having witnessed some of the positive changes, especially in Kabul, I believe that the removal of the Taliban has indeed been a blessing to many Afghans.

I only wish that the military action had been better thought out, more careful about risking civilians' lives. I know in my heart that if the war had been waged on U.S. soil, with the government trying to hunt down and kill al Qaeda and Taliban in say, Texas, it would have been done in a completely different manner. I know that massive bombs and AC-130 gunships, spewing out bullets from a rotating cannon, would not have been used. No, people would have been outraged at that. But in Afghanistan, the victims' outrage burned up and evaporated, silently, in the heat and blinding reflection of the desert. Afghans' attempts to tell the U.S. government what happened to them were dismissed, and to add insult to injury, even their children were called Taliban supporters. I would have felt very differently if the military had made an honest effort to assist civilian victims after the war, take a complete count of the dead, and offer food to their families or rebuild their clay huts. I think there would have been a lot less anger on the part of Afghans as well as in the rest of the Muslim world.

Marla Ruzicka, the American advocate for civilian victims of the U.S. wars in Iraq and Afghanistan, and Zabit Akram, the sweet commander from Kandahar, were killed within weeks of each other in Iraq and Afghanistan respectively. Both met their fate because they chose to be catalysts for change. Marla was blasted by a roadside bomb. Zabit was blown to bits when a suicide bomber targeted him in the mosque, while attending the funeral of an assassinated cleric.

My sister Sara begins to play a DVD of Farhad Darya, an Afghan pop singer whose music travels from Germany to Afghanistan, rather than the other way around. I close my eyes and begin to dance. It is as natural as a baby's suckling. I feel at once transported to a wedding with henna-painted hands clapping in an ancient Pashtun village, or to the hours of dancing amid heaps of basmati rice and spiced kabobs in the Kennedy Hotel near JFK Airport, a popular wedding hall for Afghans in the 1980s.

I am still very close to my community, attending birthdays, weddings, parties, and now political events as well. I have often considered leaving, in an emotional sense. My mother accuses women who are "too educated" of leaving their communities and marrying "others," because they think that they have become better than everyone else. I have always been keenly aware of this dilemma. But now I understand why they leave. They begin to feel lonesome, misunderstood, and disinterested in the regular affairs of a community that most resembles a small town. Still, I know I will never really leave. I witness my parents, family, and community rapidly changing. My sister Sara still chooses to wear the *hijab,* and my sister Aziza shuns jeans because they don't reflect her professional style. Neither of them expects to marry in the way I married Nadir, and my parents insist they complete their college education before they consider marriage. Even though they don't say it, I know my parents respect my path. I still struggle with some of their choices and attitudes, but as I struggle to understand them and the challenges they overcame, my love and respect for them only deepens.

Still, even with my own family, I question my simplest acts. I wonder how much helping with the cooking and cleaning is too much, especially if my male cousins or brother aren't contributing. I waver on how much I should engage in the men's conversations, how close I should sit, and what is inappropriate to say—based on Western standards, then on Afghan standards, then on what Islam and God would say, after that on what my family would prefer, and finally on what my gut says. I always come back to the same thing. I find my own way. I love to serve guests, even though it re-creates the typical scene of women serving men. In moments so perfect I feel I am completely full, I have found that it is possible to create a harmony between being a feminist and a good Pashtun girl, a Muslim and a free woman, an American and a proud Afghan. Those moments feel stolen, somehow impossible, like flying in the Afghan clouds with the defiant and freed prisoner Lena.

Notes

Chapter 4   The Little, Little Masuda

1. Danesh Kerokhel, "In Afghanistan, Marriage Is a Sentence," Knight Ridder/Tribune, July 12, 2002.

Chapter 6   A Pure Kandahari Girl

1. "Kandahar Reportedly Bombed," Associated Press, February 9, 1982.
2. "Afghan Conflict 'Could Last Until End of Century': Interview with Charles Dunbar, America's Top Diplomat in Kabul," *U.S. News & World Report*, August 1, 1983.
3. *See* John F. Burns, "Afghans: Now They Blame America," *The New York Times Magazine*, February 4, 1990; Barry Kramer, *The Wall Street Journal*, September 2, 1977, 22.

Chapter 7   A Visitor from Hollywood

1. Willem Vogelsang, *The Afghans* (Oxford: Blackwell Publishers, 2002), 124–25.

Chapter 8   The Worst Health Care in the World

1. Deborah Ellis, *Women of the Afghan War* (Westport, CT: Praeger, 2000), 106–7.

Chapter 9   An American, My Own Way

1. Robert D. Kaplan, "The Lawless Frontier," *The Atlantic Monthly,* September 2000, 66–80.
2. Amnesty International, "Afghanistan: Protect Afghan Civilians and Refugees," AI Index: ASA 11/012/2001, October 9, 2001.

Chapter 13   Changing the Rules

1. Robert Nickelsberg and Jane Perlez, "Survivors Recount Fierce American Raid That Flattened a Village," *The New York Times*, November 2, 2001.

2. Murray Campbell, "Bombing of Farming Village Undermines U.S. Credibility," *The Globe and Mail (Toronto),* November 3, 2001.
3. Michael Powell, "NY Afghan Navigates 2 Shattered Worlds: After Watching World Trade Center Collapse, Young Immigrant Documents Her Return to a Country Torn by War," *The Washington Post,* February 8, 2002, A3.
4. David Zucchino, "U.S. Addresses Iraqis' Losses with Payments," *Los Angeles Times,* March 13, 2005.

Chapter 14   An Afghan Women's Bill of Rights

1. "Nine Killed, Four Injured as Unrest Continues in Afghanistan," Deutsche Presse-Agentur, January 11, 2004.
2. Hamida Ghafour, "The Women's Group Where Attendance Can Cost Your Life," *The Daily Telegraph,* September 5, 2003.